A REAPPRAISAL *of*
FRANCO-AMERICAN RELATIONS
1830-1871

A
REAPPRAISAL
OF
FRANCO-AMERICAN RELATIONS
1830–1871

By

HENRY BLUMENTHAL

GREENWOOD PRESS, PUBLISHERS
WESTPORT, CONNECTICUT

Library of Congress Cataloging in Publication Data

Blumenthal, Henry.
  A reappraisal of Franco-American relations, 1830-1871.

    Reprint of the ed. published by University of North
Carolina Press, Chapel Hill.
    Bibliography: p.
    Includes index.
    1. United States--Foreign relations--France.
2. France--Foreign relations--United States. I. Title.
E183.8.F8B55   1980   327.73'044   79-25197
ISBN 0-313-22138-3

Reprinted in 1980 by Greenwood Press, Inc.
51 Riverside Avenue, Westport, CT 06880

Printed in the United States of America

10 9 8 7 6 5 4 3 2 1

To My Brothers

Preface and Acknowledgments

THIS MONOGRAPH IS DESIGNED to fill a gap in the diplomatic history of the United States. So far, no exhaustive study has been written about Franco-American relations in the mid-nineteenth century. Professor Donald C. McKay's brief and general historical survey *The United States and France* merely touches on this important period. Chronologically, this book follows R. A. McLemore's *Franco-American Diplomatic Relations, 1816-1836*.

The purpose of this investigation is to throw new light on the interrelationship between France and the United States during four decades of controversy, revolution, and war. Contrary to popular notions, the relations between the two countries were not friendly. Usual references to the historic Franco-American friendship from the times of Lafayette to the present conveniently ignore crucial issues and petty incidents which led to a growing estrangement between Paris and Washington in the last century. The hostility, distrust, and misunderstanding between the two nations and their governments did not grow out of any single dramatic event. No war climaxed their many differences, although several times they appeared to be close to the brink of war. Franco-American alienation in the mid-nineteenth century gradually developed and deepened as the result of a multitude of conflicting policies and viewpoints.

For centuries England and France had fought each other to secure dominance in world affairs. By the middle of the nineteenth century they began to wonder whether the irony of history had brought another competitor into existence. Between 1830 and 1870 the population of the United States tripled, reaching a total of forty million, a population somewhat larger than that of France. Already rich in resources, the Federal Union, moreover, acquired in the 1840's more contiguous territory than the British Isles and continental France together embraced. By the 1850's the total tonnage of American merchant ships surpassed that of any other nation. It was natural, therefore, that the two leading European sea powers looked upon the rapidly rising trans-Atlantic republic as a disturbing element in the world balance of power.

Judicious analysis of the available evidence leaves no doubt that ideological and religious differences, though secondary to considerations of power politics, also tended to alienate France and the United States. The success of the social and political system of the Protestant republic across the Atlantic gave the Catholic monarchs of France as much concern as its rapid territorial and economic growth. Religious differences affected Franco-American relationships to a remarkable degree. However, as far as French monarchists were concerned, next to the political and economic consequences which the rapid rise of the United States threatened to entail, the greatest danger was the possible spread of republicanism under the leadership, or with the encouragement, of the United States. This apprehension gained additional strength after the mid-nineteenth-century revolutions and was a major source of suspicion and friction. French policies concerning American expansion, the Civil War, and the Maximilian affair clearly reflected these fears. At the same time, while American statesmen did not have to worry about the infiltration of monarchical ideas into the United States, they realized that Central and South America were not immune to them. And it was of real concern to them whether the governments of Louis Philippe and Napoleon III translated their anti-republican views into anti-American policies.

Franco-American relations did not operate in an international vacuum. They felt the impact of the major nineteenth-century developments, such as the industrial revolution, the growing conflict between authoritarianism and democracy, the rising wave of nationalism, and the perennial rivalries among the European nations.

Although this monograph concentrates on the interrelationships between France and the United States, it must be kept in mind that the policies of third powers greatly influenced these relations. Whether the leaders of France and the United States were men of determination and wisdom, or of indecision and imprudence, their triumphs and failures in the Western Hemisphere depended on many factors beyond their control. Throughout this period London's attitude played a major role. In the 1860's, Berlin, St. Petersburg, and Vienna also exercised direct and indirect influences on the course of Franco-American relations.

During the period under consideration London and Paris usually sought to coordinate their policies with respect to the United States. However, even if they had not been suspicious of each other, the state of world affairs prevented them from decisively intervening in American affairs. Outstanding among the problems to which they had to turn their attention, particularly during the 1850's and 1860's, were Russia's ambitions in the Balkans and the Near East, the tensions between Austria and Italy, and the emergence of Prussia-Germany as a major power. France was deeply involved in these developments. Desiring to make France once again *la grande nation,* Napoleon III embarked upon domestic and foreign policies which actually had the effect of weakening France. The enterprising French ruler not only lacked the capacities equal to his set goal, but he also shifted his alliances so often that in the end he was outmaneuvered by the cynical master of *Realpolitik,* Otto von Bismarck. While Napoleon's ambitions were destined to lead to Franco-American complications, developments in Europe prevented him from being as active in America as he would have liked to be.

The first four chapters of this monograph are devoted to a discussion of ideological, diplomatic, and economic questions, from the outbreak of the July Revolution in France to the beginning of the War between the States. The deterioration of Franco-American relations described in these chapters reached a certain climax during the American Civil War and the Maximilian affair. In view of the anxiety which the interventionist maneuvers of the French emperor then caused American statesmen, it was not surprising that the United States welcomed the downfall of Napoleon III in 1870. America's strict neutrality in the Franco-Prussian War disappointed the French, who failed to realize that in the forty years prior to Sedan a great transformation had taken place in Franco-American relations.

To focus full attention upon separate aspects of these relations, I have chosen to make a topical presentation of my material rather than to give it a straight chronological treatment. I am, of course, aware that many of the events discussed in the first four chapters either took place simultaneously or at approximately the same period. An effort has been made to interrelate important events by way of cross references. I hope, moreover, that the careful documentation will be of particular interest to the specialists in the field.

The omission of a chapter on the cultural and intellectual relationships between the two nations in the nineteenth century was not due to a lack of interest on my part. Howard Mumford Jones's

America and French Culture dealt with these aspects so brilliantly that it is still authoritative on this subject. To go beyond its scope and to make a meaningful and substantial new contribution calls for more research than I have so far been able to complete.

* * *

I wish to express my gratitude to the following libraries and archives and their staffs: Archdiocesan Archives of New York, Archives de France (Paris), Archives du Ministère des Affaires Étrangères (Paris), Bibliothèque Nationale (Paris), Bibliothèque de l'Université de Paris, Boston Public Library, Brown University Library, Catholic University Library, William L. Clements Library, Columbia University Library, Duke University Library, Georgetown University Library, Harvard University Library, Johns Hopkins University Library, Library of Congress, Massachusetts Historical Society, National Archives (Washington), Newark Public Library, New Jersey Historical Society, New York Historical Society, New York Public Library, New York University Library, Pennsylvania Historical Society, Princeton University Library, Rochester University Library, Rutgers University Library, St. John's University Library, United States Embassy Library (Paris), University of California Library (Berkeley), University of Chicago Library, University of Colorado Library, University of Oklahoma Library, University of Pennsylvania Library, University of Virginia Library, Vanderbilt University Library, and Yale University Library.

Mr. Derick Webb has graciously permitted me access to the James Watson Webb collection at Yale University.

I am also greatly indebted to the following scholars who have read part or all of the manuscript: Lynn M. Case, of the University of Pennsylvania; Shepard B. Clough, of Columbia University; L. Ethan Ellis, of Rutgers University; Benjamin Klebaner, of the City College of New York; and Dexter Perkins, of Cornell University. I wish also to acknowledge the advice and encouragement I have received from Walton E. Bean and Lawrence A. Harper of the University of California, and Edward Fuhlbruegge of Rutgers University.

A fellowship from the Waksman Foundation in France and grants from the Rutgers University Research Council were of material assistance in the preparation of this study. I am particularly grateful to the Ford Foundation and the Rutgers Research Council for their generous contributions toward the publication of my manuscript.

HENRY BLUMENTHAL
Rutgers University

Contents

List of Tables

List of Abbreviations

AHA	American Historical Association
AHR	*American Historical Review*
AMAE	Archives du Ministère des Affaires Étrangères
CALP	Correspondence from and to the American Legation at Paris
CCC	Correspondance consulaire et commerciale (AMAE)
CDS	Confederate Department of State
CFSUS	Communications to foreign sovereigns from the President of the United States
CLFUS	Ceremonial letters from France to the President of the United States
CP	Correspondance politique (AMAE)
CPC	Correspondance politique des consuls (AMAE)
CPEU	Correspondance politique—États-Unis (AMAE)
CSA	Confederate States of America
DDCDS	Diplomatic despatches from U. S. ministers in China to the Department of State
DDEDS	Diplomatic despatches from U. S. ministers in England to the Department of State
DDFDS	Diplomatic despatches from U. S. ministers in France to the Department of State
DDGDS	Diplomatic despatches from U. S. ministers in Germany to the Department of State
FIDS	Instructions from the Department of State to U. S. ministers in France
FNFDS	Notes from the Department of State to the French Legation
FNTDS	Notes from the French Legation to the Department of State
GIDS	Instructions from the Department of State to U. S. ministers in Germany
LC	Library of Congress
MDEU	Mémoires et documents—États-Unis (AMAE)
MDF	Mémoires et documents—France (AMAE)

MF	Microfilm
NALP	Notes from the French Foreign Ministry to the American Legation at Paris
NAR	*North American Review*
NDMSC	Navy Department, Correspondence of the Mediterranean Squadron Cruise
RDDM	*Revue des deux mondes*
SMDS	Special Missions of the Department of State
USCLF	Letters from U. S. consuls in France
USCDF	Despatches from the Department of State to U. S. consuls in France

A REAPPRAISAL *of*
FRANCO-AMERICAN RELATIONS
1830-1871

CHAPTER I

Republican Ideology and Diplomacy (1830-1860)

AT THE TIME of the founding of the American republic, French statesmen were primarily concerned with questions of power rather than of ideology. Their interest in the success of the struggle for independence was motivated by their desire to embarrass and weaken the British Empire. That the new nation across the Atlantic chose to adopt republican institutions did not disturb French royalists. If anything, they believed the republican form of government was destined to keep the United States so weak and powerless that Europe would not have to be afraid of it. Their ideological prejudices closed their minds even to the speculation that a people operating under a system of self-government in a land with considerable natural resources might be so productive as to pose in time a challenge to the traditional European social and political order. As the United States grew in the nineteenth century, France, Great Britain, and other European powers made belated and by and large unsuccessful attempts to block American expansion. Inasmuch as the territorial, economic, and maritime growth of the United States benefited many European countries in various respects, they could in the end reluctantly accept the disturbing fact that across the Atlantic a great power was on the rise. The "American danger" was, after all, not acute as long as Washington continued to recognize the existing European possessions in the Western Hemisphere and to stand by its traditional policy of nonintervention in European affairs.

While North America's economic competition was a matter of concern to Europe, the United States was not expected to threaten the security of European states. European monarchs, however, did have reason to fear the impact of the model republic's successful institutions upon the security of their thrones. The governments of Louis Philippe and Napoleon III felt uneasy about the possibility that a growing number of Frenchmen might be so impressed by America's accomplishments that the idea to establish a republican system in France might gain momentum. Obviously, such a turn of events was hardly likely to come about without an effective propaganda effort and the existence of widespread dissatisfaction with the internal and external policies of the French rulers. French monarchists regarded it, therefore, as a serious challenge that the United States lent at least its moral support to the republican movement in Europe, and that some Americans actually aided and assisted it. Americans propagated democratic ideals because they deeply believed in them as the most effective way of elevating the individual and improving the conditions of mankind. At the same time, they were not unaware of the possibility that the existence of an active republican movement in France—and elsewhere in Europe—might deter the monarchs from forceful intervention in American affairs.

To meet this problem, the French monarchs did not only attempt to control republican activities at home and to deny the superiority of republican institutions, but they also pursued policies designed to frustrate the successes of the American republic and to arouse the suspicions of the Latin Americans against the United States. The Yankees, they contended, posed as friends who were interested in the welfare and political emancipation of the peoples in the Western Hemisphere, whereas in reality they sought to dominate them politically and to exploit them economically.

I

At the time of the Revolutionary War, Frederick the Great of Prussia refused to assist the infant cause of America because "his trade was to be a king." Sixty-odd years later, Louis Philippe began to wonder whether it had not been a mistake for royalist France to have been the godfather of the American republic. By then the ideological conflict between monarchism and republicanism had developed into a central issue of the age and greatly affected the relations between France and the United States. Confident that their system of self-government must at least be judged an improvement upon all others, American citizens resented anti-republican propaganda in France and elsewhere.[1]

Arguments against popular government shifted with changing conditions. In view of America's unprecedented progress and prosperity

1. See *Pennsylvania Inquirer* (Philadelphia), March 29, 1848, and *The Daily Picayune* (New Orleans), March 28, 1848.

its adversaries no longer questioned the practicability of republics. Instead, they denounced democracy as the mother of corruption, tending to debase the national mind and to enervate the public spirit. The eminent French statesman and historian François Guizot apprehended that democracy meant chaos and social war. He visualized it as a system of perpetual crisis.[2] Its success in the United States was frequently flatly denied. A French lady, for example, warned her countrymen that "American democracy is the greatest falsehood of the age."[3] Other observers agreed with her that a relentless and haughty merchant aristocracy really ruled the country. They charged that American property interests were at the mercy of political prima donnas who did not hesitate to destroy the well functioning Bank of the United States or arbitrarily to suspend specie payments during the depression of 1857.[4] Indeed, these critics blamed the depression itself on republican liberties.

Others followed the American scene with skepticism and bewilderment. They noted that the Constitution granted the President more powers than constitutional monarchs enjoyed. The war against the Mexican Republic appeared to them as wicked and ambitious as any expansionist scheme perpetrated by the monarchs of the Old World.[5] They found it difficult, moreover, to reconcile the institution of slavery with the advertisement of liberty, and the bloody disorders in Kansas with the claim of universal popular contentment. They finally questioned the moral superiority of a political system in which senators made concessions, as in the Great Compromise of 1850, for fear of unpopularity.[6] The press of imperial France took delight in portraying the "demagogic" institutions of the United States as a strange mixture of barbarism and civilization. If only the misguided Yankees would appreciate the virtues and blessings of monarchy! At least, they should not so loudly proclaim that there was no love lost for the "despots" of Europe.[7]

2. François de Guizot, *De la démocratie en France* (Paris, 1849), p. 9; see also the editorial in *Harper's Magazine*, XIII (1856), 697-700.

3. M. de Grandfort, *The New World* (New Orleans, 1855), p. 120.

4. Simon J. Copans, "French Opinion of American Democracy, 1852-1860" (Ph.D. dissertation, Brown University, 1942), pp. 95-99; W. d'Ormesson, *La grande crise mondiale* (Paris, 1933), pp. 48-49; Pageot to Dalmatié, Washington, D. C., July 13, 1839. *CPEU*, XCV.

5. Abiel A. Livermore, *The War with Mexico Reviewed* (Boston, 1850), p. 180.

6. *RDDM* (October 14, 1850), pp. 369-73; see also Eugene Newton Curtis, *The French Assembly of 1848 and American Constitutional Doctrines* (New York, 1918), p. 262.

7. Copans, pp. 16-20.

The ardent one-sidedness of these widely held views could be matched by those of the republican sympathizers. The writings of Alexis de Tocqueville and other students of American society, though extolling the virtues of equality even more than those of liberty, do not seem to have been very convincing to the great mass of French monarchists.

As a recent arrival among the exalted company of kings, Louis Philippe was very sensitive to the monarchical esprit de corps. It has been said of him that "a smile from the pettiest prince of the old stock is more grateful to him than the good will of the greatest of republics."[8] And his leading minister, Guizot, could boast of his reputation for being even more royalist than the king. Believing in "a monarchy limited by a limited number of bourgeois," he looked upon republicanism as a churchman would look upon atheism. Nevertheless, paramount interests and international customs of courtesy restrained the statesmen of the two countries from permitting their ideological differences unduly to aggravate their official relations. When royalist schemers planned to put a prince of his own family on the projected throne of Mexico, Louis Philippe disapproved. His fear of war with the United States proved to be stronger than his dislike of republics. Even Guizot was not blind to the expediency of sending a minister to Washington who "understands the democratic spirit well enough to use it without fear of becoming imbued by it."[9]

By the same token, Americans honored Prince François de Joinville as "a truly republican Prince" when he visited the United States in 1841. And Americans in Paris admired the pomp and splendor of the court so much that they literally crowded other foreigners out of many imperial festivities.[10] Their diplomatic representatives went to the other extreme. They yielded only reluctantly to the etiquette of a uniform. Associating republicanism with simplicity, they neglected to realize that uniforms carried great consideration in the Old World.

There is a certain irony in Andrew Jackson's congratulatory letter

8. Martin to Buchanan, Paris, October 31, 1846. *DDFDS*, XXX.

9. Quoted in *Revue retrospective* (March, 1848), pp. 146-47. Pageot did not disappoint his master. He resigned from his Washington post after the February Revolution.

10. The court's balls came to be known as *bals américains*. According to the *National Intelligencer* of February 3, 1862, the number of Americans presented to the Emperor and the Empress amounted to 150 in 1857 at three balls; 110 in 1858, 139 in 1859, and 109 in 1860 at two balls each. So many American citizens who visited Paris wished to pay their respects to the imperial rulers that French and American officials often found it difficult to handle this problem without giving offense. Dayton to Seward, Paris, January 14, 1862. *DDFDS*, (MF) XXXIV: 54.

to his "Great and Good Friend,"[11] King Louis Philippe, on the occasion of the July Revolution of 1830. Historically, though, it is not coincidental that this revolution occurred in France at a time when Jackson "revolutionized" American politics. In both instances the principles of popular government made distinct progress. To underline his friendly disposition towards the new constitutional monarchy, President Jackson pleased French authorities with his presence at a celebration in honor of the recent events. The public's sentimental attachment to France reached a new height with "this most wonderful revolution in the history of the world."[12] This attitude lasted as long as the notion prevailed that the constitutional monarchy was perhaps the most ideal form of government for France. As illiberal tendencies could be noted after 1832, Americans began to question whether there was an ideal governmental system for France.[13]

II

Since the Revolution of 1789 the French people had been restlessly searching for a form of government that would give them both glory and liberty. Louis Philippe satisfied them in neither respect. Many patriotic Frenchmen resented the fact that their government failed to play a leading role in the affairs of Europe. They never overcame their disappointment over its failure to aid the Poles and Italians in their struggles for independence. According to the poet-statesman Alphonse de Lamartine, "France was bored," and what was worse, favoritism and corruption added to the general dissatisfaction. With the apparent genius of Louis Philippe's government for alienating the majority of the French people, its anti-clerical policies irritated the Catholics. Representing the self-satisfied bourgeoisie, its failure to attend to the social problems created by the industrial revolution evoked much criticism among the lower income groups. Moreover, the depression which began in 1847 made many workers receptive to the socialist teachings of Louis Blanc. Still, Parisians were stunned when a revolution suddenly swept the Orleanist dynasty from the throne and a provisional government of republicans and socialists proclaimed, after some hesitation, a republic on February 24, 1848.[14]

11. President Jackson to Louis Philippe, Washington, D. C., November 20, 1830. *CPEU*, LXXXIV.

12. Rives to Van Buren, Paris, July 30, 1830. *DDFDS*, XXIV; Roux de Rochelle to Molé, Washington, D. C., October 28, 1830. *CPEU*, LXXXIV.

13. Eugene N. Curtis, "American Opinion of the French Nineteenth-Century Revolutions," *AHR*, XXIV (1924), 254. See also Robert Scott, "American Travellers in France, 1830-1860" (Ph.D. dissertation, Yale, 1940), pp. 26-34.

14. For the first reactions of Americans in Paris, see J. H. Powell, *Richard Rush:*

As a result of this completely unexpected development, Richard Rush, the highly qualified United States Minister to France, faced the necessity of making a difficult decision. Should he lend aid and advice to the infant republic or should he stay aloof from the internal affairs of another nation? It is well to remember that at that time he could not pick up a telephone to ask the State Department for instructions. It took exactly twenty-six days before his first detailed report of the revolutionary happenings reached Washington. And it required about as many days before the return mail brought the despatches from the Secretary of State. As the extraordinary events took place with breathtaking speed, Rush decided not to wait for instructions. As an experienced statesman and diplomat who for a generation had been in close contact with the political leaders of his country, he took it upon himself to act according to the principle that his government was interested in furthering republicanism wherever it came into existence. In his estimate, the United States could ill afford to disappoint the democratic movement in Europe.[15]

Somewhat cautiously he informed Washington about his course of action during the critical days of the revolution. On February 26, he reported, the provisional government intimated that it would earnestly welcome his early felicitations.[16] Two days later he officially presented the fraternal greetings of the United States. In a prepared speech he applauded the promotion of institutions in France which had proven so satisfactory to the people of the United States. But lest there be any objection to his friendly demonstration, he reiterated his government's traditional policy of nonintervention in the domestic affairs of other peoples. In this instance, the French people had made their choice. Was it not natural for the sister republic to acclaim the wisdom of their choice?

A member of the provisional government made an eloquent reply. Thanking Rush for his moral support, he frankly admitted that France had expected it from its ancient ally. Dramatically symbolizing the union of the two republics, President Jacques Dupont de l'Eure then

Republican Diplomat, 1780-1859 (Philadelphia, 1942), pp. 257-59. The first news about the revolution caused a panic at the New York Stock Exchange. Confidence returned with the expectation that the troubles in Europe would induce Europeans either to immigrate to the United States or to buy American stocks. *Courrier des États-Unis* (New York), March 25, 1848.

15. Gilbert Chinard, "Comment l'Amérique reconnut la République de 1848," *French-American Review*, I (1948), 86-89.

16. Rush to Buchanan, Paris, March 4, 1848. *DDFDS*, XXXI; see also G. T. Poussin, *Les États-Unis d'Amérique* (Paris, 1874), pp. 169-70.

grasped Rush's hand and exclaimed: "The French people holds the hand of the American nation." Outside the building the guard presented arms and the people on the streets burst into an ovation: *"Vive la République des États-Unis!"*

In the cause of republicanism, Rush had courageously taken a chance which departed from diplomatic usage. Would his government understand his prompt action? For almost two months this question preoccupied his mind. He felt greatly relieved when President James K. Polk and Secretary of State James Buchanan approved his "judicious speech." The Polk administration followed precedent, at least in so far as the United States had always recognized *de facto* governments. It was also realistic policy and perhaps good business to support republicanism abroad. The recent territorial acquisitions of the United States had yet to be consolidated before they were safe from delayed European intervention. Under such circumstances the young republic of France was less likely to join a royalist coalition of Britain and Spain against the United States than a French monarchy. It needed peace to solidify its very existence.

In an unprecedented move, the Senate dispensed with its agenda on the sixth of April and unanimously adopted a resolution "tendering the congratulations of the American to the French people."[17] Four days later the House moved by a vote of 174 to 2 that the President have this joint resolution presented to the French government. When Rush transmitted these felicitations, Lamartine once again paid high tribute to the United States whose "wise counsels serve in advance as a law to the French Republic."[18] Touched by this gesture of Congress, the French Assembly decided on the extraordinary form of a decree to express its gratitude.

III

Many Americans took pride in the fact that the French copied their system of universal suffrage. Senator Stephen A. Douglas of Illinois proudly declared that republicans throughout the world fixed their eyes upon the American model. "Our success," he said, "is the foundation of all their hopes. Shall we, then, turn a deaf ear . . . to France?"[19] Speaking in support of the new republic, Senator Daniel S. Dickinson of New York credited France with having gone a step

17. *Cong. Globe*, 30 Cong., 1 sess., p. 592.
18. Quoted in R. Rush, *Recollections of a Residence at the English and French Courts* (London, 1872), p. 485. For an interesting recent article on Lamartine, see G. Wright, "A Poet in Politics: Lamartine and the Revolution of 1848," *History Today*, VIII (1958), 616-27.
19. *Cong. Globe*, 30 Cong., 1 sess., pp. 568-69 (March 30, 1848).

beyond the American contribution to government. America demonstrated that man was capable of self-government; France, he contended, showed that a powerful monarchy may be destroyed by the sheer force of public opinion. Certainly this was an important lesson to monarchs and oppressed peoples alike.[20]

Manifestations of solidarity with free France multiplied all over the United States. The New York *Herald* urged active assistance to the French republic in case it should be attacked by the monarchical armies of Europe.[21] The Democratic National Convention adopted congratulatory resolutions.[22] At a mass meeting in New York a resolution was passed "to tender our ardent desire for Reciprocal Citizenship."[23] The future looked brighter to Americans who, like Horace Greeley,[24] interpreted the French revolution as a preliminary to a European Federation and, perhaps, a Universal Republic. Such enthusiasm led the poet James Russell Lowell to dedicate an *Ode to France*:

> And down the happy future runs a flood
> Of prophesying light;
> It shows an Earth no longer stained with blood,
> Blossom and fruit where now we see the bud
> Of Brotherhood and Right.

The optimism of the many was tempered by the skepticism of the few. Doubt about the French people's capacity to govern themselves could be found among New Englanders as well as Southerners. The *North American Review*, the *National Intelligencer*, and the *Southern Quarterly Review*, for instance, voiced the opinion of the minority which saw too many obstacles to the construction of an enduring republic in France.[25] France lacked historical foundations for a federal system, which these journals regarded as an essential condition for an effective constitution. They also took exception to the excessive self-

20. *Ibid.*, p. 456 (April 6, 1848).

21. March 22, 1848.

22. Curtis, *French Assembly*, p. 96. The Whigs deemed it politic not to draft a platform in 1848.

23. Forest to Lamartine, New York, April 4, 1848. *CPCEU*, II. The Philadelphia *Pennsylvania Inquirer* reported about other meetings in its issues of March 23 and April 25, 1848. At a meeting in St. Louis the resolution was adopted: ". . . the kings and despots of Europe who deny our brethren the enjoyment of self-government . . . are enemies of the human race." *The Daily Picayune* (New Orleans), April 12, 1848.

24. G. G. Van Deusen, *Horace Greeley: Nineteenth Century Crusader* (Philadelphia, 1953), pp. 106-7.

25. See Merle E. Curti, "The Impact of the Revolutions of 1848 on American Thought," *Proceedings of the American Philosophical Society*, XCIII (1949), 210.

confidence of the French people and the revolutionary origin of the republic. New England intellectuals, like Edward Everett and George Ticknor, privately feared that "the revolution will prove no boon for France or Europe."[26] Ticknor was not only convinced that the French were incapable and too inexperienced to exercise political power wisely but that the republican experiment might in time reduce France to "what Asia Minor and Egypt are now."[27] Such statesmen as Daniel Webster and Charles Sumner and the well known broker John E. Thayer condemned the "kingless monarchy" as the creation of communists and anarchists.[28] While many Southerners saw no reason to hail a republic which as one of its first acts emancipated the slaves in the French colonies,[29] John C. Calhoun penetrated the immediate French problem with amazing foresight. His analysis of the recent developments led him to the conclusion: "They have decreed a republic, but it remains for them to establish one."[30]

Stormy days did indeed lie ahead for the Second Republic. The April election of the Constituent Assembly disappointed the "social" republicans of Louis Blanc. The voting public clearly indicated that it was in no mood for socialist experiments. Concluding that the political revolution of February would not really bring about the social improvements they desired as much as political rights, the radical workers of Paris decided to take matters into their own hands. As a result, Paris witnessed in May and June a violent class war which led to the virtual dictatorship of General Louis Cavaignac. It was not until this insurrection had been brought under control that the bourgeois majority in the Constituent Assembly could proceed with the drafting of a constitution. These turbulent "June Days" had frightened the people and did not augur well for the future of the Second Republic.

26. Everett to Lady Ashburton, Cambridge, Mass., March 23, 1848. Everett Papers.
27. George Ticknor, *Life, Letters and Journals* (Boston, 1876), II, 234-36.
28. E. L. Pierce, ed., *Memoirs and Letters of Charles Sumner* (Boston, 1893), III, 37, 75. See also Elizabeth B. White, *American Opinion of France from Lafayette to Poincaré* (New York, 1927), p. 123; and John G. Gazley, *American Opinion of German Unification, 1848-1871* (New York, 1926), p. 247. Chapter VII of this study is devoted to American opinion of France.
29. Jean Dautry, *Histoire de la Révolution de 1848* (Paris, 1948), pp. 109-10. This emancipation ranked among the few lasting achievements of the revolution. Charles Pouthas, *Les révolutions de 1848 en Europe* (Paris, 1952), p. 72.
30. Gazley, p. 236. Calhoun believed that the Germans "have far better material to construct and maintain constitutional governments than France or any other European country." Merle E. Curti, "John C. Calhoun and the Unification of Germany," *AHR*, XL (1935), 476-78.

IV

The makers of the new constitution listened to much well-intentioned American advice. Secretary of State Buchanan expected Rush, a member of the bar and former Attorney-General of the United States, as well as an experienced diplomat, to impart valuable information to them. The history of France had clearly taught American statesmen that a central republican government would not guarantee constitutional liberties. In the past, a revolution in Paris had always decided the fate of France. Unless state governments were established this time, Buchanan questioned the survival of the Second Republic.[31]

Believing that federalism was the answer to French needs, Rush busily circulated information about the federal system of the United States. He sent his copy of The Federalist to the distinguished French economist Michel Chevalier, who publicized its leading doctrines in the French press. Whenever the opportunity presented itself, Rush conversed with the members of the constitution-making committee.[32] Several other prominent Americans also attempted to influence the drafting of the French constitution. George Bancroft, then minister to England, spent Easter of 1848 in Paris to prevail upon prominent Frenchmen to adopt a bicameral and federal system.[33] From New England, Edward Everett pleaded with his friend Tocqueville that without the adoption of these two principles the republic would be short-lived.[34] Editions of the American Constitution enjoyed a wide circulation in France. Consul Robert Walsh and French journalists interpreted its meaning to the public.[35] That Catholic leaders praised its religious benefits made it acceptable to the Catholic masses.

However, when the constitutional debate ended, habit and tradition prevailed over reason and experience. France had for too long been disposed to centralization to depart from it now. Much objection was voiced to the imitation of alien institutions. Lamartine, who

31. Buchanan to Rush, Washington, D. C., March 31, 1848. FIDS, XV.

32. Although Adolphe Crémieux, the Minister of Justice, Lamartine, and Tocqueville tried to familiarize themselves with all aspects of the American Constitution, the provisional government did not wish to be assisted in its deliberations by a group of legal experts from the United States. M. A. DeWolfe Howe, The Life and Letters of George Bancroft (New York, 1908), I, 91; see also Victor Pierre, Histoire de la République de 1848 (Paris, 1873), I, 479.

33. Eddie W. Schodt, "American Policy and Practice with Respect to European Liberal Movements, 1848-1853" (Ph.D. dissertation, University of Colorado, 1952), p. 77.

34. Everett to Tocqueville, Cambridge, Mass., May 12, 1849. Everett Papers.

35. Robert Walsh, Notes on the American Constitution (Keeseville, N. Y., 1849). See also G. Chinard, "L'Amérique et la Révolution de 1848," French-American Review, I (1948), 265-68.

favored one chamber, rested his argument on the difference that France possessed neither an aristocracy like England nor a federation like the United States.[36] In an address before the National Assembly, Félix Pyat successfully defended the troublesome doctrine of the omnipotence of the legislative body. He argued that the danger of a strong president in France was inverse to that in the United States. The American federal system required a powerful president. The centralized system of France, on the contrary, would be best served by a president with very limited powers.[37] While the final draft of the constitution established neither a federal nor a bicameral system, it provided for a bill of rights, universal suffrage, and the popular election of a president with relatively strong executive power.

V

If its structure, dissensions, and disorders weakened the Second Republic from within, its recognition abroad also produced uncertainties. The royalist loyalties of French diplomats rendered the conduct of the Republic's foreign policy especially difficult. Louis Philippe's ambassador in Washington typified this attitude when he made the vain attempt to enjoin the French Consular Corps in the United States to consider the proclamation of the Republic as null and void.[38] His replacement by Guillaume Tell Poussin became necessary and was meant to be a truly friendly gesture to the United States, where Poussin had previously served as an officer in the Corps of Engineers. However, enthusiastic French talk of "the union of our two nations"[39] sounded more intriguing than it was practical. It is more than doubtful that the bonds of republicanism would have been strong enough to correlate the foreign policies of the two republics.

Rush's prompt recognition of the Second Republic caused considerable surprise in some diplomatic quarters, consternation and opposition in others. As a matter of courtesy, Rush paid Lord Normanby a visit on February 27. The British ambassador had little hope of dissuading his American colleague from taking the unheard of step of "an individual without credentials to present himself officially to

36. Lamartine made this comment in a speech before the National Assembly on September 27, 1848.

37. *Moniteur*, September 6, 1848. For arguments in opposition to Pyat's position see Édouard Laboulaye, *De la constitution américaine* (Paris, 1850), p. 22. The legitimist *Gazette de France* warned in its issues of March 6 and June 1, 1848, against attempts to imitate foreign constitutions.

38. Forest to Lamartine, New York, April 4, 1848. *CCC New York*, XIV. See also A. de Tocqueville, *Souvenirs* (Paris, 1893), pp. 360-61.

39. Bastide to Polk, Paris, July 10, 1848. *FNTDS*, XIII.

a government which had opened no communications with his own."[40] Although he thought that Rush had already committed himself to recognize the Republic, Normanby played for some delay by suggesting a concerted move by the diplomatic corps. By the time Rush returned to the American legation, he found Lamartine's official announcement about the formation of the provisional government. The legalistic argument against recognition had thus been removed.

It strengthened Rush's lone position that the ministers from Argentine and Uruguay followed his advice by recognizing the new government one day after he had done so. On March 1, the papal nuncio followed suit with a public letter to Lamartine which amounted to recognition. It would be unwarranted, though, to exaggerate the significance of Rush's diplomatic move. Unquestionably it encouraged an insecure government. But it also antagonized several European courts which the provisional government anxiously tried to conciliate.[41] How else can one explain Lamartine's omission of any reference to American recognition in his report to the National Assembly? Could he not afford the friendship of a republican power too far away to intervene promptly in case of international complications? Or did he studiously avoid mentioning the United States in compliance with the intimated wishes of the British Cabinet?[42] Few French publications allude to Rush's role in the Revolution of 1848. It is especially noteworthy that even Lamartine ignores it in his historical writings about the revolution.

If Lamartine received American support with mixed feelings, neither was it given without some concern about its implications. President Polk commented in his *Diary* that there will be either a general war or all European sovereigns must grant more liberal institutions.[43] His Secretary of State hoped that the monarchies of Europe would not commence hostilities against France merely because it had established a republic. Still, timely counsel to avoid war seemed to be more prudent from the American point of view than to be faced with the embarrassing eventuality of becoming involved in

40. C. H. P. Normanby, *A Year of Revolution* (London, 1857), pp. 130 ff.

41. Rush's bold act exposed his colleagues at such courts as Berlin and St. Petersburg to unusual suspicions. It was also reported that as a precautionary measure the Prussian police was ordered to be on guard against American students at the universities. A. J. Donelson to Polk, Berlin, March 13, 1848. Polk Papers.

42. Henry Wikoff, "My First Week in Paris," *Democratic Review* (September, 1849), pp. 211-14; see also Donald G. Mitchell, *The Battle Summer: Being Transcripts from Personal Observations in Paris during the Year 1848* (New York, 1850), pp. 117-18.

43. M. M. Quaife, ed., *The Diary of James K. Polk* (Chicago, 1910), III, 414.

one. Polk had no intention of entering into an alliance against monarchism and cautioned Governor-General Cavaignac "to act with forbearance and magnanimity towards other nations."[44] As if to warn France not to expect the active participation of the United States in a war against the European monarchs, the Secretary of State too stressed the need for peace to preserve the young republic.

Convinced that any French aggression would inevitably lead to an overwhelming coalition against it, Lamartine issued on March 7 a reassuring manifesto: "Different forms of government can live side by side, understanding and respecting each other. They are the expression of different degrees of maturity of the genius of people."[45] Most important was his declaration that the Second Republic intended to seek peaceful modifications of the treaties of 1815. This moderation gained French leaders the respect of England. On the day Rush recognized the provisional government, Lord Normanby gave it to understand that peace in Europe and stability at home would be Britain's price of recognition. Lord Palmerston was greatly interested in peace, and he convinced himself that Lamartine offered the best guaranties for it. Accordingly, he invited the major continental powers to assure Paris that there would be peace as long as France did not break it. Although the British detested republics, they did not wish to witness a repetition of 1792.[46] On August 19, General Cavaignac received the British ambassador for the first time since the revolution. From then on, the fear of a general war diminished.

VI

The wisdom of this peaceful approach was not shared by all. Such a radical political leader as Alexandre Ledru-Rollin, for instance, would have preferred a republican crusade against the monarchies of Europe. He wanted to destroy the system of 1815 and replace it with the United States of Europe.[47] Such a course would also have appealed to American crusaders like Charles A. Dana who believed that "a war between liberty and despotism is inevitable."[48] He, like

44. Polk to Cavaignac, Washington, D. C., August 17, 1848. *CFSUS*. See also *Courrier des États-Unis* (New York), March 21, 1848.

45. A. de Lamartine, *Histoire de la Révolution de 1848* (Paris, 1849), II, 23-41; see also Louis Blanc, *Histoire de la Révolution de 1848* (Paris, 1870), I, 230-43.

46. E. de Guichen, *Les grandes questions européennes et la diplomatie des puissances sous la seconde république française* (Paris, 1925), I, 52-55; Donald M. Greer, *L'Angleterre, la France et la Révolution de 1848* (Paris, 1925), pp. 213-14.

47. Alvin Calman, *Ledru-Rollin and the Second French Republic* (New York, 1922), p. 414.

48. J. H. Wilson, *The Life of Charles A. Dana* (New York, 1907), p. 82.

others, confidently expected this last and momentous war to bring lasting peace.

The Second Republic can hardly be blamed for having shied away from the risks of war. The outcome of a military crusade against the monarchical systems of Europe was unpredictable. However, it could have chosen the alternative of becoming the militant leader of Europe's republican movement. That it did not grasp this opportunity turned out to be a failure of historic consequence. *The United States Democratic Review,* a literary and political magazine devoted to the vigorous propagation of democratic ideals, observed very keenly in December of 1852 that "France's only salvation is in becoming the head of the liberal cause in Europe."[49] Not understanding this, it went on, the future of France could be only one of illusory greatness.

The United States minister at Berlin somewhat deflated the oversimplified notion that France could conquer the world without a fight, merely by promoting republican ideas. Political liberalism and nationalism were not only related but also distinct manifestations of the age. He reported that even liberal Germans were repelled by the idea of fraternization with the French. Their nationalism superseded their republican sentiments.[50]

Experience taught the United States that economic interests, too, are not necessarily benefited by the common institutional interests of nations. One of Secretary Buchanan's first reactions to the proclamation of the Second Republic was similar to Martin Van Buren's following the July Revolution of 1830, namely, to explore the possibility of a favorable trade treaty.[51] The French consul general at New York had the same idea.[52] He suggested that his government capitalize on the friendly disposition of the United States by trying to secure various tariff reductions. The chances for such revisions were slim indeed. Jealously protecting American economic interests, Congress was not in the habit of being swayed by political sympathies. In France, General Cavaignac's precarious position did not permit him to act, and the composition of the legislature did not warrant any optimism. Its many property owners and industrialists regarded

49. *U. S. Democratic Review,* XXXI (1852), 600.

50. Donelson to Polk, Berlin, March 18, 1848. Polk Papers. Ardent French republicans believed in the United States of Europe under French leadership. Henri Delassus, *Le problème de l'heure présente* (Lille, 1904), I, 258-60.

51. Van Buren to Rives, Washington, D. C., November 8, 1830. *FIDS,* XIV. Buchanan to Rush, Washington, D. C., March 31, 1848. *FIDS,* XV. See also, Curtis, *French Assembly,* p. 92.

52. Simounet to Bastide, New York, August 30, 1848. *CCC New York,* XIV.

protection as a necessity. They succeeded in persuading the extreme left that free trade would inevitably lead to a lowering of wages. Neither did the socialist theories of Louis Blanc and his followers hold out the promise of the triumph of liberal economic principles.[53] The form of government had changed, but the substance of France's foreign trade policy remained unchanged.

VII

The meaning of revolutions usually changes with their rhythm and the passing of time. Because Americans were primarily interested in the triumph of republican institutions, they hailed the birth of the Second Republic as a welcome political event. For a long time, even Frenchmen interpreted the Revolution of 1848 in political terms. The historians Victor Pierre and Pierre de La Gorce, for example, saw in it a phase in the struggle of the French middle class for increased political power.

Certainly the revolution endeavored to advance the constitutional liberties of the people. Lamartine made the significant suggestion that the French army and people also hoped that it would be instrumental in restoring their country's position of leadership on the continent of Europe.[54] It is now generally accepted that the meaning of the Revolution of 1848 is more accurately interpreted in social rather than in military or political terms.[55] At least some contemporary Americans recognized the underlying social character of the recent revolutionary events. Charles A. Dana compared them with the Revolution of 1789 which had destroyed feudalism. In the summer of 1848 he saw in them an attempt "to destroy the moneyed feudalism and lay the foundations of social liberty."[56] Comparing the Revolution of 1830 with that of 1848, George Ticknor ventured to comment that the first gave political power to the middle class, the last "gives it to the working class." Although he erred in making this prediction on April 5, he emphatically asserted that "this is a social revolution."[57]

Without the correct diagnosis of the nature of such a major event as this revolution, contemporaries could neither intelligently follow

53. Octave Noël, *Histoire du commerce du monde* (Paris, 1906), III, 116; see also Powell, p. 268.

54. Lamartine, II, 21-22.

55. Paul Farmer, "Some Frenchmen Review 1848," *Journal of Modern History,* XI (1948), 321. See also André Maurois, *A History of France* (New York, 1956), p. 405.

56. Curti, "The Impact of the Revolutions of 1848," p. 210.

57. Ticknor, II, 230-32.

its course nor evaluate its consequences. A narrow political interpretation could not but result in political disappointments. For the failure of the republican movement in France in the mid-nineteenth century was due less to rational rejection of republican principles than to material conflicts. Neither the socialists nor the great majority of bourgeois, peasants, and workers favored political emancipation divorced from economic security. Moreover, each of these groups interpreted the meaning of security to suit its particular needs. To reconcile the divergent economic views proved to be too great a challenge to a people that had, in André Siegfried's words, "its heart to the left and the pocketbook to the right." The middle class would join forces with the proletariat to broaden the popular basis of government. But the socialist insurrections shook the faith in the Second Republic at home and abroad. The boldness of the socialists brought into existence a powerful conservative reaction of the bourgeois and peasant interests.[58] By taking an unequivocal position against socialism as being incompatible with Catholicism, the Church threw its weight into the scale of the conservative reaction. And once the struggle against the threat of economic radicalism had begun, conservative Catholics felt encouraged to fight political ultraism as well. The Catholic Church thus played a decisive role in the rise and fall of the French Republic.[59]

With respect to republican institutions, Catholics changed their opinion from hopeful acceptance in 1848 to outright rejection by 1852. They regarded the form of government as a matter of opinion rather than faith. Abbé Morel gave as valid a reason as any for the growing contempt for the republican assembly when he labeled it "a school of anarchy."[60] As one of Louis Philippe's ministers, Achille de Broglie's comments would be suspect. Still, he accused the omnipotent republican legislature of having done nothing, tried nothing, known nothing.[61] The *North American Review* was less charitable in its judgment. It lashed out mercilessly against the abstract political theorists and visionary orators. "Wholly devoid of practical talent," such doctrinaires as Lamartine and Blanc "had no business" to assume

58. A. Dansette, *Explication de la Deuxième République* (Paris, 1942), p. 69. See also Albert Guérard, *Beyond Hatred: The Democratic Ideal in France and America* (New York, 1925), p. 36; and Donald C. McKay, *The National Workshops: A Study in the French Revolution of 1848* (Cambridge, Mass., 1933), p. 3.

59. R. W. Collins, "Catholicism and the Second French Republic, 1848-1852" (Ph.D. dissertation, Columbia University, 1923), p. 106.

60. *Ibid.*, pp. 47-51, 327; see also *Catholic Magazine*, VII (1848), 218-19.

61. Albert de Broglie, "1852 et la révision de la constitution," *RDDM* (May 15, 1851), p. 607.

the leadership of the government. They discredited themselves as well as the cause they aspired to further. Their timidity and indecision disgusted advocates of free government as much as the performance of the French Assembly. The *Review* questioned the very capacity of "this noisy debating club to transact business with efficiency and despatch." Little hope could be held out for the success of the republican experiment in a country where exaggerated notions of liberty degenerated it into license.[62]

Conditions in France differed so much from those in the United States that American ideas of republicanism could not be transplanted to foreign soil with guaranties of survival. Although exceptions might be cited to challenge the validity of generalizations, certain characteristics distinguished the two nations. Monarchical traditions had left their mark on the institutions and genius of the French people, as the ways of democracy had become the habit with Americans. The manifest indifference of the French with respect to the duration of their Constitution was matched by outright American reverence for theirs. It made a great difference, moreover, that the French conceived liberty as an abstract idea, whereas Americans practiced it as a living reality. Furthermore, group particularism frustrated French society as much as respect for individual liberty vitalized the American community. And significantly, Americans stressed individual initiative in contrast to French preference for governmental paternalism.[63]

The combination of structural weaknesses, inept leadership, economic conflicts, and sociological inadequacies shook the young republic to its foundations. It had come to a people that was unprepared for it. It is even doubtful that a majority of Frenchmen wanted it. The view merits attention that, while the July Revolution was the victory of the press, that of 1848 was the victory of journalism.[64] In the first case, it issued from a popular movement; in the other, it was the result of a journalistic struggle. When many Frenchmen realized

62. Unsigned article, "French Ideas of Democracy and a Community of Goods," *NAR* (October, 1849), pp. 282-84. See also Roger Soltau, *French Political Thought in the Nineteenth Century* (New Haven, 1931), p. 118; and Leo Gershoy, "Three French Historians and the Revolution of 1848," *Journal of the History of Ideas* (January, 1951), pp. 131-46.

63. Emilio Castelar, "The Republican Movement in Europe," *Harper's New Monthly Magazine* (June-November, 1872), p. 52; Henri Cauvin, "La France est monarchique," *Constitutionel*, December 5, 1852. Senator Underwood of Kentucky commented on the instability of French constitutions. *Cong. Globe*, 32 Cong., 2 sess., p. 142 (December 23, 1852).

64. A. Cuvillier-Fleury, *Portraits politiques et révolutionnaires* (Paris, 1852), I, 71. See also *La Presse*, February 26, 1853.

that "they had made a revolution by mistake,"[65] France was mentally prepared to welcome a Bonaparte. Weary and disillusioned, it longed for a leader to give it order, stability, and military glory.

VIII

The election of Prince Louis Napoleon to the presidency of the Second Republic prompted the question: what kind of republican will the nephew of Emperor Napoleon Bonaparte make? In September of 1849, a special agent of the United States gave Secretary of State John M. Clayton this answer: "The President of France is influenced exclusively . . . by an inordinate solicitude to re-establish the Imperial Throne."[66] Finding that France had voted "like a drunken man," Dana did not doubt that "Napoleon would rather be Emperor than President."[67] Other Americans presumed quite accurately that Louis Napoleon would move towards uncontrolled executive power as rapidly as the public would permit.[68]

The Taylor administration had been conscious of the new trend in French politics. Frequently, a change of policy is accompanied by a change of personalities. In this instance, the course of events compelled the recall of an American minister who had weathered too many political storms during too short a time. Richard Rush represented the United States during the last weeks of the constitutional monarchy. He had taken a conspicuous part when the barricaded provisional government set up a republic. He was held in esteem by General Cavaignac. He witnessed the popular election of Louis Napoleon, whom he personally disliked and politically mistrusted.[69] And he tried to adjust his relations with the even greater turnover of foreign ministers.

When a Bonaparte directed the affairs of France, Washington deemed it advisable to be represented by a new envoy. It sent the Virginian statesman William C. Rives to Paris, an American diplomat who mastered the fashionable art of political double-talk practiced by the "Imperial Republic." The United States, he assured the Prince-President, wholeheartedly supported "the consolidation of her [France's] liberties upon the sure basis of order, religion, and respect for the law."[70] Unless his animosity toward his predecessor betrayed

65. NAR (October, 1849), p. 304.
66. Senate Doc., 61 Cong., 2 sess., No. 279 (Mann to Clayton).
67. Wilson, pp. 86-87.
68. Everett to Tocqueville, Cambridge, Mass., January 8, 1850. Everett Papers.
69. Powell, p. 269.
70. Rives to Clayton, Paris, November 14, 1849. DDFDS, XXXII. The British

the kind of prejudice that blinds judgment, Rives's faith in Louis Napoleon's good will contrasted sharply with what he described as the "extraordinary hallucination of Mr. Rush that there is a hostile feeling here toward us."[71]   Outwardly, President Louis Napoleon went out of his way to play up to the republican sentiments of both nations.   When, for instance, he settled a minor incident with the United States, he pointedly adverted to "susceptibilities, natural perhaps towards a monarchy, . . . but not an elder republic."

Rush returned to Washington, bitterly interpreting his recall as a disavowal of bold republicanism.   It was not long before Poussin returned to Paris, having made himself persona non grata in the United States as a result of an undiplomatic incident.[72]   It is quite likely, though, that the French president would in any case have replaced this republican diplomat with one more congenial to him.   When Poussin talked to him about close ties between the two republics, he had only a yawn for him.

The prince had his own reasons for keeping on good terms with Washington.   When the moment arrived for him to change the constitutional system of France, he wanted the United States to accept those changes at worst with reluctance rather than with defiance.   It might be difficult enough to face the reactions of a Europe that would distrust the creation of another Napoleonic empire.   He had to anticipate, moreover, unfriendly reactions from royalists and republicans at home.   The change in France came sooner than the American government expected.   Napoleon Bonaparte succeeded by the coup d'état of December, 1851, in securing his presidency for ten years.   Exactly one year later he re-established the empire.   Both times he had the audacity—or the political shrewdness—to submit his accomplished usurpations to the approval of the French people.   His name, associated with the glory of France, had an overwhelming appeal.   The coup d'état was sanctioned by 7,439,216 Frenchmen.   An even greater number voted in favor of the empire.[73]

Within the short period of five years France shifted from a kingdom to an empire via the brief interlude of a republic.   How did these spectacular institutional developments affect Franco-American relations?   Official America followed the turn of events with en-

welcomed Louis Napoleon because they expected him to bring stability to France. Franklin C. Palm, *England and Napoleon III* (Durham, N. C., 1948), pp. 151-52.

71. Rives to Clayton, Paris, January 9, 1850.   Clayton Papers, VIII.

72. For the details of this incident see chapter III.

73. Rives to Webster, Paris, January 1, 1852.   DDFDS, XXXIII.   Rives to Everett, Paris, December 1, 1852.   DDFDS, XXXIV.

thusiasm in 1848, disappointment in 1851, and resignation in 1852. In Paris, Rives protested against the measures of the coup d'état by which "the fundamental guaranties of civil and political liberty had been trodden under foot." His protest took the conspicuous form of abstention from the weekly receptions of the president. Some of his critical countrymen would have preferred, instead, his demonstrative departure.[74] This, Rives felt, would have been both an unauthorized and unwise move. On the contrary, once the French people had given its stamp of approval to the recent change, he accepted the formal invitation to the New Year's reception of the diplomatic corps. On this occasion, going down the line of the assembled diplomats, Louis Napoleon asked Rives whether he had heard from Washington since the recent developments in France. This was, of course, technically impossible. He then expressed the hope that the friendly relations between the two countries would not be interrupted.[75]

Inasmuch as in a letter to President Millard Fillmore the president of France pledged himself "honor bound to preserve the peace and to draw closer to the ancient friend and ally,"[76] it mattered little that he claimed to have saved his country from anarchy. Naturally, the Fillmore administration would have preferred to see France make a success of its republican experiment. But it understood that "the same organic laws are not calculated to secure the happiness of every nation."[77] Secretary of State Daniel Webster deplored the fact that the developments in France might weaken the faith of mankind in the solidity of popular institutions,[78] an opinion echoed by many members of Congress. But what could the United States do in view of the fact that the French nation ratified the changes in its organic law? When Emperor Napoleon III ascended the throne "by the Grace of Divine Providence," the United States faced the facts and recognized the new regime. It remained for the future to test the sincerity of the Emperor's renewed professions of friendship.

French newspapers and diplomats did their best to convey the impression that, with the exception of communists and socialists, the American people received the new order with joy. The French minister to the United States, Eugène de Sartiges, noticed a widespread and growing respect for his master. He appreciated particularly the

---

74. *National Intelligencer* (Washington, D. C.), January 7, 1852.
75. Rives to Webster, Paris, January 1, 1852. *DDFDS*, XXXIII.
76. Louis Napoleon to President Fillmore, Paris, January 12, 1852. *CLFUS*.
77. President Fillmore to Louis Napoleon, Washington, D. C., February 16, 1852. *CFSUS*.
78. Webster to Rives, Washington, D. C., January 12, 1852. *FIDS*, XV.

prayers of the bishops and archbishops for the success of Napoleon's undertakings. The Catholic Church in the United States sincerely believed that Napoleon's providential mission had saved France and Europe from atheistic socialism and anarchy. Sartiges was also gratified by the fact that independent American observers were perfectly willing to view the French scene dispassionately and fairly.[79] The New Orleans *Picayune*[80] expressed the voice of common sense when it pleaded for the recognition of Napoleon's government on the ground that it constituted the French government.

Those Americans who predicted in 1848 that mob government would make Paris the tomb rather than the temple of freedom were obviously not surprised by the unfolding of the recent events. Bitterly disappointed that the sacred republican cause had again been betrayed by a Napoleon, ardent believers in this cause doubted that the "fraudulent edifice of the unscrupulous dictator's empire would last long."[81] The Philadelphia *Inquirer*,[82] for instance, did not believe that "an adventurer who has violated every law, human and divine, will be permitted for any considerable time, to wear the Imperial purple." His fall, it ventured to predict, would be as sudden as his rise had been remarkable. Faith in the ultimate victory of popular government, even in France, did not die. The *United States Democratic Review* suggested the remedy: the French people must work for liberty with patient and earnest endeavor instead of gambling for it.[83] These opinions were supplemented by a demand from the Industrial Congress of the City of New York for the severance of diplomatic and commercial relations with France. However, when Senator Isaac P. Walker of Wisconsin introduced this memorial, the Senate tabled it by a vote of 21 to 14.[84]

The extent of the American disillusionment cannot be estimated for an age in which opinion polls were not yet developed. Indications are that it was widespread throughout the United States. The faith of Americans in the virtues of democracy made it rather difficult for them to understand the authoritarian regime of Napoleon III. They

---

79. Sartiges to Turgot, Washington, D. C., May 23, 1852. *CPEU*, CVII. Sartiges to Drouyn de Lhuys, Washington, D. C., December 26, 1852. *CPEU*, CVIII.

80. January 13, 1852.

81. White, pp. 130 ff.; Wilson, pp. 77, 398; James Schouler, *History of the United States of America* (New York, 1891), V, 237.

82. December 17, 1851.

83. Unsigned article, "Absolutism versus Republicanism: The State of Europe," *U. S. Democratic Review*, XXXI (1852), 599.

84. *Cong. Globe*, 32 Cong., 1 sess., p. 181 (January 2, 1852). See also Ben Price to Rives, New York, January 12, 1852. Rives Papers.

were not impressed by a civil order without liberty. They were, in fact, bewildered by the regime's political hypocrisy and infuriated by its ruthlessness. Imperial France offered to Americans the spectacle of a country in which the parliament, though elected by universal suffrage, was entrusted with little responsibility and exercised even less authority. It was no secret to them that the supposedly "liberal" Emperor imprisoned republican leaders and drove others into exile, persecuted those who criticized him, muzzled the press, violated academic freedom, and ousted university professors who courageously opposed him. The relaxation of these measures in 1859, a time of growing crisis both in Europe and in the United States, came too late to have any noticeable effect on American public opinion. Nor did Napoleon's social and economic accomplishments lead to a general revision of the American attitude toward him. The Emperor, after all, did try to govern in the interests of the poor and the workers, as well as of the peasants, merchants, and manufacturers. French capital and labor benefited from the expansion and modernization of industry, the rapid construction of railroads, the improvement of all means of transportation, the adoption of a liberal tariff policy, and the phenomenal growth of France's foreign commerce. The splendor of the imperial court and the gay life in the embellished French capital, moreover, created an atmosphere of social relaxation and made Paris once again a center of world-wide attraction. Few Americans appreciated these achievements. But while Napoleon continued to be the main target of frequently abusive attacks in the United States,[85] the American people never abandoned its respect for France and the French people.

At the same time, personal and anti-republican feelings of the imperial family were destined to develop Franco-American tensions in spite of outward control of such antipathies. Napoleon's and Eugénie's dislike of the American republic dated far back. Despite the hospitality which Louis Napoleon enjoyed during his sojourn in the United States in 1837, he returned to Europe with mixed feelings about the American way of life. And Empress Eugénie did not only harbor great resentment against the republic which had expanded at the expense of her native Spain; as a devout Catholic she was also concerned about the spread of Protestantism in the New World. Indeed, Napoleon and Eugénie feared the "spirit of encroachment

85. Prominent Americans referred to Napoleon III as "a born despot of the meaner order," "this weak and wicked potentate," or "an impudent scoundrel." While many continued to hold such views, others made a favorable reappraisal of the Emperor by the end of the 1850's. Gazley, pp. 265-71.

which distinguishes the American race."[86]   They were bewildered by the energetic drive of the American people which cast an ominous shadow on the existing order of the Western world. They were greatly disturbed by the emphasis on material values in American civilization. And they doubted that a country in which the social and cultural standards of the masses were dominant, while granting political rights to the individual, really provided the atmosphere in which the brilliant individual could develop himself to the highest level of his capacity. Applying the standards of an ancient civilization to the young American nation, they completely failed to understand the spirit that moved the society of pioneers in the New World. Napoleon and Eugénie were accustomed to think in terms of the glory of France, the desirability of a powerful state, special rights and privileges for a top layer of society, and the vital importance of the cultural and intellectual aspects of life. American concepts and practices conflicted too much with these ideas to be appreciated by the French rulers and many citizens of France. For Americans stressed the principle of social and political equality; they emphasized the welfare and power of the people; and necessity compelled them to think in utilitarian terms.

Occasional flattering comments about the American people notwithstanding, Eugénie's feelings about the "republican pretensions" of the United States were so deep that soon after the establishment of the Second Empire she exercised her influence to form a European league against it and, in the 1860's, to support the Emperor's scheming maneuvers in the Western Hemisphere. As far as Napoleon himself was concerned, his attitude towards the United States was also affected by the consideration that until he, a self-made emperor, demonstrated the superior benefits of his regime, the free and prospering American republic presented "a standing reproach to his usurpation."[87]

IX

The exigencies of political realities prompted the United States to do official business with the Second Empire. Many individual citizens, however, neither forgot nor forgave the French monarch for his deadly blow to free institutions. The supporters of the "Young America" movement, a group of militant democrats who advocated active intervention in behalf of European liberals, did not hide their contempt for

86. R. Sencourt, *Napoleon III: The Modern Emperor* (London, 1933), pp. 67, 269-77; see also R. Sencourt, *The Life of Empress Eugénie* (New York, 1931), p. 162; and Poussin, p. 400.

87. Buchanan to Marcy, London, October 26, 1855. *DDEDS,* LXVIII.

the emperor. A prosperous French republic would have made an ideal spearhead of republicanism in the midst of monarchical Europe. The rise of this new "despot" frustrated the international aspirations of "Young America," ever anxious to promote the spread of constitutional liberties beyond the seas.

The eager readiness of the United States to recognize and to encourage the revolutionary governments of the mid-nineteenth century earned it the reputation in conservative circles as the *enfant terrible*, against which European society must defend itself. These groups welcomed the establishment of the Second Empire as a bulwark against the infiltration of dangerous alien influences. To them, the challenge of American republicanism constituted a real threat. It was not just a topic for conversation. Had not Senator Douglas of Illinois publicly declared that the national interest of the United States might compel it to abandon its traditional neutrality in the conflicts of the Old World?[88] Political speculation had run wild ever since the Senator threatened with reference to the Hungarian revolution that "if Russia, Austria or any other country should intervene in Hungary, the United States would have to determine whether they should not act."[89] Sartiges was convinced that in 1852 the Democratic party planned "the overthrow of the conservative institutions of Europe in favor of a Universal Republic."[90] Some Frenchmen mistook the public utterances of prominent American citizens for indications of official policy. They knew that the spokesmen of "Young America" not only advocated a progressive foreign policy, but that they had also promised it to the revolutionary leaders of Europe. They were disquieted by the great interest the trans-Atlantic republic showed in the mid-nineteenth-century revolutions and by the verbal defiances it launched, particularly against Austria.[91] If the Taylor administration was suspected of being favorably disposed towards active intervention, its successor had even more reason to avenge the death of the Second Republic. The well known publicist and literary critic Émile Montégut sounded the warning signal when he asked Europe to be on guard not only against American propaganda but possible aggression as well.[92] The fear of a sudden American invasion reached such fan-

88. *Cong. Globe*, 32 Cong., 1 sess., pp. 70-71 (December 11, 1851).
89. Sartiges to Turgot, Washington, D. C., January 11, 1852. *CPEU*, CVII.
90. *Ibid.*, January 26, 1852.
91. Merle E. Curti, *Austria and the United States, 1848-1852* (Northampton, Mass., 1926), pp. 152-53, 201-2; see also *RDDM* (January 14, 1852), p. 391.
92. *RDDM* (February 1, 1853), p. 605.

tastic proportions that the republican *Charivari*[93] ridiculed those who imagined that secret American agents had already infiltrated key positions of the French empire.

Talk about the propagation of free institutions was one matter, physical support for it was another. It is noteworthy that the zealots in the opposing monarchistic and republican camps thought in terms of an eventual violent clash. Even moderate defenders of the republican cause realized the importance of physical as well as moral power to promote the progress of liberty in Europe. During the height of the revolutionary period, the American envoy to France urged the reinforcement of the Mediterranean squadron of the United States fleet "to lend moral weight for the republican principle."[94] Commodore Morgan, in command of the squadron, agreed that his force "is not altogether of the imposing character demanded by the unsettled state of the continent."[95] The total strength of the navy, however, did not permit more than a slight temporary increase of American ships in the Mediterranean. If the United States intended to play an active role in world affairs, its military and naval forces had to be considerably enlarged. It was for this reason that the American minister to The Hague pleaded for an early and effective strengthening of the navy. He was convinced that, sooner or later, self-preservation would compel his country to throw its full weight into the scale in defense of free institutions in Europe.[96]

In the meantime, George N. Sanders, a leading "Young American" from Kentucky, had offered some 144,000 old muskets to the Hungarian republicans.[97] Furthermore, the French ambassador at Madrid suspected his American colleague, Pierre Soulé, of planning to smuggle 100,000 guns into Spain in preparation for the alleged conspiracy to overthrow the Western monarchies.[98] Soulé, the temperamental republican who hated Napoleon III and his regime, had also

---

93. Consult issues of December 25, 1854, February 3 and October 19, 1853.

94. Rush to Buchanan, Paris, June 3 and 7, 1848. *DDFDS*, XXXI. See also John Reardon, "Evidences of Anti-Isolationism in American Foreign Policy, 1789-1850" (Ph.D. dissertation, Georgetown University, 1953), p. 151.

95. Commodore Morgan to Preston, flag ship *Independence*, September 24, 1849. *NDMSC*. See also Morgan to Hyatt, flag ship, November 25, 1849. *NDMSC*. Morgan to Rives, January 3, 1850. Rives Papers.

96. M. E. Curti, "Young America," *AHR* XXXII (1926), 53-54. Belmont to Sanders, The Hague, September 19, 1854. Sanders Papers.

97. Curti, "Young America," p. 41; Copans, p. 53. For a summary of Sanders' views and activities see M. E. Curti, "George Sanders—American Patriot of the Fifties," *South Atlantic Quarterly* (January, 1928), pp. 79-87.

98. A. A. Ettinger, *The Mission to Spain of Pierre Soulé* (New Haven, 1932), p. 322. Soulé, of French descent, had gained prominence as a senator from Louisiana.

economic and political weapons in his arsenal. According to Congressman Lemuel D. Evans of Texas, Soulé schemed to maneuver the United States into a war with France, Britain, and Spain over Cuba. The resulting interruption of American corn and cotton supplies, he calculated, would create social disturbances powerful enough to sweep the thrones of Europe into oblivion.[99]

Sanders and Soulé maintained contact with all the revolutionary leaders of the continent. Even James Buchanan, then Washington's representative at the Court of St. James's, joined these revolutionaries at a famous dinner party in London, drinking to "a future alliance of America with the federation of the free peoples of Europe."[100] Association with conspirators did not seem harmless to French monarchists, particularly when it was followed up with a call to violence. Although the Senate subsequently refused to confirm Sanders as consul at London, Sanders' circular letter of October 1854[101] could not but deepen suspicions against his government. In Paris it would have been unsafe to be caught in the possession of his inflammatory appeal to "strike against the tyrannical regime." Sanders' invitation to mutiny and revolution was as dramatic as it was conspiratorial. Speaking as a sympathetic friend, he urged Frenchmen to lose their apparent apathy and to regain their fighting spirit: "Hate Napoleon more and you will fear him less. Hate this conqueror of France in whose political slave camps thousands of distinguished Frenchmen suffer a corroding death of life in Africa and Cayenne. . . . Soldiers of France! Brave men of every land call upon you. . . . resist an order to mow down the helpless people. . . . Men of France! Strike once more for the Republic. Europe—America expects it of you. Strike! . . . America will ever welcome the men who fight for liberty."

The French Foreign Minister had for some time been unhappy about the demagogic interferences on the part of some American officials. Napoleon finally considered this whole matter important enough to allude to it in a private conversation with the American minister, John Y. Mason. He regretted the danger of hostility between the two countries "by circumstances trifling in themselves, but

99. J. Callahan, *Cuba and Its International Relations* (Baltimore, 1899), p. 260.

100. Basil Rauch, *American Interest in Cuba, 1848-1855* (New York, 1948), p. 283; see also Drouyn de Lhuys to Sartiges, Paris, August 24, 1854. *CPEU*, CXI.

101. A copy of this letter, dated October 4, 1854, is among the George N. Sanders Papers (Library of Congress). Victor Hugo congratulated Sanders and asked him to continue his noble mission. R. L. Hawkins, ed., *Newly Discovered French Letters of the Seventeenth, Eighteenth and Nineteenth Centuries* (Cambridge, Mass., 1933), pp. 182-84.

aggregately important."[102] The Emperor complained that the United States had sent many ministers and consuls abroad who interfered in European politics and were especially disposed against him. He mentioned specifically the American consul at Bern who contributed money to a newspaper which abused him. Worse yet, Soulé collaborated with revolutionaries who were seeking to assassinate him. Mason gave the standard reply that his government would never sanction such violation of the nonintervention principle. A similar assurance was made in Washington. There, the Secretary of State emphatically denied any intention of exporting political doctrines.[103]

But what should the Emperor's government think about such declarations when in later years American citizens still hurled insults and threats against Napoleon? In New York a demonstration was held to honor Orsini and Pierri, the two "noble martyrs" who had attempted to take the Emperor's life. The demonstrators vowed that "the day of reprisals is approaching."[104] And in the halls of Congress Representative Samuel S. Cox of Ohio said in 1859 this prayer of hatred:[105] "I pray with something of a Red Republican fervor, that France may have barricades on the Boulevards, the throne in flames . . . the dynasty he [Napoleon] seeks to perpetuate cut off, or flying from the rage of a Red Republic; . . . exiles returning from their home in pestilential swamps, . . . prisons breaking, the press free. . . . This would be a fit retribution from God for crimes and perjuries; and not at all unfit as a reward of an intermeddling policy with the republican interests of the New World!"

X

The ideological differences between Europe and the United States manifested themselves also in the Western Hemisphere. Conscious that the two continents were separated by free institutions even more than by the ocean, Washington watched with vigilance for any attempt to extend monarchical principles to the American continent.

Evidence abounds that French and British residents and officials exerted much influence to prejudice Latin Americans against republicanism and the United States. Napoleon III gave a new impetus to this policy which had already prevailed under his royal predecessors.

102. Mason to Marcy, Paris, October 29, 1854. *DDFDS*, XXXVI.

103. Sartiges to Drouyn de Lhuys, Washington, D. C., November 5, 1854. *CPEU*, CXI.

104. Sartiges to Walewski, Washington, D. C., April 27, 1858. *CPEU*, CXVIII. The New York *Times* of April 21, 1858, labeled this demonstration "a scandalous impertinence."

105. *Cong. Globe*, 35 Cong., 2 sess., p. 434 (January 18, 1859).

King Charles X, for instance, had given instructions to neutralize Washington's efforts to establish institutional conformity in the New World.[106] Ever since Louis Philippe's time French statesmen played with the idea of resuscitating the cause of monarchy in Mexico. According to a high Chilean official, who transmitted the information to the envoy of the United States in Chile, Napoleon III had monarchical designs for the various Central American states.[107] Sartiges had encouraged him in that direction when in 1854 General Rafael Carrera of Guatemala made himself president for life.[108]

In Chile and Peru monarchistic ideas had made such inroads with the help of French and British agents that the ministers of the United States employed much of their energy in an effort to check them.[109] Napoleon's chargé d'affaires in Ecuador displayed particular hostility against "the false apostles of the Universal Democracy" who preached fear of monarchies only to serve their own selfish interests.[110] This agent did not shrink from warning Ecuador against cooperation with the northern republic by asserting that after the Crimean War Napoleon would deal firmly with the Yankees. Washington was also not unaware of the Great Powers' game to enlist the aid of the Brazilian Empire for the purpose of setting up several petty South American monarchies. It counteracted such maneuvers by advising Brazil "that her true policy lies with us, and not with the old, inflated and corrupt monarchies of Europe."[111]

XI

When in 1845 war clouds gathered over Oregon, the Washington *Daily Globe* expressed the widely held conviction that the monarchies would not dare to make a war against the United States. "It would be the signal of a strife throughout Christendom of the old aristocracies with the millions."[112] According to this theory France and Britain feared the diffusing influence of its political axioms more than the territorial expansion of the United States.

So deep was the faith of Americans in the republican cause that they measured the progress of civilization by its advance. They at-

106. Charles X to Roux de Rochelle, St. Cloud, May 11, 1830. *CPEU*, LXXXIV.
107. Pollard to Forsyth, Santiago, April 10, 1859, in W. R. Manning, *Diplomatic Correspondence of the United States, Inter-American Affairs, 1831-1860* (Washington, D. C., 1932), V, 168-70.
108. Sartiges to Drouyn de Lhuys, Washington, D. C., April 9, 1854. *CPEU*, CX.
109. Manning, V, 241-46; X, 749-53.
110. Villamus to Drouyn de Lhuys, Quito, October 20, 1854. *CP Équateur*, II.
111. Manning, X, 148-49.
112. *Daily Globe*, April 28, 1845.

tributed their domestic peace and prosperity primarily to the superiority of their institutions. Their ideological enthusiasm may explain, but does not justify, the notion that popular self-government would benefit other nations as much as their own. Such self-deception reduced the capacity for dispassionate analysis. The failure of the Second Republic clearly demonstrated that political institutions must be in organic harmony with the genius of a people and the social conditions of their country. The election of a Bonaparte to the presidency of the republic and the popular approval of Louis Napoleon's coup d'état suggest that the majority of the French people, although desiring political liberty, also wanted a strong leader. There were evidently not enough republicans in France to give the Second Republic a real chance.

It should be noted that the forms of political systems, whether identical or different, had little bearing on the determination of policies. Whether a king, a president, or an emperor steered the French ship of state, Paris and Washington continued to deal with each other in accordance with their respective national interests. During the existence of the Second Republic, however, both governments realized that their identical forms at least eliminated ideological principles as an additional source of conflict.

Although both countries emphasized their ideological differences or similarities, their governments stressed the issue less than individual citizens. "Young America" gave the United States a wholly unwarranted reputation as a revolutionary and subversive power. Washington neither conspired against France nor did it possess a blueprint for the overthrow of European monarchies. While it did not sanction the suspicious activities of a fanatic minority, which reached a certain climax by 1854, the appointment of "Young Americans" to foreign posts seemed to encourage them. Actually, the United States depended more on demonstration than on agitation to propagate the ideal of constitutional liberties. It could not claim a spectacular success for its efforts. In fact, its impact on the liberal movement of Europe during this period was relatively limited.[113]

Historically, both Europe and the United States had reached a turning point by the mid-century. Both tried and failed to make the turn. A combination of complex elements delayed the victory of political liberalism in Europe. Torn between the traditions of non-interference and political mission, the United States welcomed revolutions giving birth to republics, but felt not ready as yet decisively to

113. Pouthas, I, 29.

intervene in them. Although it did not lose faith in the ultimate triumph of republicanism in Europe, it was understandably disheartened by the early collapse of the Second Republic.[114]

Faith alone did not motivate America's encouragement of republicanism abroad. The fear of a future conflict with the powerful monarchical systems was ever present, even though it remained in the background, just as fear of the republican movement at home disposed Louis Philippe and Napoleon III against the power which gave it inspiration. Even moral encouragement of this movement limited the French rulers' freedom of action. At the time of the Ostend Manifesto, for example, Napoleon was informed that American diplomats carefully estimated the degree of latitude which the internal state of affairs in the various monarchies permitted their own government.[115]

To combat the two-pronged American danger of militant republicanism and dynamic expansionism, French monarchs tried to identify the one with the other. Didn't Frenchmen understand, they suggested, that the New World giant was reaching out for the control of a major portion of the world under the pretext of advancing liberty?

114. A. J. May, *Contemporary American Opinion of the Mid-Century Revolutions in Central Europe* (Philadelphia, 1927), pp. 127-28; see also A. Whitridge, *Men in Crisis: The Revolutions of 1848* (New York, 1949), p. 284.

115. Sartiges to Drouyn de Lhuys, Washington, D. C., October 30, 1854. *CPEU*, CXI.

CHAPTER II

Franco-American Diplomatic Relations (1830-1860)

FROM THE TIME of the American Revolutionary War, France's interest in the United States was primarily motivated by a desire to check and reduce the power of its British rival. It was for this reason that Louis XVI supported the independence struggle of the English colonies, although he looked with contempt upon their republican system. And, among other reasons, Napoleon I sold the Louisiana Territory to the United States because he regarded the rise of a strong trans-Atlantic commercial sea power as the trump in French hands that "some day will break England's commercial tyranny."[1] This long-range view was based on the assumption that Britain's selfish policies would continue to justify close cooperation between France and the United States.

After the Restoration, however, French statesmen practically abandoned the concept of a powerful America allied with France. Many factors brought about this change which ultimately affected the destiny of France. The political leaders of France became increasingly concerned about the rapid territorial and economic expansion of the United States which they regarded as a potential threat to the future of their country. Moreover, both Paris and Washington found it expedient to promote a growing understanding with London. On its part, the British government was anxious to draw the United States away from France. Experienced observers could hardly fail to notice that ever since the end of the War of 1812 pacific and often mutually beneficial settlements characterized Anglo-American relations.

As a result, French diplomats concluded that France could no longer rely on America as a trustworthy ally against Britain. In case of war, they observed, it might even side with Britain if its interests demanded it. In view of the fact, furthermore, that the Whigs in the United States were oriented towards England and that the people in

1. F. Barbé-Marbois, *Histoire de la Louisiane* (Paris, 1829), p. 282.

the Northeast looked upon France as an industrial rival and a repugnant society, these diplomats regarded America's friendship as an illusion.[2] They had little faith in the gratitude and political morality of the United States.[3] They were, in fact, unhappy about spending their important lives in the "dreary abode,"[4] "where the law protects the rascal and leaves the honest man to take care of himself."[5] It should not be surprising, therefore, to find that their reports displayed as much exaggeration as they reflected personal prejudices against what they considered to be a culturally backward society of upstarts.

During the four decades from the beginning of the July Revolution to the Franco-Prussian War some forty foreign ministers or their interim substitutes were called upon to deal with Franco-American problems. Still, a continuity of policy is discernible. Such French envoys to the United States as Pageot, Bacourt, Sartiges, and Mercier contributed considerably to this continuity as well as to the great change in the relations between the two countries.

Convinced that American democracy was animated by a spirit of encroachment, these French diplomats sounded constant warnings about the global proportions of its ambitions. They feared that the annexation policies would ultimately lead to the absorption of Canada and Mexico, to the establishment of Yankee predominance in Central America, and to the conquest of the Pacific islands as stepping stones for the trade routes to China and India. They visualized that the enterprising commercial ascendancy of the United States would grow in proportion to its merchant marine and in the near future compromise the political and commercial interests of France in the Atlantic and Pacific regions.[6]

Under these circumstances, Alphonse Pageot contended in the 1840's that France could no longer pretend to be the protector of the American republic and should not consent to become its future "satellite." Unless American aggressiveness was contained, he warned,

2. Bacourt to Thiers, Washington, D. C., October 30, 1840. *CPEU*, XCVI. Pageot to Guizot, Washington, D. C., September 29, 1845. *CPEU*, CI.

3. Bacourt to Guizot, Washington, D. C., May 6, 1841. *CPEU*, XCVII. Sartiges to Thouvenel, Washington, D. C., October 9, 1852. Papiers Thouvenel, XVII. See also Nassau W. Senior, *Conversations with Distinguished Persons during the Second Empire from 1860 to 1863* (London, 1880), II, 169-70.

4. A. F. de Bacourt, *Souvenirs of a Diplomat* (New York, 1885), p. 297.

5. Sartiges made this comment in a letter dated June 28, 1857. *Papiers et correspondance de la famille impériale* (Paris, 1870-71), No. 76.

6. Boislecomte to Brenier, Washington, D. C., March 6, 1851. *CPEU*, CVI. Sartiges to Turgot, Washington, D. C., June 13, 1852. *CPEU*, CVII. Sartiges to Drouyn de Lhuys, Washington, D. C., April 3, 1854. *CPEU*, CX.

its spirit of usurpation foreshadowed a world catastrophe.[7] In the following decade, Eugène de Sartiges expressed similar views. He left no doubt in his reports to Paris that no diplomatic protestations or disinterested advice would halt the march of Yankeeism: "It will bow only to material force."[8] To overawe the presumptuous heedlessness of the United States, French diplomats in Washington urged the closest cooperation with London. Indeed, they repeated this theme as they succeeded one another: one interest must prevail among France, Britain, Europe, and Latin America; namely, "to resist the endless invasions of the North Americans."[9]

The Premier and Foreign Minister of Louis Philippe's government, François Guizot, may be identified as the architect of France's new American policy. On January 12 and 21, 1846, he discussed before the Chamber of Deputies the principles which underlay his course in Texas, California, and Oregon.[10] His central argument rested on the principle of an American balance within a system of international balance. Attributing the social and moral grandeur of Europe as being largely due to the existence of an equilibrium among a number of independent states, he argued that it was of extreme importance to France that no power establish preponderance in any part of the world. France was not expanding as fast as Russia, Britain, or the United States. It had, therefore, a special interest in preventing the exclusive domination of the American and Asian continents. Guizot noted that in Asia Britain checked Russia, but in America nobody checked the United States. Moving as fast as it did, the United States, he was concerned, might in a generation or two be a danger to France and Europe.

Guizot's American policy was also influenced by cultural and ideological considerations. He regarded the preservation of Latin civilization in the Western Hemisphere as vital to the interests of France. As he saw it, France could not stand idly by watching the American continent gradually come under the cultural influence as well as political domination of the North Americans. Also, although his faith in the monarchical system was unshakeable, he noted, nevertheless, that enlightened Europeans had always fought against the preponderance of a universal monarchy. He contended, therefore, that the triumph of democratic institutions should be blocked in

7. Pageot to Guizot, Washington, D. C., July 15 and September 29, 1845. *CPEU,* CI.

8. Sartiges to Turgot, Washington, D. C., December 15, 1851. *CPEU,* CVI. Sartiges to Drouyn de Lhuys, Washington, D. C., February 6, 1854. *CPEU,* CX. See also *Journal des Débats,* September 30, 1851.

9. Sartiges to Walewski, Washington, D. C., November 23, 1857. *CPEU,* CXVII.

10. F. P. Guizot, *Histoire parlementaire de France* (Paris, 1864), V, 1-32.

America, for "what was not good for the universal monarchy, is not good for the universal republic."

To protect himself against his critics, he made it perfectly clear that this policy was not followed with any intention to compromise good relations with Washington. France had the greatest admiration for the energy of the American nation which did entitle it to play an increasingly important role in world affairs. He was, for instance, fully aware that, while territorial questions caused legitimate differences of opinion between the two governments, Washington and Paris saw eye to eye on the internationally vital problem of the freedom of the seas.

In the perspective of history it is noticeable that France pursued two different, if not contradictory, policies with respect to the United States. In the Western Hemisphere, it aimed at checking the increasing power of the Union. In the world at large, it endeavored to use the United States to its advantage. This dualism, which runs like a thread through the record, greatly reduced the chances of far-reaching Franco-American cooperation. Having no intention of interfering with French designs in Africa and Asia or of becoming involved in intra-European controversies, American leadership expected France to reciprocate in kind. When, instead, France cooperated with Britain in an attempt to obstruct their march to the Pacific coast, Americans were as disappointed as they were determined to fight for their objective. For they regarded control of the North American continent as vital to their national security. They preferred, of course, to rely on persuasion and diplomacy to explain to France, above all other powers, the many material benefits Europe would derive from the development of Texas and California as parts of a progressive Union. No more effective course could have been chosen in this attempt to influence European statesmen than to identify American possession of the western territories with the self-interest of their own countries.

With this general trend in mind, let us specifically review the diplomatic contacts of the two countries in the Western Hemisphere and the Pacific, where their interests conflicted, as well as in the Far East and Europe, where their mutual diplomatic relations were negligible.

ZONES OF FRICTION

Texas

As long as France could not acquire Texas directly, as Americans feared in 1835 it was seeking to do,[11] or indirectly through a Franco-

11. Saillard to Broglie, New Orleans, August 16, 1835. *CPEU, LXXXIX.*

Spanish marriage scheme,[12] it favored the independence of the Lone Star Republic. This policy was designed to block the dynamic southwestern advance of the American people as well as to keep the door open for the dynastic interests of the House of Bourbon. For in Guizot's judgment, Europe had the duty to stem the flood of Protestantism and republicanism on the American continent.[13] When in the fall of 1839 France recognized Texas in exchange for a favorable trade treaty, it became the first European power to take this step.[14] From that moment on it had an additional reason to object to the annexation of this independent state by the United States. French fears in this respect were considerably intensified in 1843 when President Tyler appointed John C. Calhoun to the post of Secretary of State. It was well known that this apostle of slavery regarded Texas as vital to the security and prosperity of his section and nation.

Since England too wished to maintain the independence of Texas, it took the initiative in concerting Anglo-French policies on this question.[15] Originally, both powers opposed annexation, even if the people of Texas determined to join the Union.[16] But they had waited too long to prevent by peaceful means the ultimate triumph of American diplomacy. By the spring of 1844 they found themselves in a dilemma. If an Anglo-French plan to intervene in Texas were disclosed before the forthcoming election, it threatened to sweep the annexationists into power. Pageot feared, moreover, that, if France or England alone should try to accomplish what they planned to do jointly, Americans would resist to the utmost.[17] For a moment it appeared to have been wise on the part of the European diplomats not to have officially intervened against the treaty of annexation. Its defeat by the Senate—for sectional reasons—accomplished more, at least temporarily, than any foreign protest.

Asked about the rumors of joint Anglo-French intervention, Guizot told the American envoy, William Rufus King, that they were en-

12. N. C. Brooks, *A Complete History of the Mexican War* (Baltimore, 1848), p. 51.

13. Guizot to Pageot, Paris, February 10, 1844. *CPEU,* C.

14. J. W. Schmitz, *Texan Statecraft, 1836-1845* (San Antonio, 1941), p. 79. See also E. W. Winkler, *Secret Journals of the Senate, Republic of Texas, 1836-1845* (Austin, 1911), pp. 168-69.

15. Aberdeen to Cowley, Foreign Office, January 12, 1844. *CP Texas,* VII.

16. Justin H. Smith, *The Annexation of Texas* (New York, 1911), p. 387. For Britain's relations with Texas, see E. D. Adams, *British Interests and Activities in Texas, 1838-1846* (Baltimore, 1910); and J. K. Worley, "The Diplomatic Relations of England and the Republic of Texas," *Texas Historical Association Quarterly, VI* (1905), 1-40.

17. Pageot to Guizot, Washington, D. C., April 13 and June 27, 1844. *CPEU,* C.

tirely without foundation. Although France intended to guarantee the sovereignty of Texas, he promised that it would act independently of England. Not quite convinced of the sincerity of this declaration, the American minister reminded Guizot not to forget that it was England which encouraged Mexico's hostile attitude towards France and the United States.[18]

As far as Anglo-French military intervention in Texas was concerned, 1844 was the year of decision. Although the policies of the Great Powers have been subject to different interpretations, historians are generally agreed that the question was one of joint intervention or none. According to Justin H. Smith, the determination of the American people to resist force with force deterred France from joining Britain and Mexico in a projected war against the United States.[19] Ephraim D. Adams' research, on the other hand, led to the conclusion that Lord Aberdeen's decision in the summer of 1844 to abandon a Texan policy likely to result in costly embarrassments left France little choice but to be correspondingly careful.[20] Still another historian suggested that Britain's lack of confidence in sustained French cooperation compelled the British government to be more cautious than it desired.[21]

The underlying assumption that either Britain or France was at any time really prepared to go to war on account of Texas remains a matter of speculation. Joint or parallel diplomatic moves of these two powers did not necessarily call for eventual military cooperation. On the contrary, they wished to convey the impression of a united diplomatic front in order to make military intervention unnecessary. Then, as so often in the nineteenth century, the chances of active European interference with American affairs were greatly reduced because of the pressure of problems at home, in Europe, and the Orient.

Although Guizot made a major issue of the independence of Texas and may have considered fighting for it in unison with England, he did not lose his sense of realities. In 1842 he was willing to honor Texas' request for a tripartite mediation of its war with Mexico. But he yielded to Lord Aberdeen who refused to go along because, in the

18. King to Calhoun, Paris, July 31, 1844. *DDFDS*, XXX.

19. Smith, *Annexation of Texas*, p. 413.

20. Adams, p. 181.

21. G. L. Rives, "Mexican Diplomacy on the Eve of War with the United States," *AHR*, XVIII (1913), 285; see also R. A. McLemore, "The Influence of French Diplomatic Policy on the Annexation of Texas," *Southwestern Historical Quarterly*, XLIII (1940), 347; and Donald C. McKay, *The United States and France* (Cambridge, Mass., 1951), p. 88.

judgment of the British government, peace would have to be enforced upon Mexico. Britain was not prepared to do this.[22] By May of 1844 Guizot had arrived at a crucial decision regarding Texas. He wrote to Pageot: "We cannot and shall not go further or do more than England which disavowed all violent intervention."[23] He reiterated this basic policy in an important conference with Lord Cowley on December 2, 1844. In it he went so far as to disclose his intention of refusing to recognize the annexation of Texas by the United States. "But as a question of Peace or War," he declared, "I am not prepared to say that its junction with the American States is of sufficient importance to us to justify us in having recourse to arms in order to prevent it."[24]

The American minister in Paris kept himself well informed about the extent of Anglo-French opposition to the annexation of Texas. His realistic appraisal led him to expect no more than diplomatic maneuvers and remonstrances.[25] The Federal government was indeed fully aware of the accelerated diplomatic offensive early in 1845 to preserve the independence of Texas by all means short of war. But neither European financial inducements to Texas to remain independent nor threats to force Mexico to recognize Texas without delay were of avail.[26] The Texan Congress went ahead and unanimously adopted the annexation resolution. This action caused considerable consternation in France and hurt Guizot's personal prestige. It was of little consolation to him that Louis Philippe had loyally supported his "Stop America" policy. French critics deplored the fact that the political and economic importance of Texas to France had been greatly exaggerated.[27] Altogether, Paris was incredibly inaccurately informed about American developments. Guizot may have felt justified in meddling there rather imprudently because his agents in the New World had misinformed him. He was given to believe, for instance, that the people and government of Texas desired to remain independent, that the anti-annexationist Henry Clay rather than the annexationist James K. Polk would be elected President of the United

22. Schmitz, p. 182.

23. Guizot to Pageot, Paris, May 28, 1844. *CPEU*, C.

24. Smith, *Annexation of Texas*, p. 404; see also Mary K. Chase, *Négociations de la République du Texas en Europe, 1837-1845* (Paris, 1932), p. 180.

25. King to Calhoun, Paris, December 31, 1844, January 29 and February 27, 1845. *DDFDS*, XXX.

26. Guizot to Alleye, Paris, May 23, 1845. *CP Mexique*, XXXI.

27. *RDDM*, August 14 and 31, 1845; *Le National*, July 7, 1846.

States, and that in its session after the election Congress would not definitely settle the Texan question.[28]

Whatever considerations motivated the French government to pursue a policy which, in the opinion of Americans, placed it in the category of "unfriendly nations,"[29] the prominent French parliamentarians Antoine Berryer and Louis A. Thiers challenged them with eloquent conviction. France, these political leaders contended, had nothing to fear from the United States. They attacked the theory of the American equilibrium as one of singular inconsequence. Certainly Western civilization was not lost because Texas joined the Union. On the contrary, asserted Thiers: "In the measure in which America grows, England needs us and is more disposed towards us. . . . In the world balance the United States is for us a gift from Heaven."[30] From the contemporary point of view, the *Journal des Débats* did not quarrel with this argument. But this newspaper, which was generally friendly towards the United States, did not feel reassured about America's future role. It expressed its anxiety by asking: "Where will the rapid march of the United States stop? And if the excesses of American democracy are not contained, will it not break its ties with European society?"[31]

California and Oregon

While Europeans worried about the next move of the United States, Americans were confident that their westward march to the Pacific could at worst only be delayed. To insure the success of their pioneering social experiment, they were determined to eliminate the costly threat of war on their continent. They regarded the possible intrusion of France or Britain into any part of the territory coveted by them as such a threat.[32]

With their eyes on California, Americans felt alarmed when Frenchmen too dreamed of acquiring it. In 1839, for instance, Captain Laplace of the frigate *Artémise* displayed an eager "scientific" interest in California. Two years later Duflot de Mofras, an attaché of the French legation in Mexico, arrived in Alta California to explore the possibilities of establishing a lease for French commercial schemes in the Pacific region. Baron Alleye de Cyprey, who represented

28. Saligny to Guizot, New Orleans, November 23, 1844. *CP Texas*, VIII.

29. White, *American Opinion of France*, p. 111.

30. *Moniteur*, January 21, 1846; see also Grimblot, "Du Texas et son annexation aux États-Unis," *Revue Indépendante* (1844), pp. 614-15; and *Le Constitutionel*, January 13, 1846.

31. *Journal des Débats*, January 22, 1846.

32. Calhoun to King, Washington, D. C., August 12, 1844. *FIDS*, XV.

France in Mexico in the early 1840's, actually proposed to his government the employment of naval forces for the purpose of conquering California.[33] If these "visits" and recommendations are linked with the suspicious actions in 1844 of the acting French consul at Monterey, ambitious designs on the Pacific Coast begin to take shape.[34]

When the annexation of Texas foreshadowed a war with the United States, Mexico would rather propose a European protectorate over California than see it conquered by the Yankees. It now appeared, however, that the French government was less inclined towards such a proposal than some of its subordinate officials in America. Perhaps having been made more cautious after what happened in Texas, Guizot, in effect, rejected the offer of an Anglo-French protectorate over the Far-Western province of Mexico.[35]

Mexico was in no condition to engage the superior power of the United States in a war. Its only chance lay in European military intervention on its behalf. In that case, a local contest would have been enlarged into a world conflict for which the Union was ill-prepared. The situation was further complicated by the dispute over Oregon. Britain did not relish the prospect of seeing California and Oregon in American hands. But were these territories worth fighting for? An Anglo-American war over Oregon would, of course, have been an answer to Mexico's prayers. However, if Britain yielded on the Oregon question, it was also likely to yield on California.

As the tension grew early in 1846, the world focused its attention on the position of France.[36] Would it cut the Gordian knot of this crisis? Inasmuch as France had no special interests to protect in Oregon, it should have been a relatively simple matter to arrive at a policy decision. In reality, this "simple" question was intricately tied up with a multitude of issues, both of an international and domestic nature. The tradition of Franco-American cooperation came here into conflict with the expediency of the Anglo-French entente. To side

33. A. P. Nasatir, "The French Consulate in California, 1843-1856," *California Historical Society Quarterly*, XI (1932), 199-200, and XII (1933), 157.

34. A. P. Nasatir, *French Activities in California* (Stanford, Calif., 1945), pp. 22-25; R. K. Willis, "French Imperialists in California," *California Historical Society Quarterly*, VIII (1929), 116-29; N. A. Graebner, *Empire on the Pacific—A Study in American Continental Expansion* (New York, 1955), pp. 66-68, 74-75; Bernard De Voto, *The Year of Decision: 1846* (Boston, 1943), pp. 20, 116; H. J. Rathgeber, "Early French Trade and Settlement in California" (Master's thesis, University of California, Berkeley, 1940), pp. 38-57.

35. John S. Galbraith, "France as a Factor in the Oregon Negotiations," *Pacific Northwest Quarterly*, XLIV (1953), 72-73.

36. George Vern Blue, "France and the Oregon Question," *Oregon Historical Quarterly*, XXXIV (1933), 39-59, 144-63.

with Britain threatened to offend Washington, while to support the American claim in Oregon could not but strain the relations of the entente. To Guizot, it must be kept in mind, more was at stake than the decision of who should possess Oregon. He felt that Europe could not tolerate seeing the insatiable United States take one territory after another. He feared that the consequence would be disastrous for Europe because the all too independent trans-Atlantic giant would get completely out of control.

Guizot soon discovered that his views could not be readily implemented. For he was not an entirely free agent in the conduct of the foreign policy of France. The French Assembly's debate about Texas revealed the existence of a passionate division. When public opinion became as pronounced as on the American question, Guizot had to accommodate it with compromises. Unable to act with determination and forcefulness, he announced that France would be neutral in case of an Anglo-American war. This premature neutrality declaration had serious consequences. Intending to teach these two powers not to take France for granted, Guizot convinced them instead that they could not count on it. In his own country, he stirred up a storm of protest. Deputies attacked his Oregon policy as proof of his readiness to sacrifice the ancient alliance with the United States to the exigencies of the entente cordiale. An angry *Constitutionel* interpreted the neutrality declaration as an "oratorical intervention in favor of Britain."[37] If it was not meant to be that, statesmen like Berryer and Thiers challenged the logic by which the acquisition of Texas and California would upset the American balance, but the added possession of Oregon would not make any difference. Obviously, Guizot's policy also found public approval and strengthened the hands of the peace parties in Britain and the United States.

Whatever aspirations France had for world leadership, its divided councils caused an indecision that played into the hands of its rivals. When the Oregon war fever suddenly disappeared with the complete reversal of Britain, the Pacific triumph of Polk's administration did not help to endear "neutral" France to the United States. If Britain did not intend to deepen the growing estrangement between Paris and Washington, it could hardly have embarrassed Guizot more than by so handsomely coming to terms with the United States.[38]

37. *Le Constitutionel*, January 13, 1846; see also *Le Commerce*, February 1, 1846.

38. For French reactions to Britain's "complete retreat from Oregon," see *La Presse*, July 1, 1846, and *Le Constitutionel*, October 7, 1846. For contemporary Anglo-American relations consult Frederick Merk, "The British Corn Crisis of 1845-46 and the Oregon Treaty," *Agricultural History*, VIII (1934), 95-123; and Julius W.

Senator Sydney Breese of Illinois was one of those who had all along predicted that the European monarchs would not dare fight the American republic. "If war comes," he speculated, "it will not be a war for Oregon, but one of systems in which the dynasties will fall before the advance of republican principles."[39] Although this estimate greatly oversimplified the reasons behind Britain's decision, the Duke of Wellington indeed feared that "a war with the United States will not be with that Power alone."[40] The ambitious republicanism of "the Democracy abroad" deterred the European powers to some extent. Britain's suspicion of France, however, was the decisive factor in its final disposition of the Oregon question. At that time the interests of these two powers diverged in Egypt, Spain, Tahiti, and the Chusan archipelago. A war between them was in the realm of possibilities, particularly after Prince de Joinville's boast in 1844 that France's new steam fleet enabled it "to engage any power in the most audacious sea war."[41] With the security of its insular position thus challenged, Britain was not inclined to take a chance, no matter how much Paris tried to stress its really peaceful intentions.

In principle, Guizot endeavored to prevent the Americanization of the Mexican people with whom France shared a community of cultural ties. Even after his "defeat" in Texas he continued to make some halfhearted efforts to organize a great European coalition to block the United States from overrunning Mexico. Mexico, he contended, had the same right to seek or refuse alliances which served its interests as the United States. Despite Louis Philippe's reassuring pledges to the American minister, his government was really still undecided in June of 1846 as to its policy in the Mexican War.[42] Once again, France alone was not expected to intervene, but was more likely to resist the dynamic force of "Manifest Destiny" in cooperation with Britain.

When the Oregon question was settled peacefully, British intervention in Mexico could be discounted. London had evidently limited itself to moral persuasion in American affairs. Moreover, the Whigs, who had recently replaced the Tories, did not favor so close a co-

Pratt, "James K. Polk and John Bull," *Canadian Historical Review*, XXIV (1943), 133-48.

39. *Cong. Globe,* 29 Cong., 1 sess., p. 385 (March 12, 1846).

40. Galbraith, p. 70.

41. Prince François de Joinville, *Notes sur l'état des forces navales de la France* (Paris, 1844), p. 5. See also John W. McClearly, "Anglo-French Naval Rivalry, 1815-1848" (Ph.D. dissertation, Johns Hopkins University, 1947), pp. 167-231.

42. King to Buchanan, Paris, June 1 and 30, 1846. *DDFDS*, XXX.

operation with France as their predecessors. In France, too, even the conservative party would no longer sacrifice the ancient Franco-American unity on a British altar. The cumulative effects of these developments and the impressive initial blows which American forces inflicted upon their southern neighbor prompted France to declare its neutrality in the Mexican War.[43]

At the beginning of the war the French squadron in the Gulf of Mexico was reinforced, presumably to protect French commerce. The American press interpreted this move as a delicate matter that could easily lead to a collision of the fleets.[44] France, however, passed all tests of neutrality. In the beginning of 1847, Mexican agents in Marseilles tried to deliver letters of marque against the commerce of the United States. As soon as Guizot familiarized himself with this matter, he took prompt action against such arrangements. And again, when the American consul at Algiers reported the illegal fitting out of a privateer, the French government promised to take the proper steps to prevent such "criminal attempts."[45]

The final incorporation of California into the Union, in spite of vigorous European objections, did not enhance the prestige European statesmen enjoyed in the Western Hemisphere. By 1848 Europe began to resign itself that henceforth the United States was a Pacific as well as an Atlantic power. Reluctantly, France had to forget its dream of establishing a colony in California. Many Frenchmen, however, continued to live and prosper in the beautiful western state. For, remembering the protest of the French consul at Monterey against Commodore Sloat's taking possession of California, President Polk was anxious not to give cause for future French complaints. He instructed his military and naval commanders to pursue a conciliatory course towards all French residents in the newly acquired territory. Indeed, the President desired to cultivate harmony among all people residing on the Pacific coast. France, moreover, was permitted to open consulates in San Francisco and Monterey to develop its legitimate interests in the Far West.[46]

Mexico

The chronic financial difficulties and unsettled conditions of Mexico qualified it as the "sick man of the Western Hemisphere."

43. J. H. Powell, *Richard Rush* (Philadelphia, 1942), pp. 247-48.
44. White, *American Opinion of France*, p. 114.
45. Guizot to Martin, Paris, February 26, 1847; Martin to Buchanan, Paris, May 31 and June 16, 1847. *DDFDS*, XXX.
46. Buchanan to Pageot, Washington, D. C., July 16 and 21, 1847. *FNFDS*, VI.

When the United States withdrew its troops from the heart of Mexico in 1848, it practically announced to the world that the possession of Mexico constituted too great a liability to be desirable. It chose the lesser of two evils by tolerating the independent existence of a weak neighbor who was likely to be preyed upon by its European creditors. Mexico's financial difficulties had already in the past exposed it to European pressures. In 1838, for instance, the French occupied Vera Cruz and blockaded the Mexican coast[47] in an effort to collect compensations for considerable losses their citizens had suffered as the result of internal disorders in Mexico. At that time the United States viewed the blockade with misgivings. It offered to mediate the dispute, for besides injuries to commerce, a blockade by a European power in the American zone could not be devoid of political implications. Although this incident was finally settled, rumors about French and British designs on Mexico continued to circulate until the ill-fated adventure of Emperor Maximilian. These European powers were suspected of planning the establishment of a protectorate over Mexico in order to make certain that their financial interests would in the future be protected.[48] The expansionist ideas and adventures of certain French citizens caused concern on several occasions because they implied a more permanent threat to the integrity of Mexico. An attaché of the French legation in Mexico, for instance, published a book in 1844 in which he advocated the establishment of a Mexican monarchy with strong Catholic and European family ties.[49] This officially inspired trial balloon brought a clear warning from Congress that such an enterprise would be the signal for war.[50] Another publication attracted widespread attention in 1852. In his pamphlet about Mexico and the United States, Du Pasquier de Dommartin pleaded for the creation of vigorous French colonies in Sonora and Chihuahua which in his opinion occupied a key position from a geopolitical point of view.[51] Unless Europe acted soon, he prophesied that the United States would ultimately assume the role of absolute arbiter of the world's commerce.

It looked somewhat curious that late in 1852 the French adventurer Count Raousset de Boulbon attempted to wrest Sonora from Mexico.

47. William Spence Robertson, "French Intervention in Mexico in 1838," *Hispanic American Historical Review,* XXIV (1944), 222-52.

48. J. F. Rippy, *The United States and Mexico* (New York, 1931), p. 201.

49. E. Duflot de Mofras, *Exploration du territoire de l'Orégon, des Californies et de la Mer Vermeille* (Paris, 1844).

50. *Cong. Globe,* 30 Cong., 1 sess., Appendix, pp. 175-82 (Jan. 26, 1848).

51. H. Du Pasquier de Dommartin, *Les États-Unis et le Mexique—L'intérêt européen dans l'Amérique du Nord* (Paris, 1852), pp. 74-76.

When the first rumors about this colonial adventure reached the eastern states, Congress and the press were concerned. Unconfirmed reports spoke of the protection which the French squadron in the Pacific had rendered in the course of the undertaking.[52] The Philadelphia *Inquirer*[53] could hardly believe that the French government would expose itself to such an untenable position. In fact, the French count earned the ridicule of the world when he failed in his scheme. While Patrice Dillon, the French consul in San Francisco, had asked for the presence of a French warship in the Gulf of California "to follow the events,"[54] he reported to Paris that he had strongly urged Raousset to renounce his project. The French government disapproved of this unauthorized enterprise and actually asked the adventurer to abstain from pursuing it in the future.[55] However, as far as Mexico was concerned, the records reveal that as early as 1853 Napoleon hinted to the Mexican minister at Paris that "France will support Mexico against American inroads."[56] Interpreting this statement in his own way, the Emperor implemented it during the next decade.

Central America

A century ago Central America qualified as a sensitive area in American diplomacy. With a great deal of justification Paris and Washington either accused or suspected each other of imperialistic ambitions in this region. Many interested French citizens and officials implored Napoleon to adopt an aggressive policy to reverse the trend towards rapid Americanization of Central America.[57]

The three great maritime powers pursued somewhat different objectives in this part of the world. Britain cared primarily for the advantages of trade. Washington's responsibilities compelled it, in addition to the promotion of trade, to pay attention to strategic considerations. And interested as the French were in the economic

52. Senator Lewis Cass of Michigan suspected the French government of supporting this adventure. *Cong. Globe,* 32 Cong., 2 sess., pp. 91-92 (Jan. 15, 1853). See also *U. S. Democratic Review,* XXXI (1852), 600.

53. December 13, 16, and 22, 1852.

54. Dillon to Drouyn de Lhuys, San Francisco, March 31, 1853. *CPCEU,* IV. Dillon's personal feeling, however, was "to risk something for France." Dillon to Faugère, San Francisco, March 31, 1853. *MDEU,* XXV.

55. Drouyn de Lhuys to Sartiges, Paris, June 9 and July 7, 1853. *CPEU,* CIX. See also H. B. Metcalf, "The California French Filibusters in Sonora," *California Historical Society Quarterly,* XVIII (1939), 3-21.

56. P. N. Garber, *The Gadsden Treaty* (Philadelphia, 1923), p. 99.

57. A. Housse, *Note sur la situation des républiques de l'Amérique, à propos d'une mission projetée,* August, 1852. *MDEU,* XXV.

market, they also sought a political balance between North America and the rest of the continent.

Concerned about the possibility of European attempts to monopolize the best routes across the Isthmus, the United States took the initiative in securing guaranties for the neutrality of the projected international highways.[58] In principle, France acceded to such a proposition because it offered desirable safeguards for its own commerce. But Paris was frankly surprised when the American envoy brought the Clayton-Bulwer Treaty (1850) to its attention, with a view to concluding an analogous convention. France had not been advised of this impending Anglo-American understanding. Inasmuch as this treaty had the effect of neutralizing Central America, the French government realized that its own aspirations in this region had suffered a setback.[59]

It looked strange, therefore, when in 1858 a situation arose in Nicaragua which gave the impression that France was trying to achieve indirectly what it could not do officially. In that year, a Frenchman by the name of Félix Belly negotiated for the right of building a canal through Nicaragua and a French controlled railroad from San Juan del Norte to some point on the Pacific.[60] He made no secret of it that he hoped to teach Central Americans how to dispose of the "despicable Yankees." The extraordinary influence which this "crusader" managed to wield over Nicaraguan and Costa Rican affairs displeased the State Department considerably. But upon inquiries, France asserted emphatically that "no official character" had been conferred on Belly.[61] As long as he acted as a private speculator, the United States could do little more than warn Nicaragua that any canal through its territory must be equally open to the commerce of all nations. Although John Y. Mason, who represented the Federal government in Paris, resented Belly's "excessive impudence," he was satisfied that the French government did not give countenance to Belly's enterprise.[62] He doubted, furthermore, that the money for the construction of the canal could be raised in France alone, a view with which the New York *Journal of Commerce*[63] fully agreed.

58. Clayton to Rives, Washington, D. C., January 7, 1850. Clayton Papers. "That the United States would ever cede the control of an eventual Isthmian canal to any European power" was dismissed as "a foolish illusion." Alexandre Holinski, *La Californie et les routes interocéaniques* (Bruxelles, 1853), p. 360.

59. Sartiges to Walewski, Washington, D. C., June 7 and 8, 1858. *CPEU*, CXIX.

60. Manning, *Diplomatic Correspondence*, IV, 676-79.

61. Walewski to Sartiges, Paris, May 26, 1858. *CPEU*, CXVIII.

62. Mason to Cass, Paris, July 30 and October 12, 1858. *DDFDS*, XLIV.

63. March 17, 1859. This newspaper described Belly as "a stock-jobbing schemer, as likely to make a canal through Nicaragua as to make one in the moon."

Nevertheless, in the summer of 1858 Belly not only acquired the rights to cut a canal, but the French government was also permitted to station two warships at the termini of the canal. The Union's strong representations against such a provision met with immediate success.[64] It had reason to be satisfied, moreover, when a subsequent treaty between France and Nicaragua included a clause specifically guaranteeing the neutrality of the sea routes. But Washington regretted that this treaty also provided for the employment of French military forces in case Nicaragua requested them. Both France and Britain were ready to answer such a call if filibustering expeditions, illegally departing from the United States, should continue to threaten the integrity of Nicaragua as they had done during recent years.[65] Mutual mistrust regarding the intentions of each of the major powers in this region cast long shadows. But their jealousy helped to maintain the status quo.

Regarding the independent existence of the separate Central American states as problematical, Napoleon's government explored the possibility of their federation. In its estimate, the federated states would be in a better position to escape the fate of becoming part of the British or American empire. But while Washington did not object to the principle of a Central American federation, London preferred to perpetuate the status quo. As far as the Central Americans themselves were concerned, they were not disposed to support the project of a federation.[66]

Haiti and the Dominican Republic

The bitter struggle between Haiti and the Dominican Republic presented France with another opportunity to advance its interests in the Western Hemisphere. Fearing the military superiority of Emperor Soulouque of Haiti, the Dominicans were looking around for foreign aid and assistance. In 1843 they approached France, offering it a permanent naval base at Samana Bay in exchange for French protection. Louis Philippe was tempted to accept this offer. Only the fear of diplomatic complications restrained him from concluding such a deal.[67] In 1849, after England had declined the offer of a joint

64. C. Huberich, *The Trans-Isthmian Canal: A Study in American Diplomatic History, 1825-1904* (Austin, 1904), pp. 14-15.

65. Rippy, p. 199.

66. For references to this federation project see Drouyn de Lhuys to Sartiges, Paris, April 14, 1853. *CPEU*, CIX. Sartiges to Drouyn de Lhuys, Washington, D. C., May 30, 1853. *CPEU*, CIX. Walewski to Sartiges, Paris, January 13, 1859. *CPEU*, CXXI.

67. C. Tansill, *The United States and Santo Domingo, 1798-1873* (Baltimore,

Anglo-French protectorate, the Dominican congress renewed its proposal to France alone. Again, London and Washington successfully intimated their disapproval. Duff Green, whom the Federal government had appointed as special agent to the Dominican Republic, tried to dissuade the Dominicans from ever contemplating an association with France. He offered the poverty and decay of Martinique and Guadalupe as evidence for his contention that a connection with France would retard rather than promote the progress of the Republic.[68] Under these circumstances, the Dominicans saw no other way out than to ask the United States for a protectorate. The European powers, of course, blocked it and suggested instead a tripartite arrangement. Count Charles de Boislecomte, the French minister at Washington, hoped thus to compromise the American government "into steps that would assure the independence of the island."[69] He and his British colleague indeed maneuvered Secretary of State Daniel Webster into a cooperative measure to procure the pacification of the island.[70] The three powers tried to impress Soulouque with their joint might and demanded either peace or a ten-year truce between Haiti and the Dominican Republic. To their embarrassment, the Emperor of Haiti honored their diplomatic intervention with skilful defiance. It is hard to believe that this was a case in which the David of Haiti dared Goliath. It is more likely that for long-range reasons Napoleon hinted to Soulouque that France would not resort to arms against him.

France and the United States continued to compete for Samana Bay as a naval base, while England maneuvered to keep both out of there. However, had it not been for certain clauses involving racial discrimination, unacceptable to the Dominicans, the Pierce administration could have acquired it by treaty in 1854.[71]

South America

That France showed little respect for what it called the strange principles of the Monroe Doctrine is also borne out by its policies in South America. As far as religious and cultural ties affect the rela-

1938), p. 310; see also M. Treudley, *The United States and Santo Domingo, 1780-1866* (Worcester, 1916), pp. 232-35.

68. Green to Clayton, Santo Domingo, October 24, 1849. Special Agents, XV.

69. R. W. Logan, *The Diplomatic Relations of the United States with Haiti, 1776-1891* (Chapel Hill, 1941), p. 260.

70. Frederic L. Paxson, "A Tripartite Intervention in Hayti, 1851," *University of Colorado Studies*, I (1902), 323-30. See also B. C. Clark, *Remarks upon United States Intervention in Hayti* (Boston, 1853), pp. 18-19.

71. M. M. Knight, *The Americans in Santo Domingo* (New York, 1928), p. 4.

tionships between nations, France was in a position to exercise considerable influence in this region. To promote French interests in South America, Charles X deemed it necessary to instruct his agents to neutralize the republican and anti-Catholic ambitions of the United States in that part of the world.[72] These efforts were intensified in the decade following the acquisition of California and the opening of Japan. For it was then anticipated that the Latin American states bordering on the Pacific would be the next victims of the Yankees. Édouard Drouyn de Lhuys, Napoleon's Foreign Minister, for instance, wrote to André Villamus at Quito: "The independent states in this part of the world should fear the turbulent activities of the North Americans and their unscrupulous policies."[73] Villamus' anti-American attitude really needed no encouragement. He and his French colleagues lost no opportunity to undermine the influence of the United States in Latin America.

Their main propaganda weapon consisted of the prophecy that the Yankees would endeavor to conquer the entire continent. But France was not exactly in the position to assume the role of disinterested defender of these countries' independence. The Latin Americans looked upon the activities of France with almost as much suspicion as on those of their big northern neighbor. How could they forget the French blockades of Argentina and Mexico in 1838, the Anglo-French intervention in the Rio de la Plata, or the project of a protectorate over Haiti? The records also reveal that long before Emperor Maximilian played with the idea of inter-continental marriages, France contemplated a royal marriage with Brazil in the late 1830's.[74]

The denials of the French and the British notwithstanding, their intervention in the Rio de la Plata was widely interpreted as an attempt to secure commercial privileges rather than to pacify this region. The Brazilian minister to Paraguay, for instance, confided in 1845 to his colleague from the United States that "France intends to make a colony of Montevideo to establish exclusive European interests in this market."[75] Britain, of course, did not stand idly by to see this happen. Had it not been for this inter-European rivalry, mere protests from

72. Charles X to Roux de Rochelle, St. Cloud, May 11, 1830. *CPEU*, LXXXIV.
73. Drouyn de Lhuys to Villamus, Paris, January 31, 1855. *CP Équateur*, III. See also W. R. Sherman, *The Diplomatic and Commercial Relations of the United States and Chile, 1820-1914* (Boston, 1926), p. 96.
74. J. F. Cady, *Foreign Intervention in the Rio de la Plata, 1838-1850* (Philadelphia, 1929), p. 57.
75. Manning, *Diplomatic Correspondence*, X, 63-76.

the American governments, both in the North and South, could hardly have forestalled such a French colony.[76]

Under these circumstances the American press asked how long the two Americas would permit themselves to be the puppet of the crowned heads of Europe.[77] Calhoun, Webster, and others raised their voices in Congress against the "highhanded" and "outrageous" interference of the Old World powers.[78] The United States was, of course, not indifferent about the Anglo-French intervention. But President Polk lent only his moral support to the Argentine republic.[79] He felt relieved that at the beginning of the Mexican War the maritime powers were too preoccupied in South America to interfere with the developments in California. Besides, England and France could not convincingly accuse Washington of coercing small American states when they did it themselves. Nevertheless, in the fall of 1847 the envoy of the United States mentioned to the King of France that Washington hoped for the early raising of the protracted blockade of Buenos Aires. And when, a year later, it was partially lifted, he pleaded for its complete discontinuance.[80] In time, Britain, France, and the United States agreed to disclaim any special privileges in the Rio de la Plata region. Thanks to their mediation in 1859, Buenos Aires and Argentina re-established the Confederation.

If France found it difficult to advance its own political and commercial interests in South America, it regarded helping to check those of the United States as a positive achievement.[81] France succeeded, for instance, in getting a pledge from the American government that it would prevent any filibustering invasion of the Amazon.[82] French diplomats frustrated such deals as the attempted Yankee exploitation of guano deposits and the acquisition of the Galapagos group.[83] Above all else, their constant warnings against the North American danger made many Latin Americans suspicious of the Union.

Because they suspected the United States of preferring to deal with many weak Latin republics, Frenchmen recommended to their govern-

76. Cady, *Foreign Intervention*, pp. 76-78, 270-71. See also H. E. Peters, *The Foreign Debt of the Argentine Republic* (Baltimore, 1934), p. 21.

77. See *U. S. Democratic Review* (1846), p. 184.

78. *Cong. Globe*, 29 Cong., 1 sess., pp. 197-98 (Jan. 14, 1846).

79. St. George Leakin Sioussat, "James Buchanan," in S. F. Bemis, ed., *American Secretaries of State and their Diplomacy* (New York, 1928), V, 312-15.

80. Rush to Bastide, Paris, September 12, 1848. *DDFDS*, XXXI.

81. Georges Lafond, *L'effort français en Amérique latine* (Paris, 1917), p. 51.

82. Drouyn de Lhuys to Gréling, Paris, November 7, 1853. *CP Brésil*, XXXIII.

83. Huet to Walewski, Lima, May 22, 1857. *CP Pérou*, XXIV; Drouyn de Lhuys to Villamus, Paris, January 31, 1855. *CP Équateur*, III.

ment that it encourage the union or confederation of several states. They seriously doubted that, without manifesting solidarity in questions of common interest, the South American states could long preserve their independent existence.[84] Carried away by their imagination, they visualized the Stars and Stripes practically all over the Western Hemisphere. The truth was well expressed by John Randolph Clay, a diplomat who was particularly qualified to comment upon the Latin American policy of the United States: "We have never adopted any general policy with regard to the nations of this continent."[85]

Cuba

After the acquisition of California the American government was more concerned with securing the control of the strategic approaches to its coastlines than with any other foreign policy objectives. Originally, its avowed policy with respect to Cuba favored the status quo. But the prevailing Southern influence in its councils gradually whetted its appetite for the acquisition of this island. As part of the Union, Cuba would offer the prospect for the creation of enough slave states to perpetuate the political preponderance of the South. Since foreign and domestic policies are closely interrelated, sectional jealousies within the United States would most likely have prevented the purchase or conquest of this territory. In any case, Britain, France, and the United States watched each other very closely to keep either of the other two powers from acquiring the island.

With interests in the West Indies, France was particularly afraid that control of Cuba would so swell the commercial and political power of the United States as to threaten her own possession in this area. It preferred, therefore, the status quo of Cuba as well as that of the entire Caribbean region. This did not exclude, as has been noted, an active policy in this part of the world. Basically, however, the French government seemed to be anxious not to complicate relations with the United States by an aggressive Caribbean policy, lest Washington be provided with a pretext for aggression.

The Cuban issue developed into an acute affair through the adventurous expedition of General Lopez, a Venezuelan who had many friends in the United States. After two unsuccessful attempts to "liberate" Cuba, his hopeful group escaped the watchful eyes of the

84. S. Dutot, France et Brésil (Paris, 1859), p. 211; see also André Cochut, "Le Chili en 1859," RDDM (December 15, 1859), p. 822.

85. Clay to Marcy, Lima, December 25, 1854, in Manning, Diplomatic Correspondence, X, 749-53.

New Orleans authorities in August of 1851 only to face another disaster. As a result of these activities the interested European powers were more determined than ever to maintain Cuba's status as a Spanish possession. Alarmed by the international consequence of the attempted invasion, Sartiges asked the Secretary of State for an interview. In the course of it Daniel Webster explained to the French envoy, without convincing him, that the Federal government, too, was opposed to the annexation of the island because it feared that it would touch off a sectional conflict.[86]

Although France and Great Britain were unwilling to give Spain the guaranties it requested, they instructed their respective naval forces in the West Indies to be on the lookout for future filibustering expeditions against Cuba.[87] What made these orders undesirable to the American government was not the end they presumed to serve. The rumored method of joint action caused the usual uneasiness in Washington. The United States had no intention of invading Cuba. If at all, its acquisition would be openly negotiated. But the defiant talk of some congressmen notwithstanding,[88] even the purchase of Cuba would most likely have been blocked by the joint action of the two leading European powers. By October 3, 1851, Sartiges had as yet no knowledge of the special instructions to the French naval station in the West Indies. As soon as their existence was established, Acting Secretary of State John J. Crittenden sent a lengthy note to the French legation. In it he discounted the necessity or propriety of the orders which implied bad faith in the integrity of the American government. "The ungracious act of watching the American people as if they were fruitful of piracies," he protested, "could not but tend to produce collision or alienation."[89] He then asked the French envoy to understand that, lying near the mouth of the Mississippi River, Cuba in the hands of a powerful European nation could endanger the lifeline of the Union. The policy of the Federal government, he emphasized, must be guided by this paramount strategic consideration.[90] Sartiges replied that his government intended to preserve the

86. Sartiges to Baroche, Washington, D. C., August 26, 1851. *CPEU*, CVI.

87. Rives to Webster, Paris, September 18, 1851. *DDFDS*, XXXIII. The French Minister of Marine disliked the idea of employing his available resources in this kind of indefinite operation. Ducos to Turgot, Paris, March 20, 1852. *CPEU*, CVII.

88. *Cong. Globe*, 32 Cong., 2 sess., p. 19 (Dec. 23, 1852).

89. Crittenden to Sartiges, Washington, D. C., October 22, 1851. *CPEU*, CVI.

90. It should be remembered that in 1847 Lord Bentick asked the House of Commons to acquire Cuba "to cut the trade of America in two." Perry Belmont, "La question cubaine, 1852-1856," *Revue d'histoire diplomatique* (April-June, 1935), pp. 239-41.

peace and not to offend or admonish the United States. Lest there be any misunderstanding, he asserted with unmistakable clarity that France had issued the orders to its West Indian squadron spontaneously and without consulting London. They applied, moreover, only to illegal maneuvers against which the United States had pledged the watchfulness of its own navy.[91]

Sartiges did not inspire confidence in his political trustworthiness by denying Anglo-French cooperation in this matter. On November 10, 1851, Rives's latest despatch arrived in Washington. It contradicted Sartiges conclusively. The United States minister in Paris reported that a distinguished French admiral confided to "a gentleman of the highest respectability" that France and England cooperated closely on the Cuban question. Since discreetness is not a social habit, this confidential remark traveled promptly across the ocean. For that matter, the Spanish Foreign Minister, the Marquis de Miraflores, declared before the Spanish Cortes on July 16: "All I can say . . . is that at the present time the naval force of England and France, and the state of our relations with those countries, offer us the uncertain means of preserving the integrity of our valuable island."[92]

When Rives went to the Quai d'Orsay to ascertain the facts, the French Foreign Minister, Pierre Baroche, tried to stress the point that France and Britain did not cooperate *"in virtue of any formal stipulations."* As a diplomat Rives knew the delight of his profession in hiding behind flimsy technicalities. He continued to question Baroche until the Foreign Minister finally admitted that an express understanding had been reached between him and the British ambassador. They had agreed on a system of intercommunication between their West Indian naval forces for the purpose in question.

In the course of a dinner conversation with Rives, Louis Napoleon alluded to Cuba. He suggested that in the interest of world peace France, Great Britain, and the United States engage in a joint agreement regarding Cuba. After dinner Baroche continued to talk about the advisability of such a tripartite arrangement. However, Rives was not responsive to this project because he felt that it would meet with insuperable objections. Reiterating that his country had no illegitimate designs on Cuba, he emphasized in his informal talk with the French statesman that the people of the island must be free to assert their independence. Baroche saw no objection to this statement. All

91. Sartiges to Crittenden, Washington, D. C., October 27, 1851. *FNTDS*, XV.
92. Rives to Crittenden, Paris, October 23, 1851. *DDFDS*, XXXIII.

he desired was a simple declaration by the three great maritime powers that would allay the apprehension caused by recent filibusters.[93] This idea of a tripartite convention coincided with England's view. More than that, it seems to have originated with Palmerston who proposed it to Count Walewski in August of 1851.[94] It was expected that if it rejected the idea the United States would be morally condemned in case of aggression. Advised of this project, Sartiges had no illusions about its chances. He believed that the Senate of the United States would not give its assent to such a declaration. In his judgment, no collective agreement would deter the aggressive intentions of the American republic. Only concerted action on the part of England, France, and Spain might possibly save Cuba.[95] This view was shared by Count Walewski, the French ambassador at the Court of St. James's, who wanted it made clear to Washington that the maritime powers would not tolerate its annexation of Cuba.[96]

Once the governments of France and Great Britain decided to explore the tripartite project, Sartiges discharged his assignment with his usual zeal. On April 23, 1852, he and the British ambassador presented identical notes to Secretary of State Webster, proposing the mutual renunciation of the acquisition of Cuba. The importance of Webster's prompt answer to this communication lay in the meaning between his lines. He promised that the President would give "mature consideration" to the momentous proposal. But he warned Sartiges not to expect the United States to deviate from its policy of nonentanglement, nor "to acquiesce in the cession of Cuba to an *European* power."[97] In an impatient reply Sartiges paraphrased these words by advising Webster that France and Great Britain could not be expected "to acquiesce in the cession of Cuba to *any* maritime power."[98] In the hands of a strong maritime power, he argued, the island could be used to paralyze the commerce of other nations.

On December 1, 1852, Secretary of State Edward Everett officially rejected the tripartite proposal. The United States, he wrote, desired to live in harmony with the rest of the world. But the time had come

93. Rives to Webster, Paris, October 2, 1851. *DDFDS*, XXXIII.

94. A. A. Ettinger, "The Proposed Anglo-American Treaty of 1852 to Guarantee Cuba to Spain," *Transactions of the Royal Historical Society*, XIII (London, 1930), 153-65.

95. Sartiges to Baroche, Washington, D. C., October 20, 1851. *CPEU*, CVI.

96. Walewski to Turgot, London, January 29, 1852. *CPEU*, CVII.

97. Webster to Sartiges, Washington, D. C., April 29, 1852. *FNFDS*, VI. Italics inserted.

98. Sartiges to Webster, Washington, D. C., July 8, 1852. *FNTDS*, XV. Italics inserted.

for the leading powers of Europe to realize that they were not the only ones who had a right to expand. Neither the establishment of French colonies in North Africa nor the growth of the world-wide British Empire created uneasiness in America. Why then should the European powers object to America's expansion? To them Cuba was a distant island in another hemisphere, just another possession. To the United States it would mean improved national security. America's past expansion, Everett contended, has benefited the rest of the world. Let France remember that "every addition to the territory of the Union has given homes to European destitution and gardens to European want. . . . What would have Europe's condition been in these trying years, but for the outlet we have furnished to her starving millions?"[99] If London and Paris could induce Spain to remedy the deplorable conditions in Cuba which caused many unlawful expeditions, then, Everett lectured France, their influence would be employed in a worthwhile fashion. The tone of this message surprised French statesmen as much as the refusal to underwrite the perpetual neutrality of Cuba. They saw in this immoderate interpretation of the Monroe Doctrine an attempt to substitute for general principles of international law an exclusively American law.[100]

Ironically, all the busy Anglo-French concern over Cuba created a suspense on which the Pierce administration determined to capitalize. It suddenly decided to purchase the island or to "detach" it from all dependence on any European power, including Spain. An incident that occurred at Havana on February 28, 1854, offered a convenient pretext for action. On this day, the Cuban authorities seized the American steamer, *Black Warrior,* for a violation of customs regulations which had previously not been enforced. According to the expansionists, this seizure demonstrated the risks and intolerable humiliation to which the present rulers of Cuba exposed American commerce. Sensing an immediate attack, the French envoy held a long conference with Secretary of State William L. Marcy. In an effort to prevent the violation of the island's integrity, he stressed the purely commercial nature of the Havana incident. Before he left, he informed Marcy that France would insist on the observation of the principles laid down in the tripartite project.[101]

But the outbreak of the Crimean War in April of 1854 made it very unlikely that the entente cordiale would resort to action on account

99. Everett to Sartiges, Washington, D. C., December 1, 1852. *FNFDS,* VI.
100. Drouyn de Lhuys to Sartiges, Paris, December 23, 1852. *CPEU,* CVIII. See also X. Raymond, "Diplomatie anglo-américaine," *RDDM* (April 15, 1853), pp. 298-333.
101. H. L. Janes, "The Black Warrior Affair," *AHR,* XII (1907), 280-98.

of Cuba. Since few Americans could be better informed about European affairs than the three American ministers at London, Paris, and Madrid, Secretary of State Marcy recommended their consulting together about the safest way of acquiring Cuba. Meeting at Ostend, Belgium, in October, 1854, they agreed that their government should first try to buy the island for $120,000,000. In case Spain should decline to sell it at all, they counseled the adoption of the aggressive course of wresting it from Spain.[102]

These recommendations were not kept secret and, once informed about them, startled the European cabinets. Ever since the conquest of California they had been aware of the danger that the next phase of American expansionism would center on Cuba and Hawaii. But in spite of the often defiant and militant attitudes of the youthful American republic toward the monarchies of the Old World, the powers of Europe could hardly believe that Washington would be so reckless as to risk a war on account of Cuba. France and Great Britain left little doubt that the Crimean War would not deter them from going to Spain's assistance in order to prevent America's acquisition of Cuba. Contrary to previous estimates, the prospect of war with Spain became so real that Marcy "brusquely abandoned" his representatives abroad.[103] So soon after the Mexican War, he had no intention of plunging the nation into another military adventure. The secretary knew that the vital place of Cuba in the framework of the Union's security assured the continued search for a settlement of the Cuban question. History has demonstrated that fundamental international issues have a way of perpetuating themselves for centuries, if necessary. Counting on time to remove European obstructions from the course of America's life-lines, Marcy yielded temporarily to superior force. But France and Britain had only won a Pyrrhic diplomatic victory, bought at the cost of America's growing mistrust of Europe.

Southerners saw to it that the issue was kept alive. Neither foreign nor domestic objections to the acquisition of Cuba dismayed them. That Congress was not united on the Cuban question was evidenced by a minority report of the House Committee on Foreign Affairs. Some of its members did not like the idea of strengthening Catholic influences in the United States by adding a predominantly

102. For the Ostend Manifesto, see *House Ex. Doc.*, 33 Cong., 2 sess., No. 93, pp. 127-36. This consultative meeting of the three American diplomats in Europe caused a considerable stir in Europe. Robert L. Scribner, "The Diplomacy of William Marcy" (Ph.D. dissertation, University of Virginia, 1949), pp. 198-99.

103. Ettinger, p. 396.

Catholic population. Others took exception to the argument that Cuba was needed to bolster the Union's security. They raised the pertinent question: what would happen to the "civilized world" if all powers alleged that their neighbor's territory was required for their security?[104]

In 1859, in the course of a Congressional debate on the acquisition of Cuba, Southern Senators showed little patience for any disagreement with their views. If the United States wished to purchase the island and Spain would be willing to sell, they protested that it was none of England's or France's business to meddle in the matter. "So far as a threat is implied of their combined intervention," declared Senator Trusten Polk of Missouri, "it has no terrors for me."[105] For good measure, Senator Robert Toombs of Georgia dared Europe to interfere; he expressed the super-patriotic notion that "we are able to maintain our independence against England and France thrown in the scale with Spain, at any moment."[106] The Buchanan administration obviously did not share this confidence.[107]

The effect of Great Britain's policies upon the mid-nineteenth-century relations between France and the United States in the Western Hemisphere can hardly be overemphasized. As an enterprising commercial sea power Britain was as much concerned with the protection of its considerable interests in the Americas as with the relative distribution of power in the world. For any major accretion of power in the Western Hemisphere by the United States, France, or Great Britain was destined to alter this distribution. Thus, while Paris usually joined forces with London in an effort to contain the United States, it was significant that these two European powers also watched each other in an effort to block their respective ambitions in the New World. The strong position Great Britain then occupied in the Caribbean region enabled it to exercise an influence which French and American statesmen could not afford to ignore. Even so, France strengthened its cultural, diplomatic, and economic ties with many nations in Central and South America. But despite the

104. Senators Zachariah Chandler of Michigan and Jacob Collamer of Vermont also raised the religious question. They doubted that the devoutly Catholic people of Cuba would respect the religious freedom of Protestants. *Cong. Globe,* 35 Cong., 2 sess., pp. 1081, 1183 (Feb. 17 and 21, 1859). The Jackson *Mississippian* of December 5, 1854, anticipated the "cunning scheme of the Know-Nothings to appeal to the dominant Protestant feeling in the South against Catholic Cuba."

105. *Cong. Globe,* 35 Cong., 2 sess., pp. 1085-86 (Feb. 17, 1859).

106. *Ibid.,* p. 542 (Jan. 24, 1859).

107. B. Willson, *John Slidell and the Confederates in Paris, 1862-1865* (New York, 1932), p. 18.

adventurous activities of many Frenchmen and the often demonstrated readiness of the French government to defy the principles of the Monroe Doctrine, during the period under consideration France did not make territorial gains in the Western Hemisphere. Anglo-American opposition to French expansion in the New World evidently proved to be more effective than Anglo-French opposition to the westward movement of the United States.

The two European powers were more successful in resisting United States penetration of Central and South America. Britain, however, rather than France, may claim the credit for this accomplishment. For that matter, Washington had no intention of "penetrating" South America. And it actually contributed to the pacification of Central America with its ratification of the Clayton-Bulwer Treaty (1850). This treaty established not only Anglo-American cooperation in regard to the construction and use of an Isthmian canal, but it also contained a mutual, though ambiguously phrased, pledge against aggression in Central America. Inasmuch as the taming of America's "Manifest Destiny" was a major policy objective of France, it obviously welcomed such a pledge. It would have felt even more reassured about the independence of the Central and South American states if its statesmanlike suggestion of regional federations had been favorably acted upon. From the French point of view, such federations would have been ideal barriers to the ambitions of the British, as well as of the North Americans.

The Pacific Region

While these three powers thus competed in the Western Hemisphere, they were simultaneously trying to check each other in Hawaii. Hawaii's location made it an objective which the major powers eyed with jealous temptation. Up to the 1830's France displayed great timidity and pettiness in the Pacific region.[108] From then on the enterprising activities of the Anglo-Americans alerted French statesmen to the necessity of accelerating their empire plans in the Pacific. When they realized that they were falling behind in the global distribution of power, they also made another discovery. Religion was an issue in the Pacific because Protestant missionaries from North America and Britain had "conquered" the souls of the natives before the merchants conquered the markets.

When in the summer of 1827 French missionaries and artisans at-

---

108. J. P. Faivre, *L'expansion française dans le Pacifique de 1800 à 1842* (Paris, 1953), p. 276.

tempted to lay the foundation for a colony in Hawaii, a bitter religious conflict developed, in many respects reminiscent of the religious wars of the sixteenth century.[109] American missionaries had inculcated the Hawaiian people with Protestant concepts. To them, the arrival of Catholic priests was like the coming of the plague. Catholicism, they prophesied, would bring alcoholism, immorality, and war to the islands.[110] Taking these warnings of their influential American advisers seriously, the native chiefs banned or otherwise persecuted Catholics. They regarded the adoption of a religious faith other than Protestantism as amounting to insubordination. Moreover, because many of their political opponents collaborated with Catholics, as far as the native chiefs were concerned, Catholicism assumed the character of treason. The religious persecution reached a climax with the ordinance of 1837 which forbade the teaching of "the peculiarities of the Pope's religion."[111]

Assuming the role of the modern secular protector of the Catholic faith, France decided to teach the Hawaiians and their Calvinist American missionaries to respect its religious and commercial interests or suffer the consequences. With a show of force, threatening extermination in case of refusal, Captain Laplace negotiated a treaty with Hawaii in 1839. It recognized the rights of Catholics and secured favorable conditions for the importation of French wines and brandies.[112] The imposed end of prohibition and the use of force did anything but contribute to the popularity of the French minority. The alcohol question henceforth created considerable friction with the French. This was complicated by the fact that the American missionaries succeeded in convincing the Hawaiians that French wines and brandies were the devil's brew. For the protection of the natives' health, the government, supported by the Protestant missionaries, preferred the prohibition of all intoxicating liquors. The King dramatized this issue when in 1842 he became president of the Hawaiian Temperance

---

109. Among the excellent studies which have thrown considerable light on these religious conflicts are: H. W. Bradley, *The American Frontier in Hawaii—The Pioneers, 1789-1843* (Stanford, 1942); J. I. Brookes, *International Rivalry in the Pacific Islands, 1800-1875* (Berkeley, 1941); Charles A. Julien, *Histoire de L'Océanie* (Paris, 1951); Aarne A. Koskinen, *Missionary Influence as a Political Factor in the Pacific Islands* (Helsinki, 1953); R. S. Kuykendall, *The Hawaiian Kingdom, 1778-1854* (Honolulu, 1938); and B. Smith, *Yankees in Paradise* (New York, 1956).

110. Bradley, *The American Frontier in Hawaii*, pp. 184-85, 296.

111. Kuykendall, pp. 57, 151; see also C. Gessler, *Hawaii* (New York, 1937), p. 78.

112. Kuykendall, pp. 150-67; Bradley, pp. 311-18.

Society.[113] But the French would not yield and threatened eternal war against this temperance movement.[114]

Many psychological factors explained the gradual progress the priests achieved in spite of all obstacles. Above all else, they sympathized with the natives' desire to preserve their own culture, while the Yankees introduced alien ways. Also, Catholic services appealed to the Hawaiians. They were more colorful, less abstract, and shorter than those of the Protestants; and instead of collecting money, the priests handed out gifts, especially to children. In contrast to their Protestant competitors, moreover, they did not hesitate to recognize human weaknesses. If the natives liked to smoke or drink, they saw nothing sinful in it.[115]

Helpful as their understanding of human nature was, the French missionaries needed assistance in their uphill struggle to assert themselves. Envisioning a far flung system of French possessions in the Pacific,[116] Guizot saw to it that they received diplomatic and naval support. The arrival at Honolulu of a French naval vessel caused considerable alarm in 1842.[117] In order to forestall French seizure of the islands, a British naval officer hastily arranged a British protectorate which lasted only until July of 1843 because London disapproved of this unauthorized step. To avoid any future collision of this kind, France and Great Britain signed four months later an agreement pledging "never to take possession, under any form, any part of the islands."[118] Much to their regret, the United States refused to underwrite this declaration, although the Tyler administration disclaimed any desire to seek exclusive control over Hawaii. As a constructive way of avoiding a conflict over it, Daniel Webster suggested that the commercial advantages the islands offered be made available to all powers.[119]

In spite of all these promises, the governments which made them

113. Smith, *Yankees in Paradise,* p. 248.

114. Perrin to Turgot, Paris, January 12, 1852. *CCC, Honolulu,* I.

115. Smith, *Yankees in Paradise,* pp. 234, 326-29. The same situation prevailed in the South Sea region. A growing number of natives preferred the pomp and ceremonies of the Catholics to the austerity of the Anglo-American Puritans. Koskinen, p. 94.

116. H. W. Bradley, "Hawaii and the American Penetration of the North-Eastern Pacific, 1800-1845," *Pacific Historical Review,* XII (1943), 284.

117. G. V. Blue, "The Project for a French Settlement in the Hawaiian Islands, 1824-1842," *Pacific Historical Review,* II (1933), 85-99.

118. Brookes, p. 137; see also S. K. Stevens, *American Expansion in Hawaii, 1842-1898* (Harrisburg, Pa., 1945), pp. 15-19.

119. Webster to Brown, Washington, D. C., March 15, 1843. *SMDS,* I.

apparently continued to suspect each other of aggressive designs. Future developments justified such distrust. On August 13, 1849, French naval forces suddenly landed at Honolulu and occupied the fort and two buildings for two days.[120] Unwilling to yield to French demands for special privileges, the Hawaiians asked for immediate Anglo-American intervention. It was not forthcoming. At that time, the discourtesies of the French minister in Washington, Guillaume Tell Poussin, had already strained the relations between France and the United States. The Taylor administration did not want to become involved in another controversy with republican France. It did little more, therefore, than speak up in favor of Hawaiian independence. Disgusted American citizens clamored for the State Department "to growl a little at the French." But the Hawaiians had to wait for several months before Washington as much as promised them aid.

The American government acted quite wisely on this occasion. Why should it complicate its relations with Paris when it could reasonably count on the jealousy of the United Kingdom to stop France in Hawaii? Lord Palmerston indeed cautioned the French repeatedly not to drive the islanders into the hands of the Americans. Furthermore, Dr. Gerrit P. Judd, the Hawaiian agent in Europe, received assurances of London's good offices. The British government would have preferred an arrangement whereby France, Great Britain, and the United States would bind themselves to respect the independence of Hawaii. However, as in the case of Cuba, the American government refused to become a party to a tripartite agreement.[121]

In the summer of 1851 intelligence reached Washington that French naval forces intended to renew the demands which had not been granted in 1849. The situation worried the American Board of Missions in Hawaii so much that it requested President Fillmore to dispatch a naval force for the protection of American residents. This time the State Department served France prompt notice that any attempt to subjugate the Hawaiian government would result in grave consequences.[122] This warning, based, as he claimed, on false rumors, hurt the foreign minister of France. He deplored the fact that his country had to take recourse to an "energetic tone of negotiation" to obtain equal treatment with the other, more influential foreign powers

120. J. M. Callahan, *American Relations in the Pacific and the Far East, 1784-1900* (Baltimore, 1901), pp. 118-19. It should be noted that Consul Dillon rather than the French government was behind this aggressive move.

121. Stevens, pp. 51-55.

122. Webster to Rives, Washington, D. C., June 15, 1851. *FIDS*, XV.

in Hawaii. To the gratification of Secretary Webster, Baroche not only promised not to tamper with the independence of the islands, but also to turn down a protectorate if they asked for it.[123]

Although in 1851 the French government reached a fairly satisfactory agreement which safeguarded its interests in Hawaii, it complained that the progress of the negotiations had been obstructed by the United States. France also attributed to the United States the defiant spirit of the native population towards France which found its expression in commercial, cultural, and religious discrimination.

The Hawaiian question continued to assume a growing international complexity. In view of the latest French pressures the Hawaiian government prepared a secret proclamation placing the islands under the protection of the United States.[124] Without authorization from his government, the American commissioner at Honolulu privately promised to defend them and actually discussed a course of action with the captain of the *U. S. S. Vandalia*. Because they transacted five-sixths of their commerce with the not so distant Union, the islands preferred to come under its control rather than live in a permanent state of insecurity. But while Washington could not accept such a proposition without inviting the interposition of the maritime powers, it promised to send a naval squadron to the Pacific strong enough to guarantee Hawaii's safety.

Those Americans who, after Commodore Matthew C. Perry's expedition to Japan, envisioned growing contacts with Asia realized that Hawaii would make an ideal base in the Pacific. Indeed, in his inaugural address President Franklin Pierce had already hinted at the desirability of acquiring "certain possessions not within our jurisdiction eminently important for our protection." The attention which his Secretary of State paid to the Hawaiian Islands clearly indicated that they were among those possessions. For this reason the British and French ministers at Washington thought that the islands were even more exposed to an American *coup de main* than Cuba. Secretary of State Marcy knew that these diplomats cooperated closely to prevent such a move. But he gained the impression that their governments would not go so far as to use force in a showdown. Nor was he much concerned about intimations that Russia had made a vague offer to lend support to the entente in this issue.[125] As if to test Sartiges, Marcy asked him whether he would not prefer to see the islands in

123. Baroche to Rives, Paris, July 17, 1851. *NALP.*
124. R. S. Kuykendall and A. Grove Day, *Hawaii: A History* (New York, 1948), p. 73.
125. Marcy to Mason, Washington, D. C., December 16, 1853. *FIDS,* XV.

American rather than in English or Russian hands. The French diplomat was not embarrassed for his reply: "You know very well that Russia cannot, France will not, and Britain has declined to annex Hawaii."[126] He labored strenuously to impress upon Marcy "that such a transfer would be forcibly resisted by a coalition of all maritime powers, the great and the small ones."[127] That this was no idle threat was demonstrated in the fall of 1854 when combined Anglo-French naval forces moved into Hawaiian waters to protest against the impending annexation.[128] If Hawaii could not be neutralized, Sartiges recommended the establishment of an Anglo-French protectorate as an alternative.[129]

Nevertheless, Marcy continued to be optimistic about Europe's eventual acquiescence in a negotiated transfer of Hawaii. Anxious to act soon, he consulted his assistants in London and Paris in an effort to ascertain how great the risk would really be. James Buchanan, who ranked as his top adviser, did not expect that England would fight, despite Lord Clarendon's public warning that "there is no portion of the two hemispheres with regard to which the policy of the two countries [France and Great Britain], however heretofore antagonistic, is not now in entire harmony."[130] He thought, however, that "it would be consistent with Napoleon's character to attempt to humble us."[131] The consideration which led to the decision against annexation at that time was the American government's realization that it could not defend the islands against a strong naval assault. Fearing that overextension might weaken, if not humiliate, the United States, the Pierce administration respected, as in the case of Cuba, the realities of power politics.[132] Many French diplomats believed that this restraint really involved no sacrifice because Americans had already annexed Hawaii in a more or less disguised way.[133]

Before the mid-nineteenth century, American influence extended from the Pacific to the China coast. While Britain too showed much interest in this region and developed a sizable trade with the Far

126. Sartiges to Drouyn de Lhuys, Washington, D. C., November 21, 1853. *CPEU*, CX.

127. *Ibid.*, June 7, 1853. *CPEU*, CIX.

128. Callahan, p. 122.

129. Sartiges to Drouyn de Lhuys, Washington, D. C., November 27, 1853. *CPEU*, CX.

130. Quoted in Stevens, p. 66.

131. *Ibid.*, p. 69.

132. R. Van Alstyne, "Great Britain, the United States, and Hawaiian Independence, 1850-1855," *Pacific Historical Review*, IV (1935), 22-23.

133. Berthemy to Moustier, Washington, D. C., March 18, 1867. *CPEU*, CXXXVIII.

East, the French suffered the fate of the late-comer. By the time Guizot decided to extend French influence to the region of the Philippines[134] (1845) and to step up French activities in Hawaii, Americans were already too entrenched to be easily dislodged from there. In Oceania the British enjoyed the same advantage of a headstart. When Catholic missionaries, a majority Frenchmen, set out to explore the Pacific area, they soon learnt that there too religious rivalry marched side by side with worldly competition. They were convinced that their expulsion or nonacceptance by natives had been instigated by Anglo-American heretics. They tried, therefore, to enlist the support of their government and were gratified when a French naval force arrived in Oceania. Paris had not only embarked on a search for an equilibrium of power in the Pacific; it hoped that its active policy in this part of the world would also be a source of moral encouragement to Catholics in Latin America.[135]

The United States viewed French successes in Tahiti, the Marquesas, and New Caledonia with a certain satisfaction. For this march into Oceania created disputes between the European contenders from which America was likely to draw benefits. The French at least helped to slow down the advance of the British Empire.

The Far East

While the United States rejected the idea of a political balance in America, it worked for one in the Far East. Realistically seen, only Britain and Russia were then in a position to establish a preponderance in China. It took the positive assuredness of bias for Sartiges to accuse the United States of planning to transform China into an "American India."[136] It was perhaps natural that the major powers competed jealously for the promising market of 300,000,000 souls. Thus, in the year following the Nanking Treaty between China and Great Britain (1842), France and the United States promptly secured similar commercial privileges as well as permission to practice and teach the Christian religion in China.[137]

134. Bernard d'Harcourt, "Négociations relatives à un projet d'établissement colonial français en 1845," *Revue d'histoire diplomatique*, I (1887), 546.

135. Brookes, pp. 78-90, 111-12; see also Faivre, pp. 276, 373, 479; G. Goyau, *La France missionnaire dans les cinq parties du monde* (Paris, 1948), II, 393-406; and J. M. Sédès, *Histoire des missions françaises* (Paris, 1950), pp. 30-72.

136. Sartiges to Drouyn de Lhuys, Washington, D. C., July 3, 1854. *CPEU*, CXI.

137. See T. Dennett, *Americans in Eastern Asia* (New York, 1922), p. 178; P. Renouvin, *La question d'Extrême-Orient, 1840-1940* (Paris, 1946), pp. 29-30; and John K. Fairbank, *Trade and Diplomacy on the China Coast, The Opening of the Treaty Ports, 1842-1854* (Cambridge, Mass., 1953), I, 197.

On other occasions British and American officials saw to it that France would not get away with unilateral acts detrimental to other foreign powers in China. In 1849, for instance, the French consul at Shanghai wanted to compel foreigners first to apply to him before acquiring land in the French settlement. The American consul, supported by his British colleague, immediately protested against such an arrangement and finally succeeded in having land-titles registered in the consulate of the owner's nationality.[138] Similarly, when in the early 1860's the French demanded a concession at Ningpo, Anson Burlingame, the American expert on China, insisted that treaties with China conceded to the treaty powers jurisdiction over their own citizens, but never over the territory of China. He took strong exception to the French demand on the ground that any concession of territory to another government would, to that extent, abridge already granted treaty rights of American citizens to buy, sell, and live in any part of any treaty port.[139]

In spite of their mutual distrust, the most effective way of locally enforcing respect for the "Western barbarians" was by Western unity. American merchants in China regarded closest cooperation with the British and French as a matter of imperative necessity.[140] Much to their regret they found that the government in Washington, backed by public opinion, did not understand their special problems. Ever since Webster's instructions to Caleb Cushing, the first American commissioner to China, the United States did not wish "to enter into controversies between China and any European State."[141] In fact, its officials in China and Japan carefully avoided identifying their interests with those of the Europeans.[142]

While all Western naval forces in the China Seas took concurrent steps to restrain the piracies against their commerce,[143] during the critical years from 1856 to 1860 Washington rejected several Anglo-French requests for concerted naval operations against China. President Buchanan sympathized with their war aims, but he deplored the use of force to gain the right of diplomatic residence at Peking,

138. H. B. Morse, *The International Relations of the Chinese Empire* (London, 1910), I, 349.

139. Burlingame to Seward, Peking, November 12, 1862. Seward Papers.

140. E. Griffin, *Clippers and Consuls* (Ann Arbor, 1938), p. 176.

141. P. H. Clyde, *United States Policy toward China, 1839-1939* (Durham, N. C., 1940), pp. 9-12.

142. Drouyn de Lhuys to Sartiges, Paris, June 15, 1854; see also John F. Cady, *The Roots of French Imperialism in Eastern Asia* (Ithaca, N. Y., 1954), pp. 110-11.

143. Parker to U. S. residents in Canton, Macao, April 6, 1857. *DDCDS*, II.

as well as additional commercial and religious privileges.[144] For that matter, contemporaries speculated that firm Anglo-French control of the coast of China might be contrary to the long-range interests of the United States in the Pacific. The position of neutrality which the Buchanan administration adopted in this conflict served as a reminder to London and Paris that other powers reserved the right to have their own policy with regard to China. America's abstention from military intervention in this war enabled it to render precious diplomatic services as the only available contact between the Europeans and the Chinese.[145]

The United States did not become a party to the peace treaty which concluded this conflict. But once peace was restored, it obtained the same benefits for which France and Britain had fought.[146] China granted them not just to reward American forbearance and nonintervention, but also to hold the growing European influence in the Far East at bay. Peking continued to pursue the policy that advantages Europeans had secured by treaties would be extended to Americans. China's reliance on the good intentions and fair sense of the United States led it to go so far in 1868 as to entrust Anson Burlingame with the mission of representing it as its ambassador to various Western governments. The French minister in Washington interpreted this extraordinary assignment as an attempt by the Chinese to implement their favorite proverb: "Oppose the barbarians with barbarians."[147] Whether this speculation was right or wrong, the French government deplored the fact that it did not feel free to discuss Far Eastern problems with this American spokesman for China as profoundly as it would have desired.[148] During this decade, however, France was greatly pleased with Washington's cooperation in the enforcement of the existing treaties with China and Japan. For soon after Americans had succeeded in ending Japan's isolation,[149] the European powers sought to negotiate treaties by which Japan would extend to them rights and privileges similar to those granted to the United States.[150] American influence in Asia could thus be kept

144. Henri Cordier, L'expédition de Chine de 1857-58 (Paris, 1905), pp. 170, 296; Morse, p. 485; Renouvin, pp. 36-37.

145. For the importance of these diplomatic services, see Henri Cordier, L'expédition de Chine de 1860 (Paris, 1906), pp. 252-54; see also Cady, The Roots of French Imperialism, pp. 258-59.

146. Clyde, p. 59.

147. Berthemy to Moustier, Washington, D. C., March 5, 1868. CPEU, CXLI.

148. Moustier to Berthemy, Paris, February 13, 1868. CPEU, CXLI.

149. J. H. Gubbins, The Progress of Japan, 1853-1871 (Oxford, Eng., 1911), p. 48.

150. Yosoburo Takekoshi, The Economic Aspects of the History of the Civilization of Japan (London, 1930), III, 301-25.

within bounds, to the satisfaction of Frenchmen who watched American activities in the Orient with bitter jealousy.[151]

Their first exposures to Western civilization taught the Japanese the rather strange lesson that distrust and fear may be used as instruments of international policy. Although historically the disintegration of its feudal system may have been the chief reason why Japan decided to establish contact with the West, it signed the treaty with the United States after having been frightened with the possibility of a French attack against the Loo Choo Islands. Since America was a Pacific power which had not expanded beyond its continental frontier, cooperation with it offered a certain assurance against European aggression.[152]

The Japanese considered the American envoy's attempt to negotiate a tariff by which Japan would tax American goods 5 percent, those of the British 20 percent, and French wines 35 percent as just another American intrigue against Europeans.[153] But what appeared to Westerners to be legitimate competition looked to Orientals like the Achilles heel of the white race. Also religious rivalry between Catholics and Protestants bared a weakness of Western civilization they did not fail to appreciate.

Nevertheless, when necessity required it, here as in China, the United States cooperated with the Europeans in the defense of common interests. Through identical diplomatic protests, for instance, Westerners tried to convince Japan that it could not hope to divide them in matters involving the observance of treaties.[154] When in 1868, in violation of existing treaties, the Mikado prohibited "the Christian and other evil religions," foreign Catholics and Protestants in Japan temporarily forgot their rivalries in order to protect their religious treaty rights.[155] Similarly, in 1864 one American ship joined the Dutch, English, and French in the chastisement of the Prince of Nayato for his attacks against foreign ships. As a result of this successful undertaking the diplomatic agents of these four powers secured additional Japanese guaranties for their ships.[156]

In 1867 Secretary of State William H. Seward took the initiative

---

151. H. Rouhaud, Les régions nouvelles (Paris, 1868), p. 199; see also Griffin, p. 9.

152. P. J. Treat, Diplomatic Relations between the United States and Japan, 1853-1895 (Stanford, Calif., 1932), I, 54, 72; see also Stephen King-Hall, Western Civilization and the Far East (London, 1924), p. 31.

153. Dennett, p. 359.

154. Drouyn de Lhuys to Mercier, Paris, July 2, 1863. CPEU, CXXX.

155. Berthemy to Moustier, Washington, D. C., July 25, 1868. CPEU, CXLII.

156. Drouyn de Lhuys to Geoffroy, Paris, January 5, 1865. CPEU, CXXXIII.

in inquiring whether France would be disposed to concerted action with the United States for the purpose of compelling Korea to establish treaty relations with them.[157] Recent Korean acts of violence against French missionaries and the American merchantship *General Sherman* seemed to justify a demand for certain contractual safeguards against the recurrence of such barbarities. Since Korea was expected not to yield to such a demand voluntarily, forceful "persuasion" would have become necessary. Whatever political considerations motivated Secretary of State Seward when he made this overture, the French were not in the mood at this time to organize a joint Franco-American naval expedition. The French government gave assurances, however, that it would "applaud any new progress toward civilization the United States might make in those distant regions."[158]

Europe

It is noteworthy that France and Britain encouraged America's involvement in Asia but discouraged it with respect to European affairs. France welcomed the often stated American principle of nonintervention as far as it applied to the European continent. It also saw in the nonexistence of an effective military organization in America a welcome guaranty for the pacific and passive role it wished the United States to play in the Old World.

France reacted with disapproval to any sign of America's growing interest in Europe. This involved more than resentment against its republican propaganda and the willingness of prominent American citizens "to lend an ear to the desperate cries of the oppressed of the Old World."[159] It was particularly sensitive about any interest the United States displayed in the Mediterranean region. Paris felt "considerable anxiety" when in 1830 the American minister to France made the following comment with reference to the Algerian question: "We have important interests in the Mediterranean which do not admit of our being altogether indifferent to the future destiny of any portion of its borders."[160] Information to the effect that in 1853 the United States was about to conclude a financial deal with Turkey, as a result of which it might become Austria's troublesome "neighbor" in the Mediterranean, prompted Foreign Minister Drouyn de Lhuys to

157. Berthemy to Moustier, Washington, D. C., March 3, 1867. *CPEU,* CXXXVIII; see also Dennett, pp. 418-21.
158. Moustier to Berthemy, Paris, March 29, 1867. *CPEU,* CXXXVIII.
159. *Journal des Débats,* August 24, 1853.
160. Rives to Van Buren, Paris, July 17, 1830. *DDFDS,* XXIV.

urge Vienna that it nip such a possibility in the bud.[161]   Later attempts of the United States to establish a coaling station in the Mediterranean were still regarded as an undesirable interference with the interests of European powers.[162]   The government of Napoleon III was, moreover, annoyed when in 1855 the Sultan of Morocco requested the United States to mediate his dispute with France.   Count Walewski, who was then in charge of the French Foreign Ministry, promptly let it be known that he would decline such mediation.[163] Supported by Britain, France also objected to America's willingness to honor Persia's request for the protection of its ships.[164]   Nor did the two great European sea powers like the idea when Washington took the initiative in the successful fight against the payments of dues in the Danish Sound.[165]

The discreet burial of Secretary of State Marcy's offer to end the Crimean War through his friendly mediation is of considerable historical importance.   Sartiges transmitted it to Paris on June 26, 1854. It did not come as a surprise to Drouyn de Lhuys.   As his pencil-marks on the margin of Sartiges' letter indicate, Soulé had previously informed him about the Russians' overtures to enlist the aid of Washington.   "Elude it politely" was the Foreign Minister's advice to Sartiges.   "The United States," he commented, "can hardly hope to solve the Eastern Question for which the European powers have been unable to find a solution during the last twenty-five years.   But should it succeed, it would, contrary to established principles, become deeply involved in European affairs."[166]   He advised, therefore, that Marcy not make his offer officially.

The growing understanding between Russia and the United States foreshadowed a development of the most disturbing nature to France. Interpreting the entente cordiale as directed against them both, the governments of Tsarist Russia and the American republic acted as if the bizarre project of their alliance lay in the realm of concrete possibilities.   Talk about such an offensive and defensive alliance was at least considered to be useful.   London and Paris were concerned about it at the time of the Crimean War.   Although they expected the United States to observe a strict neutrality in the war, their appeal was

161. Drouyn de Lhuys to Walewski, Paris, December 8 and 13, 1853.   Confidential. *MDF*, 2120, Nos. 98 and 99.

162. *La Patrie*, December 4, 1866.

163. Walewski to Boilleau, Paris, August 23, 1855.   *CPEU*, CXIII.

164. Boilleau to Walewski, Washington, D. C., December 16, 1855.   *CPEU*, CXIII; see also Miller, *Treaties*, VII, 453-70.

165. *La Patrie*, February 12, 1857.

166. Drouyn de Lhuys to Sartiges, Paris, July 20, 1854.   *CPEU*, CXI.

not entirely heeded. The United States was officially neutral, but not morally. While Americans sympathized with Turkey in its conflict with Russia, they leaned towards Russia in its struggle with the maritime powers. They feared that Russia's defeat might expose them to increased Anglo-French pressure. America's friendly attitude towards Russia manifested itself in many ways. The Russian legation at Washington received innumerable requests from Americans who wished to arm privateers under the Russian flag.[167] The French government, furthermore, knew about Russian naval construction orders in New York.[168] It was also disappointed about the Pierce administration's rejection of its complaint regarding the sale of Russian ships to Americans when the war overtook these ships in American ports.[169] Since the United States and France had been drifting apart, Napoleon III counted heavily on the conclusion of the war before the Russian fleet could receive American aid.

In at least one instance during the Crimean War, France had reason to be grateful to the United States. It is little known that after the unsuccessful attack on Petropavlovsk the French fleet sailed into the harbor of San Francisco. Although not driven in by distress, it brought a prize and some prisoners of war with it. But instead of giving signs of uneasiness at this "unneutral" visit, the local population gave their guests a very cordial reception.[170]

Traditionally, Franco-American understanding existed on the issue of the freedom of the seas.[171] In view of Britain's naval superiority all other powers had a special interest in liberal maritime principles. However, up to the Crimean War the United States discouraged all great combinations for the purpose of regulating maritime problems. It was finally willing to revise this position when at the beginning of that war France and Britain declared that they would respect the American principle that free ships make free goods. Had it not been for the principle of abolishing privateering, which was an integral part of the Declaration of Paris with respect to neutral rights, Washington would have adhered to the declaration. Secretary of State Marcy was even ready to yield on this point if the other powers would have adopted the principle of the immunity of private property on land

167. A. G. Jomini, *Diplomatic Study on the Crimean War* (London, 1882), II, 76.
168. Sartiges to Drouyn de Lhuys, Washington, D. C., January 8, 1854. *CPEU*, CX.
169. Walewski to Mason, Paris, December 27, 1855. *NALP*.
170. Marcy to Mason, Washington, D. C., December 13, 1854. Confidential. *FIDS*, XV.
171. Boilleau to Walewski, Washington, D. C., November 9, 1855. *CPEU*, CXIII.

and at sea.[172] The French were disappointed that in the end the Union did not accede to the convention. They thought that the proposed modification could have been the subject of future negotiations. But the arithmetic of power politics made this procedure unacceptable to Washington.[173] Without other guaranties, its national security called for continued reliance on privateers to supplement its small navy in case of war.[174]

The frictions and suspicions which characterized Franco-American relations during these decades taught both powers not to take each other for granted. The essentially negative policy of France, aiming at the containment of the dynamic United States, was, however, not as narrowly conceived as it might appear. Fundamentally constructive as America's growth has been, it was destined in time to change the distribution of power in the world to such a degree that the aspirations of France as a major power would be detrimentally affected by it. The persistence of France's containment policy was not matched by an equal determination to implement it forcefully. While this approach condemned French policy to partial failure, it should be noted that it also resulted in the avoidance of a really deep-rooted antagonism between the two countries.

172. F. Piggot, *The Declaration of Paris, 1856* (London, 1919), pp. 142-49, 209; see also C. Savage, *Policy of the United States towards Maritime Commerce in War* (Washington, D. C., 1934), I, 63-73.

173. Pellisier de Reynaud, "Le droit maritime selon le congrès de Paris," *RDDM* (February 15, 1857), pp. 923-26.

174. The American ministers at London and Paris advised against giving up the right of privateering.

CHAPTER III

Franco-American Incidents
(1830-1860)

I

ALTHOUGH MINOR INTERNATIONAL INCIDENTS may not be significant in themselves, they do occasionally lead to unpleasant complications. The crisis growing out of the so-called spoliation claims, for instance, led France and the United States to the very brink of war.

Prior to the July Revolution of 1830, France was not disposed to settle American indemnity claims dating back to the Napoleonic wars.[1] Originally, the United States demanded compensations for seizure, confiscation, or destruction of ships and goods amounting to 92,000,000 francs. To many Frenchmen this "outrageous" demand reflected on the character of the "ungrateful" and "greedy" American people. While France made sacrifices in those wars, they charged, the neutral United States made profits. And now it had the bad taste of asking for more money! The commission Louis Philippe created to investigate the claims soon discovered that neither the Ministry of Marine nor the Customs Administration was in the possession of adequate records. The French Treasury thus lacked the necessary information to check on the validity of the claims.

In the course of the bargaining negotiations, France finally offered, and the United States accepted, the sum of 25,000,000 francs, equal in value to $5,000,000. The details of this agreement were stipulated in the Treaty of July 4, 1831. To facilitate speedy ratification of this treaty, the United States not only agreed to six installment payments, it also reduced duties on French wines for a period of ten years in

1. For an elaborate discussion of the spoliation claims, see R. A. McLemore, *Franco-American Diplomatic Relations, 1816-1836* (Baton Rouge, 1941). See also Samuel F. Bemis, *John Quincy Adams and the Union* (New York, 1956), pp. 305-22; and Glyndon G. Van Deusen, *The Jacksonian Era, 1828-1848* (New York, 1959), pp. 101-2.

exchange for an equivalent French reduction on American short staple cotton.[2]

Ugly rumors accompanied the French ratification. Opponents of the Orleanist regime insinuated that Louis Philippe's ministers had a personal stake in this financial settlement.[3] The embarrassment of the king's government reached truly uncomfortable proportions when the first installment draft, presented on February 7, 1833, was not honored. Although Washington knew about the failure of the French Chamber to appropriate the money for the draft, it decided that it had no right to question the good faith of the French government. Appropriation of the necessary funds or failure to do so was an exclusively internal problem which could have no legal bearing on the international validity of the treaty.[4]

Foreign Minister Achille de Broglie was stunned by the incomprehensible vote of 176 to 168 by which the Chamber rejected the financial implementation of the Treaty of 1831. This vote was not only likely to result in bitter reactions in Washington, but it also raised delicate constitutional questions affecting the prestige of the French executive branch. As soon as Count Louis Sérurier, the envoy of France to the United States, received the bad news, he acted to prevent any precipitate move on the part of the United States. He paid an unusual Sunday afternoon visit to the Secretary of State in the course of which Louis McLane confided to him that the Chamber's vote struck President Andrew Jackson like a thunderbolt. As Sérurier was riding home, he noticed that Henry Clay had stopped his horse in front of the legation. "Well," Clay greeted him, "this means war . . . and you'll have it if your Chamber continues to shower us with insult and contempt."[5] In reality, the object of Clay's visit was to urge France not to make a collision inevitable. He agreed with Jackson that this was not a miserable money affair, but a question of honor between two countries as well as of the sanctity of a treaty.

The President disregarded all advice not to threaten France or to question her good faith. To those who cautioned him not to use irritating language in his forthcoming annual message, he supposedly replied: "No, gentlemen, I know them French! They won't pay unless they are made to."[6] Accordingly, he recommended to the Con-

2. Miller, *Treaties*, III, 641-51. France agreed with great reluctance to pay an added interest of 4 percent on these installments.

3. Marcel Marion, "Un épisode oublié des relations pécuniaires franco-américaines," *RDDM* (November 1, 1926), p. 50.

4. Livingston to Broglie, Paris, November 11, 1833. *CPEU*, LXXXVII.

5. Sérurier to Broglie, Washington, D. C., May 11 and 20, 1834. *CPEU*, LXXXVIII.

6. Charles Peck, *The Jacksonian Epoch* (New York, 1890), p. 248.

gress the passage of a law authorizing reprisals upon French property in case of another refusal to honor the pledges made by the king's government. News of this recommendation angered Paris. Edward Livingston, representing the United States in France, pleaded in vain with French authorities that the reprisal message was an intergovernmental communication of which foreign governments had no right to take official cognizance. "If consultation between two branches of government involves the risk of war," he wrote to the Foreign Minister, "then it cannot take place."[7] Livingston misjudged the situation if he believed that his references to legal formalities, no matter how true, would restrain a France whose dignity had been offended by a formal menace.[8]

France promptly recalled Sérurier and offered Livingston his passports. Under the circumstances, his recall had become a matter of course. Before long, this affair also contributed to Broglie's temporary exit from the Foreign Ministry. From Washington, Sérurier reported: "War is possible."[9] He actually recommended engagement of American naval forces at the first indication of the imminence of war. Anticipating this possibility, Livingston warned Commodore Patterson to be on guard against surprise attacks on American naval units in the Mediterranean.[10] The crisis reached its high point of absurdity when Sérurier prophesied a war of thirty years, ending without glory or compensation. On the American side, a belligerent congressman from New York believed, on the contrary, that ten thousand American whalers could sweep the entire naval power of France from the ocean. At least one National Guard unit tendered its services to the President and solicited the honor of being entrusted with dangerous assignments.[11]

More sober minds prevailed in Congress.[12] They refused to support the formal declaration of war for which Senator Bedford Brown of North Carolina had asked. Congress looked upon a war with France, of all nations, as a most deplorable calamity. Also, common sense could not justify a war likely to cost several times as much as the "paltry 5,000,000 dollars" at issue. Under the leadership of Henry Clay the Senate postponed legislative measures which would further

7. Livingston to Rigny, Paris, January 29, 1835. *CPEU,* LXXXIX.

8. *Le Constitutionel,* January 9, 1835.

9. Sérurier to Rigny, Washington, December 25, 1834, and March 1, 1835. *CPEU,* LXXXVIII and LXXXIX.

10. See Richardson, *Messages,* II, 1359-60.

11. Pageot to Broglie, Washington, D. C., May 26, 1835. *CPEU,* LXXXIX.

12. See *Register of Debates,* XI, 106, 571-74, 1508, 1538-43 (January and February, 1835).

aggravate the crisis. This delaying action paid dividends of peace. It eased the emotional situation in which two sensitive nations had permitted themselves to become involved.

In France, such leading organs of public opinion as the *Revue des deux mondes, Le Journal des Débats,* and *Le Constitutionel* interpreted the potential tragedy as a political comedy. They reassured a panicky Bourse of the artificiality of the official irritation. After a lively debate the Chamber voted 289 to 137 for the money but adopted the qualifying Valazé amendment that payments be made only under the condition that President Jackson offer satisfactory explanations. Such a condition, perhaps dictated by a false pride, seemed to add new insults to old injuries.[13] Jackson was hardly the man to apologize for an injury his country had suffered. In his message to the Congress on December 7, 1835, he went so far as to state, however, that he never intended to menace or insult the government of France. For the sake of peace the French decided to interpret this comment as meeting the requirements of the Valazé amendment.

Although this controversy was thus peacefully settled, more than verbal concessions prevented the outbreak of a most ridiculous and impolitic war. All of the great powers had domestic and international reasons to urge conciliation. France, Great Britain, and Russia wished to avoid disturbances of world trade. At the height of the crisis Thiers suggested to Louis Philippe the desirability of England's mediation.[14] Lord Palmerston offered his good offices because the prospect of a French blockade of American ports would have greatly upset Britain's economy. Among other interests, British insurance companies urged their government to mediate the dispute, for having only recently sold many new policies, they were anxious to avoid the losses a war would impose upon them. For that matter, the business interests of France, especially those of Bordeaux, Le Havre, and Lyons, deplored the imprudence of the rejection of the funds.[15] The French consul in New York posed the pertinent question to his foreign minister: "In case of a conflict, where are we going to find a market for the 32,000,000 francs of silks sold this year to the United States?"[16] In addition to these economic considerations, France and Great Britain

13. This view was held by the New York *Evening Post* and the Washington *Globe* of May 29, 1835.

14. Georges Roux, *Thiers* (Paris, 1948), pp. 58-59. See also Charles K. Webster, "British Mediation between France and the United States in 1834-1836," *English Historical Review,* XLII (1927), 58-78.

15. *Journal des Débats,* January 18, 1835.

16. Forest to Rigny, New York, December 8, 1834. *CPEU,* LXXXVIII.

feared the possible international effects of a Franco-American war on the Near Eastern problem. Furthermore, the French consul at Tangiers had informed his government about several American attempts to obtain a naval station on the African coast. Louis Philippe did not want to give the United States a pretext to establish such a foothold. "One must avoid this," he thought, "rather than provoke it."[17] Besides, his throne was not secure enough to risk a war with the American republic.

In the United States, too, much more was at stake than the collection of past claims or the satisfaction of national honor which neither side had deliberately set out to offend. Not all the consequences of war could be foreseen. Would it be fatal to republican institutions? Would an unpopular war with France speed up the secession movement rather than divert the people from domestic complications? Contemporaries speculated about such consequences.[18] Moreover, as 1836 approached, the Van Buren forces could not ignore the effects of a war on the presidential election.[19] Neither war nor appeasement served their interests. A peaceful, but honorable solution would and did enable them to praise the skill with which Jackson conducted the foreign relations of the country.

II

Pride and prejudice had another international rendezvous during the Second French Republic. This did not speak well for the caliber of the French envoy who sacrificed his standing in Washington over a trivial issue. Guillaume Tell Poussin used such haughty and offensive language in his correspondence with the State Department that he suffered the embarrassment of having to retract certain inadmissible passages.[20] One such incident had just been closed when Poussin again failed to observe the propriety expected of a diplomat. In May of 1849 he complained to the State Department that Commander Carpender of the warship *Iris* had acted highhandedly by detaining the stranded French ship *L'Eugénie* off Vera Cruz. He demanded the punishment of the officer who, for a time, had thought that he was entitled to the right of salvage. As soon as the commander learned about the complications that might arise, he released the ship which he had saved from imminent peril. But he did not expect that censure rather than thanks would be his reward. Although his explanations

17. Webster, "British Mediation between France and the United States," p. 75.
18. Sérurier to Rigny, Washington, D. C., January 12, 1835. *CPEU*, LXXXIX.
19. Pageot to Broglie, Washington, D. C., May 28, 1835. *CPEU*, LXXXIX.
20. Clayton to Rives, Washington, D. C., September 14, 1849. *FIDS*, XV.

were legally backed by the Attorney General of the United States, Poussin pressed the issue without regard to consequences. Not satisfied with his insistence on a "severe reprimand" of the officer, he badly misjudged the American sense of fairness by his contemptuous sneer that "the commander's explanations are of little interest to us." And finally he transformed this insignificant affair into an international incident by his ill-considered protest against "the strange salvage doctrines to which the United States government seems to subscribe."[21]

When this communication was brought to the attention of the French Foreign Minister, Alexis de Tocqueville, he did not cherish the idea of being drawn into a delicate decision involving the career of a French diplomat. He would have preferred that the affair be concluded in Washington where it originated.[22] That was no longer possible. As far as the Taylor administration was concerned, Poussin's obnoxious notes disturbed the amity between the two republics. Poussin's position was further weakened by the fact that "the ladies of General Taylor's family thought they had good grounds for declining social intercourse with Madame Poussin."[23] Under these circumstances Tocqueville's wisest move would have been a face-saving diplomatic reshuffle. When, instead, he took Secretary of State John M. Clayton to task for his imperious treatment of the French envoy, President Taylor and his Secretary of State resented the fact that the French Foreign Minister appeared to sanction Poussin's discourteous statements. To uphold the dignity of the American government, the State Department now notified Poussin that it would cease to correspond with him and that "every proper facility for quitting the United States will be promptly given you."[24] The Taylor administration did not expel the French envoy outright. Nor did it break relations with France. A minister was to be put in his place, not his country.

Anxious weeks followed during which talk of war filled the air. When Poussin arrived in Paris, the President of the Council of Ministers received him with the words: "We have been ready to go to war for you."[25] But American diplomats in Paris advised their government to be firm. They warned that the slightest concession in this affair might be a precedent to "the representatives of imperious and presumptuous powers, and even those of puny states . . . to address on

21. Poussin to Clayton, Washington, D. C., May 30, 1849. *FNTDS*, XIV.
22. Tocqueville to Rush, Paris, August 9, 1849. *NALP*.
23. B. Dyer, *Zachary Taylor* (Baton Rouge, 1946), pp. 349-52.
24. Clayton to Rives, Washington, September 14, 1849. *FIDS*, XV.
25. G. T. Poussin, *Les États-Unis d'Amérique* (Paris, 1874), p. 189.

the most trivial occasions, offensive statements . . . to our government."[26] Governor John J. Crittenden of Kentucky too urged the Secretary of State "not to recede one inch. If they want war, let them have it. Europe is now pale before its despots, and we want the world to know that there is one people in it who do not fear them and are ready to kick them when they misbehave."[27]

It became quite obvious that Poussin had to leave Washington. As a matter of fact, the Quai d'Orsay had intended to replace him.[28] France had enough problems on hand without seeking a *casus belli* with the United States. Although the incident engendered a certain degree of tension, both countries really desired peace. The difficulty for France lay in finding a method by which this end might be achieved without giving the impression of a diplomatic defeat. It was finally found in the declaration that Boislecomte's appointment to the Washington post preceded any knowledge of the American rupture with Poussin.[29]

On its part, the United States made a conciliatory gesture enabling France not to suffer a loss of prestige. It too appointed a new minister. Unfortunately, however, Rives's arrival in Paris before the Poussin incident had been completely settled proved to be ill-timed. In the meantime, Tocqueville had sent a strongly worded letter to Secretary of State Clayton in which he blamed him for the existing state of affairs. He complained specifically about the State Department's failure to advise the authorities in Paris of Poussin's undesirability before asking him to leave the United States.[30] In view of this offense to the dignity of France, he decided neither to send Boislecomte to Washington nor to receive Rives's credentials until the United States offered its apologies. The Taylor administration reacted to this demand with firmness. It would not have hesitated to bring about a total suspension of relations with France. "Diplomatic intercourse with France," wrote Clayton, "is not so important to us as to make it necessary to submit to indignity."[31] He sent confidential

26. Mann to Clayton, Paris, October 25, 1849. *Sen. Doc.*, 61 Cong., 2 sess., No. 276, pp. 48-50.

27. Crittenden to Clayton, Frankfort, September 29, 1849. Clayton Papers, VI.

28. Clayton to Rives, Washington, D. C., September 14, 1849. *FIDS*, XV.

29. Rives to Clayton, Paris, October 10, 1849. *DDFDS*, XXXII.

30. Tocqueville to Clayton, Paris, October 11, 1849. *FNTDS*, XIV. On the other hand, the New York *Journal of Commerce* of October 10, 1849, severely criticized Clayton for not having dismissed Poussin as soon as the offending remarks had been made.

31. Clayton to Rives, Washington, D. C., January 1, 1850. Clayton Papers, VIII. In their judicious writings about American institutions Poussin and Tocqueville really admired the United States. It was unfortunate that President Taylor and Secretary

instructions to Rives to go to Prussia or Russia in case of further complications. This did not become necessary because the incident took an anticlimactic turn when President Louis Napoleon suddenly decided in the spring of 1850 that it was an unimportant misunderstanding. Official relations were fully resumed—without apologies.

III

A few years later, another crisis developed. This time, Patrice Dillon, the French consul at San Francisco, played the leading role. He had twice declined to testify in the course of criminal proceedings against his Mexican colleague. This was his privilege under Article II of the Franco-American Consular Convention of 1853. However, on the application of the Mexican consul, claiming that Dillon's testimony was material to his defense, the United States Court subpoenaed him. Although duly served, Dillon paid no attention to the subpoena, thus making his arrest inevitable. Upon protest, he was released after half an hour, during which he was treated with respect. But Dillon continued to consider himself a prisoner of the United States because the order of the arrest was not withdrawn. To demonstrate against this "insult to the honor of France," he hauled his flag down as soon as he reached his consular residence.

Exaggerating the "gravity" of this "serious" incident, the French minister in Washington immediately suggested the kind of satisfaction his government would offer in such a case. It would hasten to offer an apology, censure the guilty officials, and salute the consul's flag with twenty-one guns.[32] Believing this incident to be harmless, Secretary Marcy displayed a conciliatory spirit. Only Sartiges' tendency to magnify the controversy worried him. This fear was enhanced when the news arrived of a complication in San Francisco. Dillon had in the meantime been arrested and held on bail to the sum of $10,000 for violation of the Neutrality Law of 1818. He was indicted, brought to trial, and found guilty of hiring troops in the United States for service with a foreign power. Only the ten to two vote of the jury saved him from punishment. Sartiges looked upon this proceeding as a wanton aggravation. To him, it appeared so grave a matter as to be likely to disturb the peace. In a private note, written in English,

Clayton did not control their personal feelings in this incident. See Mary W. Williams, "John Middleton Clayton," in Bemis, ed., *American Secretaries*, VI, 19-31.

32. Sartiges to Marcy, Washington, May 29, 1854. *FNTDS*, XVI. Although the Quai d'Orsay accused the United States of having violated principles of international law in this case, it warned Sartiges not to exaggerate the episode. Drouyn de Lhuys to Sartiges, Paris, June 15, 1854. *CPEU*, CXI.

he begged Marcy "not to let the question slip from our diplomatic and friendly hands into the robust arms of our two peoples."[33]

The Secretary of State did not comprehend that the French government would take the case seriously. He was, therefore, interested in shifting its settlement from the excited French gentlemen in San Francisco and Washington to the world-wide policy makers at the French capital.[34] To show his government's good will, he not only expressed its regrets at the unfortunate dispute, but also assured the French government of reasonable satisfaction for any injury. Sartiges' specific suggestion, however, offended the sense of America's national honor. No wanton outrage or premeditated personal insult had been committed. If the punishment was to fit the crime, the issues involved in the case had to be cleared before judgment could be rendered.

The underlying question of this case involved the legality of Dillon's arrest. It did not lend itself to a ready decision due to conflicting interpretations of the consular convention and the Constitution of the United States. The French Foreign Minister asserted that a convention establishes privileges which sometimes derogate from the Constitution. If the convention did not take precedence over the Constitution, he asked, what guaranty would the consuls have against the invasion of their office and personal liberty?[35] Marcy, on the other hand, maintained that the Constitution was a higher law than the convention. In practical terms, this amounted to a declaration that Washington considered itself exonerated from all responsibility for Dillon's brief arrest.

The legalistic approach offered no hopeful solution to the affair. The arrest of Dillon may at best have been legally doubtful, but the judge who ordered it did not intend to offend the Emperor or the consul. What, then, did France want? Washington had expressed its regret for an incident not of its making. It felt that nothing more was called for. It certainly considered a formal salute of the consular flag as unduly humiliating. What could France possibly gain by it? France might be proud, but so could the United States. For over one year a voluminous correspondence and numerous official talks kept the statesmen of two great nations quibbling over an almost childish episode. While in Europe the Crimean War made history, the French minister to the United States fought for a salute to his consular flag.

When both governments realized that important material interests should not be jeopardized by petty, time-consuming quarrels, common

33. Sartiges to Marcy, Washington, D. C., July 31, 1854. *FNTDS*, XVI.
34. Marcy to Sartiges, Washington, D. C., September 13, 1854. *FNFDS*, VI.
35. Drouyn de Lhuys to Sartiges, Paris, November 23, 1854. *FNTDS*, XVI.

sense prevailed. French commercial interests were not served by a closed consulate. A compromise was finally worked out by which French and American naval forces exchanged salutes in the harbor of San Francisco. Count Walewski, the new nominal head of the Foreign Ministry, promised that this ceremony would obliterate all recollection of the incident.[36] His last minute maneuver, however, to restore Dillon's good standing with the authorities at San Francisco did not succeed. The United States had the last word in this case. Dillon had become *persona non grata*.

IV

In the fall of 1854 a second incident occurred, this time across the Atlantic. Suspicious of Pierre Soulé, the American minister to Spain, whose associations with the revolutionary leaders of Europe may have included gun-smuggling, French officials barred him from "penetrating into France" on one of his trips from London to Madrid. In this situation, Soulé could have chosen two alternatives of action. He could have waited in Calais for the go ahead signal. If it did not come soon, Washington would have considered his treatment a national insult. Or he could have immediately returned to London, angrily accusing Napoleon's government of a deliberate anti-American snub. He chose to return to London.

As soon as the American legation in Paris received this news, it demanded satisfactory explanations for this "most unusual and humiliating" proceeding. John Y. Mason, the American envoy to France, warned Washington to be prepared for trouble.[37] If duty and honor demanded it, he would ask for his passports. Although this discourteous treatment of an American minister indicated an unfriendly, if not hostile, disposition on the part of the French government, the Pierce administration deferred comments until Paris was given adequate time to investigate the matter. This dignified reserve was not shared by the American press. The Richmond *Enquirer* resented this latest affront to the national honor. The New York *Tribune* counseled retribution: "Recall our Minister and suspend commercial intercourse with France!"[38] On the other hand, the Portland *Transcript* ridiculed the fuss made over the affair. It supported the French

---

36. Walewski to Mason, Paris, August 7, 1855. *NALP*. For a discussion of the legal aspects of the Consular Convention of 1853, see the comments in the *American Journal of International Law*, XXIII (1929), 172-79.

37. Mason to Marcy, Paris, October 30, 1854. *DDFDS*, XXXVI.

38. Gazley, *American Opinion*, p. 91.

view that the very appointment of Soulé was a provocation to Spain and France.

Napoleon had been unsuccessful in persuading Madrid to refuse Soulé's reception prior to the presentation of the envoy's credentials.[39] Did he now want to compromise the diplomat by making his position untenable? By calling public attention to Soulé as a controversial figure, his usefulness as an American minister to a European country was likely to be put in question. Ironically, if this was Napoleon's scheme, Soulé's hasty departure from Calais played right into the Emperor's hands. Soulé had hardly left that port when the French Minister of the Interior telegraphed his instructions which took the sting out of the first reports by permitting Soulé to pass through France. But Paris refused to authorize his stay in France beyond the time needed for the transit. Apologizing for the original misunderstanding, Foreign Minister Drouyn de Lhuys attempted to justify his colleague's telegraphic order. He distinguished "between the simple passage and the stay of a foreigner whose antecedents could not but give concern to the authorities charged with the domestic security of France."[40] While Secretary Marcy rejected this distinction between a native-born and a naturalized American minister, he did accept the apology.

V

Were it not for the fact that foreign nations are often judged by the conduct of their citizens, the following episodes would hardly merit the attention of the historian.

After about a year of residence in the United States, Count de Sartiges received a note from former Congressman John Barney who had just written a letter to his old friend Prince Napoleon Bonaparte, the President of the French Senate. As an act of perverted courtesy he sent a copy of it to the man whose "infamous character" he desired to expose.[41] Officials on both sides of the Atlantic may have chuckled when they read the defamatory gossip about Sartiges' preference for pretty ladies. Newspapers found it entertaining and published it. But the bachelor-diplomat seemed concerned about the effect of the tragic humor of Barney's deranged mind. Public libels have their way of damaging a man's reputation and career. They spread faster than the exoneration from them. The Fillmore administration handled the

39. S. Webster, "Marcy and the Cuban Question," *Political Science Quarterly*, VIII (1893), 10.

40. Drouyn de Lhuys to Mason, Paris, November 1, 1854. *NALP.*

41. Barney to Sartiges, Baltimore, May 3, 1852. *FNTDS*, XV.

case with admirable expedition. Within two days the State Department expressed the President's deep regret and his hope that "a gentleman of Sartiges' respectability" might best consult his own dignity by allowing the affair to pass into oblivion.[42] The French diplomat indeed appreciated this prompt apology which dispelled any false notions which his own government might have developed from Barney's accusations.

Also disputes over protocol and rank frequently offended national sensibilities. The failure of an American naval officer to pay his proper respects to a French rear-admiral at Naples was as much regarded as a lack of civility as the abstention of the United States consul at Tripoli from observing the anniversaries of the kings of France.[43] Upon complaint of the French government, American naval commanders were expressly instructed to salute the flag of France as the sovereign power on the Gaboon. In that part of Africa the French were particularly sensitive regarding the observance of protocol because they suspected American missionaries of encouraging the natives to throw off their allegiance to France.[44]

VI

On the basis of these few incidents hardly more than tentative general conclusions may be drawn. Reaction to these affairs was frequently based on long standing personal prejudices and preferences rather than on objective analysis. Although they stirred up political emotions, public opinion in both countries was so divided that it restrained the governments from taking extreme actions.

It is noteworthy that in the drawn-out incidents initial insult and insistence yielded in the end to courtesy and conciliation. No doubt paramount interests dictated a course which would not permit insignificant grievances to interfere with them. In this process a practical approach usually succeeded where the legalistic argument had failed.

If time is an element that warrants analysis in a study of incidents, so is distance. The central figure in most of these incidents appeared to be more excited than his government at a distance from him. Because these affairs looked smaller from a distance, dispassionate officials at the highest echelons were more inclined to seek satisfactory adjustments than the subordinate representatives abroad. The

42. Hunter to Sartiges, Washington, D. C., May 22, 1852. *FNFDS*, VI.

43. Pageot to Buchanan, Washington, D. C., August 7, 1846. *FNTDS*, XII.

44. Commodore Skinner to Bancroft, Staunton, Va., September 3, 1846. *CPEU,* CII. Copy.

very distance from their country and the desire for importance caused many of these agents to lose the proper perspective of their position.

One of the most striking observations that can be made is that a public incident often ends a diplomatic assignment. Poussin, Dillon, and Soulé learnt this lesson through experience. The prestige of other key figures in foreign affairs of this period suffered more than it gained from the manner in which these incidents were disposed of. Even temporary withdrawals of ministers turned out to be harmful gestures contributing to the gathering of war clouds.

It would be erroneous, if not naïve, to assume that these officials approached the incidents without ulterior motives. Completely extraneous matters often complicated the situation. The dynamic rise of nationalism in the mid-nineteenth century heightened the sensitiveness of nations. It was considered to be good domestic politics to show much bravado in foreign political talk. Strong language in external affairs also tended to accentuate or to cover up internal weaknesses in both countries. Domestic opposition to the Orleanist regime and to the Jackson administration used the spoliation claims for purposes of political embarrassment. The desire of the United States to strengthen the republican movement in Europe raised the Poussin incident to one of high policy. Similarly, Sartiges suggested a remedy in the Dillon case that would make North America lose face in Latin America and Europe.[45] A possible war over the spoliation claims was connected with alleged American projects in the Mediterranean. Even the Gaboon flag salute question was tied up with French colonialism.

Finally, the protracted and often obstructive diplomatic exchanges enabled both governments to study the political barometer of their mutual relations. The uncooperative spirit which delayed the immediate settlement of the incidents reflected the growing coolness between France and the United States. Truly friendly governments, though sometimes unable to avoid the sudden existence of embarrassing situations, manifest their good will promptly.

45. Sartiges to Drouyn de Lhuys, Washington, D. C., July 3, 1854. *CPEU*, CXI.

CHAPTER IV

Economic Relations
(1830-1871)

I

IT WAS WELL UNDERSTOOD during this period that the economic relations
between the two countries mattered a great deal more than their various
diplomatic maneuvers. American statesmen tried to appease French
opposition to their expansionist policies by emphasizing the economic
benefits France would derive from the rapid development of the Union.
French governments indeed realized the general potentialities of the
United States as a market and supplier of raw materials and foodstuffs.

The contractual basis of Franco-American trade relations was the
commercial treaty of 1822. It stipulated the conditions under which
the commerce and navigation of both countries could mutually operate.
The vital role which consular agents played in the promotion and protection of commercial interests was further safeguarded by the Consular Convention of 1853.[1] The French envoy, Eugène de Sartiges,
had taken the initiative in its negotiation. It defined the rights and
obligations of consuls, the extent of their authority with respect to
crews and passengers of ships, and it specified many reciprocal
privileges.

As Frenchmen had every opportunity to open commercial enterprises in the United States, American individuals or partnerships could
do business in France. Their activities were protected by local and
international law. However, France did not extend this privilege to
corporations. American corporations had to wait until August 6,
1882, before they were permitted to conduct operations.[2] Although
these foreign firms in France and in the United States were instrumental in stimulating import-export relations, they obviously were not
the only ones to be engaged in foreign trade.

1. Miller, *Treaties,* VI, 169-96.
2. Charles G. Loeb, *Legal Status of American Corporations in France* (Paris, 1921),
pp. 39-55.

II

During the first three decades of the period under consideration France pursued a protectionist policy. Her high tariffs and restrictions were designed to protect her agriculture, industry, and navigation against competitors whose industrial and technological development progressed faster than that of France. For a long time this trade policy enjoyed strong popular and parliamentary support. Every attempt to lower French trade barriers met with successful opposition in the Chamber of Deputies.[3] The willingness of Louis Philippe's government to moderate the tariffs was countered with new restrictions. Against the hopes of the American government, the Second Republic also showed no inclination to liberalize its trade system. The legislature received proposals to that effect with a storm of protest. Under the protectionist leadership of Thiers, a large majority rejected various liberalizing measures at the assembly's session of June 28, 1851.[4] When in 1856 Napoleon III asked the Chamber to consider the adoption of a moderate tariff, he, too, encountered the traditional reaction. Anticipating this inflexible attitude, Napoleon took advantage of emergency situations, such as poor crops in 1853 and the Crimean War, to lower duties by decrees which the Chamber reluctantly approved afterwards in 1856. These decrees reduced tariffs for such raw materials as fats, oils, cotton, wool, and hides. They permitted the import of grain, flour, rice, dried vegetables, and pulse at nominal fees. Furthermore, the ships carrying them were exempted from tonnage dues.[5] The United States obviously welcomed these measures. They foreshadowed a new era of French economic policy from which a country exporting raw materials could only benefit.

Another few years passed before France officially broke with its protectionist tradition. The French free trade movement did not grow in as favorable an atmosphere as the English. France possessed neither the industrial nor the maritime might of Britain to welcome

3. For a contemporary scholarly treatment of this question, see L. Amé, *Étude sur les tarifs de douanes et sur les traités de commerce* (Paris, 1876), I, 253 ff.; see also Shepard B. Clough, *France—A History of National Economics, 1789-1939* (New York, 1939), pp. 123-35, 180-88.

4. Noël, *Commerce du monde*, III, 118. During the revolutionary days of 1848 the Association for Free Trade marched to the Hôtel de Ville and asked for the free entry of foodstuffs and raw materials. A member of the Provisional Government congratulated this pilgrimage for its devotion to a wonderful ideal. He regretted, however, that he could not hold out hope for early action. Charles Lavollée, "De la législation commerciale en Europe," *RDDM* (April 1, 1856), p. 650.

5. F. A. Haight, *A History of French Commercial Policies* (New York, 1941), pp. 28-30; see also G. Martin, *Histoire économique et financière* (Paris, 1927), p. 367.

foreign competition. Nevertheless, British free traders influenced a growing number of Frenchmen, among them many economists, who found in Frédéric Bastiat an able theoretical leader.[6] Bastiat and Michel Chevalier, who played a dominant role in French economic thought of the mid-nineteenth century, maintained direct contact with Richard Cobden, the renowned English economist. The influence of Chevalier and the Manchester School—and perhaps also the desire to appease England's anger over his Italian policy—led Napoleon to negotiate the celebrated Anglo-French Treaty of Commerce of 1860. By this treaty Britain agreed to admit most French goods free of duty and to reduce rates on others. In exchange, France abolished her system of prohibitions and reduced her duties to a maximum rate of 25 percent by 1865.[7]

France thus moved from high protectionism towards a liberal position. The tariffs of the United States, on the other hand, shifted between 1828 and 1862 from one high level to another, via the relatively moderate rates between 1842 and 1860.[8] The opposite tendencies of the French and American tariffs were destined to cancel potential trade possibilities.

Frenchmen never ceased to protest against the restraining effects of even moderate American tariffs on their exports. Their diplomatic and commercial agents kept in closest contact with members of Congress, although they realized that foreign pressures had little chance of influencing tariff legislation. In 1842 French business regarded a duty of 20 percent as "an act of violent commercial aggression against the commerce of France." Until then, they dismissed American threats of discriminatory rates "on the wines and silks of the aristocracy" as republican propaganda. Now they knew that those republicans meant business. The industries of Lyons and Paris felt hurt. The chambers of commerce in Le Havre and Marseilles called for retaliation against such prejudices. The Department of Commerce actually recommended the denunciation of the Franco-American Trade Treaty of

6. Clough, *France,* pp. 135-37; Noël, *Commerce du monde,* III, 99-100. Bastiat leaned on Carey's optimistic sociological premises, but drew different economic conclusions from them. A. Sartorius von Waltershausen, *Die Entstehung der Weltwirtschaft* (Jena, 1931), p. 304.

7. For a discussion of this treaty consult A. L. Dunham, *The Anglo-French Treaty of Commerce of 1860* (Ann Arbor, 1930) pp. 98-102, 351. Several studies stress the political character of this treaty. See M. Marion, *Histoire financière de la France depuis 1715* (Paris, 1928), V, 417; and J. Hartmann, *Die Wirtschaftspolitik Napoleons III* (Berlin, 1938), pp. 89-91.

8. Davis R. Dewey, *Financial History of the United States* (New York, 1920), pp. 303-4. The tariff of 1864 further raised the average rate from 37.2 to 47 percent.

1822. The French government, however, abstained from following these recommendations for fear of the consequences of a resulting tariff war.[9]

Since 1831 Congress had drifted with great indecision with respect to foreign trade principles. In 1842, the protectionists in the Senate won out by only one vote. In 1846, the decision for somewhat reduced rates was again made by the narrow majority of one. It is ironic that the conservative newspaper *La Patrie*,[10] conveniently ignoring prevailing trends at home, volunteered the advice that France and Britain must help the free traders in America. Even the protectionist Thiers asserted, were he an American, he would be a free trader.[11] At first the French approved the change from specific to ad valorem rates, which the American tariff law of 1846 instituted, because it permitted the proportioning of the duty according to the importance of the product. After two years of experience with this system, Frenchmen no longer liked it. They discovered that arbitrary valuations left the unhappy importer at the mercy of the American authorities.[12] On the other hand, falsified invoices deprived the United States of legitimate revenue.[13] In the late 1850's France feared that the depressed economic situation would bring about the end of the basically liberal American tariff of 1857. Nobody expected, however, such an "ugly beast" as the Morrill tariff of 1861. French commentators understood that the necessities of war called for drastic fiscal expedients. They even found some consolation in the hope that their sacrifice might at least bring emancipation to millions of slaves.[14] Still, to them this tariff was a blow to liberal principles, inopportunely following the Reciprocity Treaty of 1860.

The vaunted liberality of this treaty was disputed by Henry C. Carey, the distinguished American protectionist. Carey made an enlightening comparison of the French and American tariffs which led him to the conclusion that many rates under the Morrill tariff

9. Archives Nationales, F 12-2688. This bundle of documents contains significant material on Franco-American trade relations. See also D. L. Rodet, "Tarif et tendances du commerce des États-Unis," *RDDM* (July 1, 1843), pp. 139-59.

10. September 6, 1846. See also *Journal des économistes* (September, 1846), pp. 199-208.

11. J. Lacour-Gayet, *Histoire du commerce* (Paris, 1952), V, 107-10.

12. Simounet to Drouyn de Lhuys, New York, December 26, 1848. *CCC New York*, XIV.

13. U.S. Consul to Marcy, Bordeaux, March 25, 1854. *USCLF Bordeaux*, V.

14. J. E. Horn, "Le protectionisme en Amérique," *Journal des économistes* (August, 1862), p. 325.

TABLE I

COMPARISON OF FRENCH AND AMERICAN TARIFF RATES IN 1860

Name of Article	Quantities	French duties under the Reciprocity Treaty	U. S. duties under the Morrill tariff
Iron, old broken wrought.....	ton	$ 6.35	$ 6.00
Iron, railroad................	ton	13.68	12.00
Iron, sheet..................	ton	25.41 to 31.28	20.00 to 25.00
Steel, in bars of all kinds......	lb.	1.00	0.0125 to 0.02
Steel, in sheets under 1/12 of an inch thick.............	lb.	0.0262	0.025
Tin, pots and pans...........	ton	58.62	56.00
Lead, pigs, bars, plates.......	ton	5.86	22.40
Locomotive engines..........	ton	29.32	38.60
Refined sugar................	lb.	0.035	0.02
Cotton tissues, weighing 3.5 oz. to sq. yd..............	100 sq. yd.	1.00	1.00
Cotton tissues, 2 to 3.5 oz.....	100 sq. yd.	0.02	2.00 to 3.00
Cotton tissues, 1 to 2 oz.......	100 sq. yd.	0.0025	4.00
Cotton raw..................		free	free
Wool, unmanufactured.......		free	0.03 and 0.09
Silk, in cocoons..............		free	free
Silk tissues.................		free	25% and 30%
Cordage, cables, fish-nets.....	lb.	0.025	0.02 and 0.03
Beer.......................	gal.	0.0175	0.25
Clocks and watches..........		5%	30%
Glassware..................		10%	55%
Leather manufactures.......		10%	30%

SOURCE: H. C. Carey, *French and American Tariffs*, pp. 8-9.

were in fact lower than those under the Reciprocity Treaty.[15] Carey contended that this treaty upheld the principle of protection by putting a low duty on only such superior quality goods in which French manufacturers could safely defy competition. In other instances, he observed, schedules were carefully determined by the measure of threatened competition or the need for raw materials which provided work for the French people. The Anglo-French Treaty of Commerce affected Franco-American trade relations only slightly. It did contribute to the growing political tensions during the Civil War. The French government attributed the cotton crisis of 1861-62 to the very much resented Northern blockade, although one of its real causes was the import of cotton goods from Britain, made possible by the Reciprocity Treaty of 1860.[16]

15. H. C. Carey, *The French and American Tariffs Compared* (Philadelphia, 1861). M. Chevalier, to whom these comments were addressed, refused to be drawn into specific comparisons. Instead, he stressed the opposite historic tendencies of the two tariffs. See *Journal des économistes* (March, 1862), pp. 484-87.

16. See chapter V.

III

The relation between tariffs and trade volume is modified by many factors,[17] not the least of which then was navigation. The United States possessed several advantages in its trade relations with France. Its economy could much better exist without the French market than France could manage without the American outlet. As an exporter of needed raw materials, the United States was in a strong position. French luxury goods were beyond the reach of the great masses of the American people and often not to their taste. The heavy and bulky type of goods, moreover, which American ships carried allowed a more economical utilization of shipping facilities than, with the exception of wine, the great number of small sized French articles. Partly as a consequence of this difference, the United States merchant marine grew considerably in size and efficiency, whereas stagnation reduced the French marine to a place of inferiority.[18] A comparison of the effective tonnage of the three great maritime powers shows the relative decline of the French merchant marine.

TABLE II

COMPARISON OF MERCHANT MARINE TONNAGE

Date	Great Britain	United States	France
December 31, 1830......	2,531,819	1,191,000	665,164
December 31, 1856......	4,841,000	4,871,652	998,996

SOURCE: E. B. Le Beuf, "Du commerce de la France," *Journal des économistes* (1859), pp. 50 ff.

Although France increased its tonnage during this period by 50 percent, Britain's grew by 91 percent, and that of the United States by 309 percent. In an age in which rapid steam transportation came to be preferred, France suffered the additional disadvantage that its steamer tonnage of 72,000 constituted in 1857 only one tenth of that of the United States. Throughout these decades the American marine operated between 84 and 86 percent of the transports between France and the United States, leaving only 8 to 12 percent to French ships,

17. French industrialists contended that their railroads neutralized the effect of tariff legislation. They took particular exception to the fact that the Germans paid lower transit rates for the goods they imported from America than Frenchmen with whose money the railroads had been built. Ch. Lavollée, "Commerce extérieur de la France d'après les documents officiels," RDDM (April, 1859), p. 985.

18. J. Tramond and A. Reussner, *Élements d'histoire maritime et coloniale contemporaine, 1815-1914* (Paris, 1947), p. 35. French vessels of all descriptions, however, were of a high quality, and the skill of their captains was judged to be of a superior order. Vesey to Marcy, Le Havre, May 8, 1854. *USCLF Le Havre.*

and the remainder to others. Americans derived additional profits from their efficient system of operation. In their trade with France they employed 28 men per 1,000 tons, in contrast to 47 men per 1,000 tons which the French required in their trade with the United States.[19] Thus, quite aside from their high cost of materials for naval construction, the French were in no position to compete with New World navigation.

Certain maritime problems headed the list of important issues for which the two governments sought up-to-date solutions. The merchants and shippers of both countries complained about the high tonnage duties in French and American ports. The problem went back to the Franco-American Trade Treaty of 1822. Prior to the negotiation of this treaty, the United States offered France the same liberal terms other nations had already accepted. But Paris preferred to maintain the protective principle also in respect to shipping. The treaty authorized tonnage dues which were exorbitant for "modern" conditions. It required French vessels in the ports of the United States to pay ninety-four cents per ton. The equivalent charge was five francs per ton for American vessels in French ports.[20] If a 2,300 ton steamer like the *Argo*, for example, made yearly twelve crossings to France, the 138,000 francs it paid annually for tonnage dues would have represented a reasonable profit on the total investment in the ship. Washington endeavored, therefore, to save American shipping interests such large expenditures by adopting a policy of greatest liberality.[21] The relative decline of its merchant marine led France, on the contrary, to contemplate a policy of discrimination in favor of French ships. Guizot was bluntly warned to expect retaliation in that case.[22]

One form of already existing discrimination against American vessels caused particular resentment. American consuls in France protested vigorously against the injurious effect of discriminatory dues. In Le Havre, for instance, a Russian ship paid eighty-seven centimes per ton; an English ship one franc and six and one half centimes; but an American paid altogether five francs and eighty centimes. The

19. H. Boucher, *La marine marchande américaine de 1585 au 11 novembre 1918* (Paris, 1923), p. 181; see also J. G. B. Hutchins, *The American Maritime Industries and Public Policy* (Cambridge, Mass., 1941), pp. 304-5.

20. Mason to Cass, Paris, September 11, 1857. *DDFDS*, XLII. Cass to Mason, Washington, D. C., May 3, 1858. *FIDS*, XV.

21. Charles M. Depew, *One Hundred Years of American Commerce, 1795-1895* (New York, 1895), I, 39.

22. King to Buchanan, Paris, January 29, 1847. *DDFDS*, XXX. Pageot to Guizot, Washington, D. C., December 20, 1846. *CPEU*, CII.

difference in charges hardly protected French shipping. It rather had the effect of favoring British navigation.[23] French attempts to diminish the preponderance of American navigation between the two countries failed, no matter what method of resistance was tried. "France did as yet not understand that in the new age, commercial had taken the place of political ambition; and that it would be much wiser to adopt, rather than combat, the American shipping example."[24]

IV

Southern cotton and tobacco producers joined Northern business-men in putting pressure on their government to end various other kinds of French discrimination. It did not make sense that Washing-ton granted a preferential status to French silks at the cost of Indian and Chinese silks, while France was collecting 4 and 5 percent more duty on American cotton than on Egyptian.[25] As far as Ameri-can tobacco growers were concerned, they were convinced that the French government's monopoly on the purchase, manufacture, and sale of tobacco discriminated against their products. A specific compli-cation arose when early in 1846 a regulation stipulated that only French ships should be given the privilege of carrying tobacco to France. Guizot did not admit the legal point of the American pro-test against "this violation of the Convention of 1822." Nevertheless, he promised that his government would discontinue this restriction in the future.[26]

These and other problems called for an early general review of Franco-American trade relations. Actually, ever since the Van Buren administration the negotiation of a new reciprocal trade treaty with France took a place of priority. In those days, trade talks were con-ducted on the highest level of diplomacy. In the course of such dis-cussions French statesmen displayed an ignorance about their trade relations with the United States that surprised, and sometimes dis-mayed, American diplomats.[27] Evidently preoccupied with European

23. The U. S. consul at Le Havre reported another objectionable condition. American shipmasters were obliged to employ a ship-broker for transactions with any official agency, unless they were familiar with the French language. This additional expense caused a great deal of resentment. Vesey to Marcy, Le Havre, June 27, 1854. *USCLF Le Havre.*

24. King to Buchanan, Paris, June 30, 1846. *DDFDS*, XXX.

25. U. S. Consul to Marcy, Marseilles, December 25, 1853. *USCLF Marseilles*, V.

26. King to Buchanan, Paris, January 29, 1846. *DDFDS*, XXX. Guizot to King, Paris, February 25, 1846. *NALP.* See also B. Duncan, "Franco-American Tobacco Diplomacy, 1784-1860," *Maryland Historical Magazine*, LI (1956), 273-301.

27. Cass to Webster, Paris, February 13, 1840. *DDFDS*, XXIX. Faulkner to Cass, Paris, October 8, 1860. *DDFDS*, XLVIII.

affairs, they devoted little time to the study of business opportunities with America. The economic reports which French envoys sent from Washington were not too helpful either in enlightening the gentlemen in Paris. They showed an inclination to stress day to day problems more than long range possibilities. The noticeable exception in this respect was made by the consuls general of France at New York. They distinguished themselves by a keen grasp of the important issues.

The envoys of the United States to France, representing above all the commercial spirit of their country, took the initiative in the promotion of a treaty that would not only promise the mutual expansion of trade, but also equalize the trade balance between the two countries. The French governments from Louis Philippe to Napoleon III did not refuse to negotiate. But one delay after another postponed the conclusion of a treaty, with the result that none was signed by the time the Civil War broke out. Contrary to public assurances, within their own official family Frenchmen argued against a new trade convention. The prejudice prevailed that commercial treaties were practically impossible with countries in which the legislature is the last resort in tariff questions. Violation of such a treaty, they were afraid, might possibly lead to political complications. Also the argument carried great conviction that in view of the really generous treatment of French economic interests by the United States, a comprehensive trade treaty would compel France to grant considerable concessions.[28]

The time for serious trade talks came when the conditions were ripe for them. The American minister in Paris, John Y. Mason, had reason to believe that Count Walewski, the head of the French Foreign Ministry in the late 1850's, would favor the liberalization of Franco-American trade relations. For that matter, Napoleon III was more inclined towards principles of free trade than "ancient prejudices" of France permitted him to reveal. By 1857 signs were not missing that imperial France saw advantages in relaxing many trade regulations. The Emperor's desire to enlarge the French merchant marine encouraged Mason, moreover, to think that France might even be interested in a reduction of tonnage dues.[29]

On the domestic front, the growing consumption of food by the French people brightened the prospects for American agriculture. Their new eating habits called for more meat than France produced.

28. Pageot to Guizot, Washington, D. C., September 13, 1845. *CPEU*, CI.

29. In 1857 the French government granted subsidies for three trans-Atlantic steamship lines. A. Vialatte, *L'activité économique en France de la fin du XVIIIe siècle à nos jours* (Paris, 1937), p. 143.

The western and southwestern states of the Union were only too eager to fill the bill. All France had to do was to open its ports. Furthermore, the cotton factories of France expanded steadily, a development that called for changes in the tariff. The French government charged a duty of 20 francs per 100 kilograms on American cotton. This amounted to an unnecessary burden which either reduced the manufacturer's profits or lightened the purse of the consumer.

Under these circumstances, Mason found the time opportune to proceed with his plans. Paris had already proposed the partial modification of tonnage dues. This was not entirely satisfactory to Washington. For the Buchanan administration preferred a general review of trade problems instead of discussing merely one single issue.[30] In 1857 Mason began to conduct preliminary discussions for a treaty of commerce and navigation. In the course of them he discovered that French bureaucracy played the game of postponing decisions as well as that of any other nation. Many times the Foreign Minister simply was too busy to pay attention to trade matters. Memoranda had to be prepared and studied. Interviews were referred to subordinates. Discouraging hints were dropped that the question of American adherence to the maritime Declaration of Paris would, of course, enter the negotiation of a trade treaty. Finally it was decided that the whole problem really fell into the jurisdiction of the Minister of Agriculture and Commerce.[31] This turned out to be a constructive move. Although it was understood that the Foreign Ministry would negotiate the final treaty, the trade experts were much better prepared to work on its details than the diplomatic staff. Eugène Rouher, the resourceful and powerful Minister of Agriculture and Commerce, demonstrated a remarkable acquaintance with Franco-American trade.

Interdepartmental communications clearly evidence that competent French authorities had carefully studied Mason's propositions before the negotiations took place. Their analysis by the Director General of Customs permits a rare glimpse of the informal and confidential views of this high official.[32] Mason had asked for the establishment of complete reciprocity, reduction of tonnage dues, change of the tobacco system, reduction of duties on cotton, free admission of American

30. Cass to Mason, Washington, D. C., May 3, 1858. *FIDS*, XV.
31. Mason to Cass, Paris, August 30 and November 6, 1858. *DDFDS*, XLIV.
32. *Report of the Director General of Customs to the Minister of Finance regarding a treaty with the United States, Paris, March 16, 1859.* Archives Nationales, F 12-6529.

cereals and fresh and salted meats, as well as changes in court procedures affecting American business in France.

According to the Director of Customs, Frenchmen would be in a better position to compete for the Atlantic shipping trade without the existing 10 percent surtax on goods not originating in France or the United States respectively. He saw definite advantages in the acceptance of Mason's first point, particularly in view of the growing preoccupation of some of his enterprising countrymen with the creation of trans-Atlantic liners. Regarding tonnage dues, he pointed out that the French treasury collected 1,125,825 francs from American ships entering French ports in 1857, while the twenty-eight French ships destined for the United States paid only 65,625 francs. The existing system, he concluded therefore, benefited the fiscal agencies, but not the merchant marine. He also observed that these dues could not be classified as a profitable tax because the American captain raised his freight charges in proportion to the tax. Higher cost of transportation meant higher prices for the French people. In the last analysis, it was they who paid the dues, not the American shipowners.

By far the weightiest argument in support of the suppression of these dues found its basis in the cotton question. Cotton accounted for more than 80 percent of the American exports to France. Because of French tonnage dues, every 100 kilograms of cotton reaching Le Havre were taxed seventy-five centimes. The Director General suggested that, without this additional charge, France might attract a part of the important re-export trade. Le Havre could then become a transit center for the shipment of cotton to Russia, Holland, Belgium, and Germany, who bought great quantities from England. Abolishing tonnage dues, however, would not have been sufficient to challenge Britain's cotton export position. The British textile industry enjoyed the additional advantage over its French competitors of tax-free importation of cotton. France could not go that far, considering that this American staple supported its treasury with about sixteen million francs yearly. The Director of Customs recommended a compromise sacrifice of four million francs, provided adequate compensations could be negotiated.

Since the favorable treatment of American cereals was extended to 1859, tobacco remained the major item which awaited a new solution. But the French government completely closed its ears to any suggestion that tobacco should be permitted to be traded in the open market. They derived from this monopoly an annual average income of twenty-eight million dollars. However much the monopoly weighed upon American producers, even the partial loss of this source of revenue could not be entertained by any French government. It constituted an untouchable system, regardless of the type of government that was in power.

Rouher was willing to go beyond these recommendations. He thought that French textile interests would be served by a 50 percent reduction of the duties on raw cotton. It would greatly strengthen their competitive position in Europe. But this business view was opposed by the Department of Finance which worried over the loss of revenue. It insisted that even an agreeable 25 percent reduction must be part of a general settlement and not an isolated concession. It cautioned Rouher: "We must not give more than we receive."[33]

Empowered to negotiate,[34] Mason held two decisive interviews with Rouher on July 18 and 25, 1859. As Mason had been instructed not to conclude a treaty without keeping the State Department fully informed, so Rouher clarified his function as that of an adviser to the Foreign Ministry rather than its negotiator. Quick agreement was reached on the principle of perfect reciprocity for all products directly imported by the ships of either country. Rouher also accepted the proposition that the maximum amount of tonnage dues be reduced to one franc. He admitted that ultimate benefits would result from such a measure, but he expected American equivalents to make up for the immediate loss of 1,200,000 francs to the French treasury. He also approved the opening of French markets to American foodstuffs. Flour was to be admitted at two francs per 100 kilograms. He was willing to permit free entry to the French Antilles of American salt fish in exchange for admitting French codfish free of duty to the United States, a privilege Washington had previously granted to British fishing interests.

Anticipating no changes in the monopolistic tobacco system, Mason thought of a method which offered at least some chances for improvement. He suggested that the French monopoly be tightened. Instead of buying tobacco through intermediaries, he saw advantage to both countries if the French government bought the tobacco directly. But Rouher did not comment on this idea.

The negotiations came to an impasse over the cotton arrangement. France offered to reduce the duty on American cotton from twenty to fifteen francs per 100 kilograms, provided that the United States found

33. *Ibid.*, July 29, 1859.
34. Cass to Mason, Washington, D. C., June 13, 1859. *FIDS*, XV.

ways and means of compensating the treasury for the annual loss of 4,000,000 francs. If Washington would accept the proposal of specific equivalents, Rouher promised to make the attractive concession of a gradual reduction of the duty on cotton until after five years it would amount to not more than five francs per 100 kilograms. In exchange, he expected relative tariff reductions on the import of French wines, silks, and Parisian specialties, until they reached the level of one-fourth of the existing duty. This conditional offer brought the constitutional system of the United States once again into the sphere of diplomacy. Mason reminded the French minister that the treaty-making power of the executive branch did not extend to modification of tariff laws. That was a matter for Congress to decide. Taken as a whole, these various agreements and proposals indicated a mutual desire to come to terms. Mason estimated that Rouher had asked for more than he offered in return. In the long run, however, American business stood to gain from the resulting stimulation of trade.[35]

When the prospect for a commercial treaty became real, the unforeseen happened. The man whose diplomatic skill and convincing earnestness engineered the progress of these trade negotiations suddenly passed away. Charles J. Faulkner, who succeeded him, lacked the intimate knowledge of facts and personalities which the late Mr. Mason used with advantage. As time went on, conditions changed. Personnel had also shifted in France. Édouard Thouvenel replaced Walewski as Foreign Minister, and Rouher was no longer available to resume the trade conversations with Faulkner. Such personnel questions affected the future course of the discussions. Faulkner showed little enthusiasm for a general treaty. He believed that the exchange of commodities between the two countries should not be permanently hamstrung by a system of equivalents. To his way of thinking, the key to improved trade relations lay in the establishment of free navigation. The new situation which had arisen since Mason's death added strength to this argument. On January 5, 1860, the Emperor surprised the world with his enunciation of a liberal international trade policy, the principles of which were embodied in the Anglo-French treaty of 1860. Furthermore, by the spring of 1860 French manufacturers had succeeded in inducing their government to repeal the duties on raw cotton. There were also many indications that the duties on foodstuffs, which for the last few years had been suspended as an expedient of temporary relief, would not be restored.[36]

35. Mason to Cass, Paris, August 3, 1859. *DDFDS*, XLV.

36. Faulkner to Cass, Paris, March 29, August 23, and November 20, 1860. *DDFDS*, XLVI, XLVII, and XLVIII.

The drawn-out deliberations and hesitations on the part of the French exposed them by 1860 to the unenviable position of granting concessions without exacting any in return for them. Under these circumstances, Washington no longer saw any reason to conclude a general treaty that would, in effect, secure a privileged status to French luxuries. French officials demanded in vain a comprehensive regulation of all commercial matters. Within a quarter of a century the respective positions of the two governments had been completely reversed, not only as far as tariffs were concerned, but also with respect to the scope of their trade talks and the desirability of a new treaty. The Civil War interrupted these trade conversations. After it, France still desired a convention on liberal terms.[37] But Congress was not in the mood to accommodate a power whose diplomacy had caused the Union great anxiety during the critical Civil War years.

V

The diplomats negotiated for a quarter of a century and had little to show for it. In the meantime the importers and exporters in both countries succeeded in expanding their overseas trade. By and large, Franco-American trade rose absolutely from 1830 to 1860. The rise continued after a temporary decline during the Civil War.

It is noteworthy that advertising seems to have contributed little to this increased trade volume. Improved transportation since the 1850's facilitated a series of international expositions in England, France, and the United States.[38] However, French and American manufacturers did not attach much importance to the display of their wares in far-away lands. The organizers of the New York Universal Exposition of 1853, for instance, were very much disappointed about the absence of some French industries. Visitors, who would have liked to appraise French machinery, were shown beautiful Gobelin and porcelain samples. Poorly as the cotton industry was represented, the consul general was not a little surprised by the few displays of French silks.[39] How could this industry hope to attract new customers, he

37. See *Annuaire Diplomatique*, X (1867), 235-36; XI (1868), 176-77; XII (1869), 173. In 1869 the two countries concluded a trade-mark convention. It forbade the reproduction of trade-marks affixed to prove the origin and quality of certain merchandise. Malloy, *Treaties*, I, 534-35.

38. Different concepts about the functions of government manifested themselves in the organization of these exhibitions. In the United States, private enterprise took the initiative in planning and financing them. In France, the government organized and subsidized them.

39. Lacoste to Drouyn de Lhuys, New York, November 10, 1853. *CCC New York*, XVI. See also references to this exposition in Archives Nationales, F 12-3168.

TABLE III
Exports and Imports from and to the United States, 1830-1871[40]
(In thousands of dollars)

Year	Exports from the U. S. Total	Exports from the U. S. To France	Imports into the U. S. Total	Imports into the U. S. From France
1830.........	71,671	11,806	62,721	8,240
31..........	72,296	9,882	95,885	14,737
32..........	81,521	13,244	95,122	12,754
33..........	87,529	14,424	101,048	13,962
34..........	102,260	16,111	108,610	17,557
35..........	115,216	20,335	136,764	23,362
36..........	124,339	21,441	176,579	37,036
37..........	111,443	20,255	130,473	22,498
38..........	104,979	16,252	95,970	18,087
39..........	112,252	18,924	156,497	33,234
1840.........	123,669	22,349	98,259	17,908
41..........	111,817	22,235	122,958	24,187
42..........	99,878	18,739	96,075	17,223
43..........	82,826	12,472	42,433	7,836
44..........	105,746	16,133	102,605	17,952
45..........	106,040	16,144	113,184	22,070
46..........	109,583	15,826	117,914	24,331
47..........	156,742	19,818	122,424	25,100
48..........	138,191	20,413	148,639	28,288
49..........	140,351	15,782	141,206	24,459
1850.........	144,376	20,183	173,510	27,636
51..........	188,915	28,635	210,771	31,767
52..........	166,984	24,512	207,440	25,969
53..........	203,489	27,044	263,777	33,524
54..........	237,044	32,861	297,804	35,972
55..........	218,910	33,554	257,809	31,802
56..........	281,219	42,511	310,432	49,016
57..........	293,824	39,226	348,428	48,000
58..........	272,011	33,663	263,339	35,536
59..........	292,902	45,107	331,333	41,447
1860.........	333,576	63,050	353,616	43,364
61..........	219,554	25,171	289,311	34,393
62..........	190,671	21,562	189,357	8,020
63..........	203,964	18,542	243,336	10,675
64..........	158,838	18,985	316,447	11,685
65..........	166,029	16,519	238,746	6,829
66..........	348,860	63,090	434,812	23,444
67..........	294,506	45,382	395,761	31,630
68..........	281,953	47,440	357,436	27,428
69..........	286,118	44,045	417,506	36,469
1870.........	392,772	54,808	435,958	48,755
71..........	442,820	28,632	520,224	29,990

40. The total U. S. export and import statistics have been taken from U. S. Census Bureau, *Statistical Abstract of the United States* (Washington, D. C., 1946), p. 982. For trade with France from 1830 through 1855, see *House Ex. Doc.*, 34 Cong., 1 sess., No. 47, I, 778-80; for that from 1856 through 1871, see the yearly volumes of U. S. Census Bureau, *The Foreign Commerce and Navigation of the United States, 1856-1871* (Washington, D. C.).

asked Paris, without showing its products? He also lamented that the silk producers had failed to create designs that would appeal especially to American tastes.

Anxious for a spectacular success of the Universal Exhibition of 1855, the Imperial Government invited the cooperation of Washington to encourage participation. But neither the publicity campaign launched by the State Department nor French inducements in the form of special exemptions for normally prohibited goods had much effect.[41] The disappointment about the London and New York shows was still too fresh in the minds of American manufacturers to convince them that it would be worthwhile to exhibit in Paris. They were quite satisfied with their home market and did not see much usefulness in competing with European industries. As a result, only 130 of the 10,148 exhibitors represented the United States. Frenchmen commented harshly on the lack of dignity that made Americans send only agricultural machinery, in which they excelled, while avoiding comparative judgment in regard to other types of machinery. Still, McCormick's reaper was hailed as a great contribution, opening a new era in agriculture. The products of America's rubber industry also found the highest recognition. Other displays from the United States attracted much interest. Visitors admired such tokens of American ingenuity as a machine that produced 1,500 paper bags per hour, and machines to split leather, to cut stones, to sew, to imprint carpets, and to make matches. The public did not seem to tire watching a carving machine that produced miniature copies of art works. Europeans were especially surprised about the high quality of American musical instruments. This accomplishment somehow did not fit in with their notion that the materialistically minded Americans had neglected to develop an appreciation for the arts.[42] On the occasion of the Paris Exhibition of 1867, Frenchmen again criticized the limited participation of American heavy industry. They also noted that the exhibited goods indicated emphasis on production rather than perfection. They did not fail to observe, however, that the United States continued to excel in labor-saving machinery.[43]

41. Sartiges to Marcy, Washington, D. C., July 14, 1853. *FNTDS*, XVI.

42. Napoléon Joseph Bonaparte, *Visites et études de S.A.I. le prince Napoléon . . . à l'exposition de 1855* (Paris, 1856), pp. 195-212. For a discussion of this exposition, see also M. Curti, "America at the World Fairs, 1851-1893," *AHR*, LV (1950), 841; *Journal des économistes* (November, 1855), pp. 309-15; and Dwight D. Morrow, Jr., "The Impact of American Agricultural Machinery on France, 1851-1914" (Ph.D. dissertation, Harvard, 1957), pp. 102-73.

43. Curti, "World Fairs," pp. 843-46; U. S. Commissioners to the Paris Universal

Perhaps one of the most salutary effects of these fairs, particularly the exposition in 1855, was the reassurance to Frenchmen that their industrial progress enabled them to face the competition of the rest of the world. One of the strongest arguments in favor of high protection thus lost considerable ground.[44]

An analysis of the import-export statistics shows that during the first thirty years of this study the trade balance was predominantly in favor of France. The Civil War and Reconstruction period was too unsettled to permit the tempting conclusion that the different tariff policies of the two countries account for the unfavorable balance for France during the 1860's. The emergency which compelled the American people to reduce the importation of the type of goods France had to offer unquestionably contributed to this reversal, if it is correct to call it such. For according to the French Department of Agriculture and Commerce, France continued to maintain its favorable balance.

TABLE IV

Exports and Imports from and to France, 1827-1871[45]

(General Commerce—in millions of francs)

Yearly average for the period	Exports		Imports	
	To all countries	To the U. S.	From all countries	From the U. S.
1827-36..........	698.4	120.6	667.4	83.7
1837-46..........	1,024.0	142.7	1,088.4	150.2
1847-56..........	1,668.4	282.5	1,467.7	179.3
1857-66..........	3,292.8	233.8	2,986.5	183.8
1867-71..........	3,676.6	281.1	3,971.0	183.2

Source: Département de l'Agriculture, du Commerce et des Travaux Publics, *Annales du commerce extérieur* (Paris), March, 1859, pp. 40-43, and April, 1874, pp. 607-9.

It is a truism that statistics must be used with caution. Official French and American trade figures are at best approximate. In addition to the direct trade between Le Havre and New York, many French shipments were sent indirectly via Liverpool. A French director of customs has estimated that in the 1850's nine-tenths of the cargoes which the Cunard Company moved from Le Havre to Liver-

Exposition in 1867, *Reports* (Washington, 1870), I; J. M. Usher, *Paris: Universal Exposition, 1867* (Boston, 1868); E. C. Cowdin, *Paris Universal Exhibition of 1867* (Albany, N. Y., 1868), p. 19. See also D. D. Morrow, Jr., "The Impact of American Agricultural Machinery on France," pp. 174-222.

44. L. C. A. Knowles, *Economic Development in the Nineteenth Century* (London, 1932), p. 246.

45. For a convenient summary of these data, see Octave Noël, *Histoire de*

pool were ultimately destined for the United States.[46] By the same token, many French shipments to the United States were ultimately destined for Mexico and South America.[47] Furthermore, price fluctuations complicate the comparison of yearly trade data. It must be kept in mind that during the depressions of 1837 and 1857 prices fell in both countries. The uncertain conditions in France at the time of the Second Republic also contributed to their decline. On the other hand, prices rose almost 45 percent between 1851 and 1857, a period of rapid expansion. During the Civil War they soared again in the United States, but rose only mildly in France.[48]

The bulk of American exports to France included the work-providing staples of cotton and tobacco, as well as such articles of foreign produce as sugar, coffee, teas, cocoa, and spices. The French sent in return such luxuries as silks, wines, brandies, and fancy goods. Cotton was absolute king among exports to France, representing between 75 and 85 percent of all exports. It provided profits for producers and manufacturers and helped New Orleans and Le Havre to develop into flourishing communities. American cotton exports to France doubled between 1830 and 1845 and had more than tripled by the time the Civil War brought a disturbing interruption. During most

TABLE V

AMERICAN COTTON EXPORTS TO FRANCE, 1830-1869

Period	Volume[49] (in pounds)	Period	Volume (in pounds)
1830-34	289,103,400	1850-54	784,868,205
1835-39	404,298,400	1855-59	968,198,886
1840-44	575,551,200	1860-64	344,305,844
1845-49	696,347,400	1865-69	386,312,432

SOURCE: *House Ex. Doc.*, 34 Cong., 1 sess., no. 47, I, 127. (1830-1844). Montholon to Thouvenel, April 6, 1860. Corr. Commerciale, N. Y., v. 19. (1845-1859). U. S. Census Bureau, *Statistical Abstract of the United States* (Washington, D. C., 1878), pp. 117-18. (1860-69).

commerce extérieur de France (Paris, 1879), p. 365; see also Claire Pohly, "Les exportations de la France vers les nouveaux pays industriels" (Ph.D. dissertation, Université de Genève, 1939).

46. Report of March 16, 1859. Archives Nationales, F 12-6529.

47. The French were keenly interested in establishing warehouses in the United States from which they could conveniently distribute their merchandise in Central and South America. Forest to Guizot, New York, March 8, 1847. *CCC New York*, XIV.

48. Shepard B. Clough, *Economic History of Europe* (Boston, 1941), pp. 503, 662; Dewey, p. 293.

49. The figures for the years from 1830 through 1844 were originally compiled by French authorities. The difference between the American and French pound, too, serves as a reminder of the relative nature of these statistics.

of this period, however, France absorbed only about 10 percent of the entire cotton production of the South. Occasionally, the authorities at Le Havre complained about fraudulent attempts to increase the weight of the bales by adding a mixture of sand and dust.[50] Such isolated instances of dishonesty, however, did more harm to the machines than to the total trade volume. This volume could have been considerably enlarged. But the charges on the import of this raw material and prohibitive tariffs on cotton goods prevented French industry from taking advantage of extraordinary re-export possibilities.

Frenchmen were particularly disquieted by the growth of American cotton manufacturing which, by the 1850's, had already overtaken their own. Americans produced low cost quality goods with which French cotton manufacturers could not compete. The French also feared that, if American industry should ever consume most of its domestic cotton production, their own textile factories would be without adequate cotton supplies. They would have preferred to buy their raw cotton from different sources or cultivate it in Corsica or Algeria. However, even production of cotton in Egypt, Turkey, India, and Brazil did not seem to be large and suitable enough to assure the stability of this French industry.[51] Still another reason underlay this search for non-American cotton sources. France wanted to put some pressure on the United States to abstain from competing with French staples. When during President Jackson's time Americans began to manufacture silk and silk wares and to produce wine, pessimists saw the ruin of Lyons and Bordeaux. But this concern was as little justified as the frequent complaints of Southern tobacco growers that France discriminated against them by growing its own tobacco.

American diplomatic despatches from Paris conveyed the impression that the French government's tobacco monopoly practically excluded American tobacco. This was completely misleading. For the decade of the 1850's tobacco accounted for about 14 percent of the imports from the United States. Up to the Civil War it took care of nearly 75 percent of the entire consumption in France, while local production remained almost stagnant.[52] According to the consul general at New York, between 1845 and 1859 France increased its

50. Treilhard to Cass, Washington, D. C., January 16, 1860. FNTDS, XVII.

51. A. Cochut, "Production et commerce du coton," RDDM (October, 1853), pp. 300-304; see also Sérurier to Sébastiani, Washington, D. C., February 24, 1832. CPEU, LXXXVI.

52. House Ex. Doc., 34 Cong., 1 sess., No. 47, I, 127-29.

tobacco imports from the United States by 38 percent.[53] In addition to the growing consumption, the unusually large amount of over 20,000,000 kilograms of tobacco sent to France in 1855 was probably destined for the fighting forces in Crimea. With prices ranging then, on delivery to the factories of the government monopoly, from 9.5 cents per pound for Maryland tobacco to 7.5 cents for Missourian, Southern planters regarded the French tobacco administration (régie) as a good customer. They had no doubt, of course, that a less restrictive system would have enabled them to increase their exports to France.

With the exception of emergency situations, such as poor crop years, American wheat and cattle producers did little business with France. Normally, France depended on continental breadstuffs. When they were scarce, it bought them from America. The farming interests of both countries aided each other more by exchanging technical information and by supplying breeding stock and seeds than in any other way. Frenchmen cooperated, for instance, with American dairy producers by teaching them certain methods of making and preserving butter and cheese calculated to resist the deteriorating influences of time and climate.[54] They willingly forwarded requested information about the fabrication of sugar from beet-root, and they made available the results of experiments to ascertain the comparative productiveness of different breeds of poultry.[55] The importation in 1839 of the first Percheron horses from France contributed to the breeding of the sturdy American draft horses, the horsepower of a by-gone age.[56] France, in turn, began to introduce labor-saving agricultural machinery which American ingenuity had perfected.[57] French agriculture also benefited from several outstanding American contributions to insect control.[58]

Efforts to promote the interests of western cattlemen were crowned

53. Montholon to Thouvenel, New York, April 6, 1860. *CCC New York*, XIX.

54. Rush to Bastide, Paris, October 11, 1848. *CALP*.

55. Derosne to Niles, Paris, October 4, 1830. *DDFDS*, XXIV. U. S. Department of Agriculture, *Agricultural Report for 1861* (Washington, D. C., 1862), p. 328.

56. U. S. Department of Agriculture, "Breeds of Draft Horses," *Farmers' Bulletin*, No. 619 (Washington, 1954), p. 7. See also Mary L. Riley, *The Imprint of France on the United States* (New York, 1948), p. 104.

57. E. Tisserand, *Considérations générales sur l'agriculture* (Paris, 1867), pp. 8-9; see also C. Hubbard, "Exposition Universelle de 1855," *Journal des économistes* (October, 1855), p. 59; and D. D. Morrow, Jr., "The Impact of American Agricultural Machinery on France."

58. H. B. Weiss, *The Pioneer Century of American Entomology* (New Brunswick, N. J., 1936), pp. 155-210; see also R. O. Cummings, "American Interest in World Agriculture, 1861-1865," *Agricultural History*, XXIII (1949), 122.

with merely limited success. Native competition and different tastes constituted a barrier that broke down only during hard times. The French people considered American meat as inferior to theirs. American mess pork was too fat for them. The quality of French veal, one of their favorite dishes, seemed to be incomparable. They explained that the difference was due to the fact that they kept calves until almost four months old, while in America it was more profitable to kill them after one month.[59] Like Americans, they bred sheep for wool rather than mutton. Cured American ham was an exception. Its excellent quality secured it a place on the table of many French families.[60]

Such important preferences made themselves also felt in the French West Indies to which American pork merchants shipped great quantities of fat salted meats as soon as the duties were lowered in 1855. Prior to this date salted meats were burdened with a duty as high as $5.58 per 100 kilograms to protect local salters. When between 1852 and 1854 salted meat prices rose nearly 45 percent, it became politically necessary and expedient to provide cheaper meat by drastically lowering the duties to 9.5 cents. Vested interests, making the chambers of commerce of Cherbourg and Morlaix their spokesmen, made futile protests against this reduction. The government of the Emperor was too much concerned with the social implications of the meat crisis to listen to their complaints. Crowds flocked to the shops to buy the much less expensive American hams and, by doing so, forced the reduction of French prices.[61] As a result of the decree of September, 1855, the United States supplied France during the next two years with 9,797,000 kilograms, or about 75 percent of the imported salted provisions. Once the meat crisis had passed, Frenchmen returned to eating French products. Imports of American meat dropped in 1858 to the insignificant amount of 102,110 kilograms.[62]

There hardly existed another commodity which French political and commercial agents promoted as zealously as silk wares. Silk was to France what cotton was to America. The important difference was that the United States sold raw cotton and imported primarily manufactured silk goods, thus providing employment for a large

59. Henry H. French, "Observations on English Husbandry," in *Report of the Commissioner of Patents for the Year 1860* (Washington, D. C., 1861), II, 161-165. The author presents a comparison of English, French, and American agriculture.

60. *House Ex. Doc.*, 34 Cong., 1 sess., No. 47, I, 136.

61. *Merchants' Magazine*, XXXII (1855), 762.

62. *Reports of the Director General of Customs, Paris, March 16 and July 29, 1859*. Archives Nationales, F 12-6529.

proportion of the industrial population of France. Silks represented an average of 40 percent of the Union's total imports from France.[63] The favorite status which French silks enjoyed in the United States in the 1830's was gradually threatened, though, by the beginnings of an American silk industry, the competition of cheaper Chinese products, and the inroads made by the Prussians and Swiss. The Germans' willingness to lower their duties on Southern tobacco in exchange for equivalent reductions on their silks greatly alarmed the merchants of Lyons.[64] They also worried about competition from low cost Chinese silks which found not only a good market in the New World, but were re-exported from there to the Baltic countries of Europe.[65] Despite these developments, the French managed to maintain in the Union a profitable outlet for their high quality wares.

Although the United States usually figured as France's second best customer for wines, wine shipments seldom exceeded 5 percent of all its imports. Various kinds of liqueur and brandy were even less in demand. In spite of special concessions granted to French wines in the Treaty of 1831 and tariff reductions in 1857—10 percent for wines and 70 percent for liqueurs—consumption remained small and stationary. Preference for other and cheaper alcoholic drinks rather than competition from Florida and California wine producers accounted for this negligible trade. From the standpoint of the French wine industry, it was displeasing to know that some wine shipments from France to America were not of French origin and that in 1867 direct German sales were four times as large as its own.[66] Occasionally, brandy firms at La Rochelle imported cheap American whiskey to mix with their own products for the purpose of sending them to the United States at a lower price.[67] For as long as the alcoholic products of France were identified as expensive luxuries, overseas demand for them was likely to remain small.

Another challenge came from the American temperance movement. When its members advocated the abrogation of the wine concessions of 1831, French merchants became so alarmed that they shipped their merchandise to America only on consignment instead of on their own

63. These percentages are specifically mentioned in the yearly volumes entitled: France, Douanes, Direction Générale, *Tableau général du commerce et de la navigation*.
64. Pageot to Guizot, Washington, D. C., December 13, 1843. *CPEU*, XCIX.
65. A. L. Dunham, *The Industrial Revolution in France, 1815-1848* (New York, 1955), pp. 378-79.
66. U. S. Census Bureau, *The Foreign Commerce and Navigation of the United States* (Washington, D. C., 1867), p. 257.
67. *House Ex. Doc.*, 34 Cong,. 1 sess., No. 47, III, 93-95.

account.[68] They also suggested that behind the ostensible and pious promotion of health and morals lurked materialistic selfishness, pure and simple. As far as they were concerned, the temperance movement did not raise its voice against coffee and tea because these articles were carried in American ships, while wines and brandies were usually transported in French ships.[69]

The rate of acceleration of the Franco-American trade did not keep pace with that of the two countries' total foreign trade. During the

TABLE VI

COMBINED IMPORTS AND EXPORTS FROM AND TO FRANCE AND THE UNITED STATES,
1827-1871
(Expressed in percentages relative to their trade with all foreign countries)

Period	GENERAL COMMERCE	
	French Trade with U. S.	U. S. Trade with France
1827-36..................	14.9%	17.2%
1837-46..................	13.8%	17.9%
1847-56..................	14.7%	14.4%
1857-66..................	6.6%	11.1%
1867-71..................	6.0%	10.3%

These percentages are based on Tables III and IV.

period under consideration, the relative decline of the trade volume between France and the United States is as significant as its absolute rise. It shows a remarkable parallel with their political developments. In both instances, their relations appeared to be better than they actually were.

It is especially noteworthy that the relative downward trend coincides with the ascendancy and reign of Louis Napoleon. That political considerations influenced French commercial policy is indicated by the relative increase of French trade with Great Britain and Turkey during periods of close political cooperation. Indeed, while the combined trade of France with Spain, the Netherlands, Russia, and Turkey then roughly equalled that with North America, for political reasons Paris paid more attention to the European countries than to its best or second best customer across the Atlantic.[70] Although Napoleon

68. After the passage of the "temperance law" in the State of New York, the State Department assured French merchants that their rights under the Treaty of 1831 would be protected by American courts. Marcy to Sartiges, Washington, D. C., May 16, 1855. *FNFDS*, VI.

69. Simounet to Bastide, New York, December 5, 1848. *CCC New York*, XIV; see also Archives Nationales, F 12-2689.

70. The combined trade of France with all European countries obviously over-

III talked about the promotion of trans-Atlantic trade, he continued to treat the United States as a politically passive factor in world affairs. This attitude, the growing political estrangement between the Second Empire and the American republic, as well as tariffs, wars, and depressions, were detrimental to the full development of Franco-American trade relations.

VI

Much as the business world sought the advantages of international trade, the consequences of the resulting interdependence could not be avoided. In his remarkable study on economic crises, Juglar stressed these interrelationships by pointing out that a major economic crisis or period of prosperity in one important country usually reflected itself in others.[71] The depressions of 1837 and 1857 substantiated this contention.

The fact that the United States and France went through a depression in 1837 does not warrant the conclusion that the panic in America caused the economic crisis in France, or vice versa. The degree of Franco-American interdependence was not so great as to be capable of bringing about such a disastrous result. But while the causes of this depression must be sought in such domestic conditions as overexpansion, speculation, monetary policies, and poor crops, certain developments in one country contributed to the economic crisis in the other.[72]

The depression of 1837 was more serious in the United States than in France. It affected particularly those French communities and industries which greatly depended on the American market. In the departments of Dordogne, Doubs, Enre, and Gard, for instance, workers were compelled to work reduced hours or to become public charges. French watchmakers and stocking manufacturers, suddenly faced with the loss of their vital American market, were concerned that a prolonged crisis might seriously prejudice their existence.[73] Business failures brought losses to French creditors who were accustomed to advancing short-term credits to American firms. On March 5, 1838, the Minister of Commerce went so far as to address a circular to the chambers of commerce, warning about the risks of doing business with American firms. This kind of talk, issuing from

shadowed that with the United States. W. H. Walker, "Franco-American Commercial Relations, 1815-1850" (Ph.D. dissertation, University of Iowa, 1928), p. 135.

71. C. Juglar, *Des crises commerciales* (Paris, 1889), pp. 17, 279.

72. Dunham, *Industrial Revolution*, p. 367.

73. E. Levasseur, *Histoire du commerce de la France* (Paris, 1912), II, 210-11.

such a highly placed person, could not but aggravate the crisis. Exaggerated rumors about "the total bankruptcy of the greater part of the banks in five eastern states and of the sad misery which affected all classes" aroused such bitter resentment in the United States that the French Foreign Minister considered it necessary to express his regrets about these indiscretions.[74]

The crisis left a lasting shadow. The monetary and commercial disorders, ruined banks, and suspended payments made French investors wary of investments in America, even though occasional prospects of 30 to 40 percent profit appeared tempting. French consuls never tired of cautioning their fellow countrymen that "the cheap money policy of the United States might result in another disaster like the one of 1837."[75] When in 1848 financial embarrassment of several important European banking and business houses compelled some French and American merchants in New York to suspend payments, or when in 1855 a short crisis led to temporary financial difficulties, commentators promptly recalled "the worst days of 1837."[76]

England, France, and the United States experienced another depression in 1857. Its causes were complex. In all three countries speculation and overexpansion led to an imbalance in the economy. The boom and bust in the United States have been attributed to easy credit policies. Several factors, such as poor harvests from 1852 and 1856, the failure of the silk crop in 1856, and the speculative incentive which the Crimean War provided, strained the financial structure of France to the breaking point. The cost of this war and the purchase of large amounts of foreign grain drained France of its specie reserves at a time when the financial demands of business and industry were very heavy. This situation was further complicated by England's large exports of specie to the Orient.[77]

The sensational news in the spring of 1857 that Greene & Company, the well established American bankers at Paris, had suspended their

74. Cass to Forsyth, Paris, March 21, 1838. *DDFDS*, XXVIII.
75. Forest to Guizot, New York, January 30, 1847. *CCC New York*, XIV.
76. J. G. Courcelle-Seneuil, "Crise commerciale aux États-Unis," *Journal des économistes* (January, 1855), pp. 112-15.
77. For a discussion of this depression consult G. W. Van Vleck, *The Panic of 1857* (New York, 1943), pp. 41-53; H. Rosenberg, *Die Weltwirtschaftskrise von 1857-1859* (Stuttgart, 1934), p. 131; A. Clément, "Des crises commerciales," *Journal des économistes* (February, 1858), pp. 161-91; Achille Viallate, *L'activité économique en France de la fin du XVIIIe siècle à nos jours* (Paris, 1937), p. 153; and the *American Railroad Journal* (January, 1857).

payments was an early sign of coming troubles.[78] Embarrassments of business houses in all three countries multiplied and produced a disastrous chain effect. When in the fall of 1857 a panic struck New York, respectable firms in Paris felt the impact of American payment suspension very badly. Leading exporters suddenly dropped their transactions by 50 to 75 percent within a few weeks. Prices of many commodities fell as much as 20 percent. For weeks no vessels left Marseilles with cargoes for the United States. Under these circumstances, manufacturers reduced or suspended their operations. Thousands of workers were laid off.[79] These developments merely aggravated the French crisis; they did not basically cause it. At the same time the inability or hesitation of French firms to extend new short-term credits to American enterprises and their panicky attempts to collect outstanding ones did not help to improve the situation in the United States. Nor did the liquidation of American securities in France and England contribute to a speedy American recovery.

France withstood the shock of this catastrophe better than Britain and the United States. However, in the fall of 1860 the cash reserves of the Banks of England and France dropped sharply and compelled these institutions once again to raise their interest rates. The *Revue des deux mondes*[80] promptly looked to "the land from where the crises come to us" to explain the temporary shortness of specie. This observation did not fully accord with the facts because another poor European crop was at the root of this difficulty. It necessitated the importation of a considerable amount of American wheat which caused a drain on the gold market in London and Paris. The situation was different with the financial crises of France in 1861 and 1864. They could be traced to the American Civil War and large exports of silver to India and Egypt to pay for cotton.

VII

Trade constituted only one, though the most important, aspect of the economic relations between France and the United States. While the French government was anxious to foster trade, in view of its ambitions in Africa and Indo-China it preferred French capital and manpower to develop its own colonies. Although the government did not channel investments abroad, it recognized their political potentialities in Europe. On the other hand, it did not look with

78. *Bankers' Magazine* (May, 1857), p. 899.
79. Levasseur, II, 266; Martin, pp. 383, 399.
80. November 15, 1860, p. 496.

favor upon the export of French capital or the emigration of its citizens to America.

Any attempt to determine the extent to which French capital took its risks in the United States is best limited to stocks and bonds. In spite of the unavailability of complete records, at least some light can be shed on this type of investment. Evidence for direct investment in property, business, or industry is as yet too spotty to permit any estimate.[81]

The French government prohibited the negotiation of all foreign securities as far back as 1785. It relaxed this decree in 1823 and permitted the quotation of foreign government bonds.[82] But it continued to bar all other types of foreign securities. The Paris stock exchange began to quote the bonds of the Bank of the United States in 1836. In the following years several other American bonds were officially offered to French investors, such as the 6 percent Illinois and Ohio bonds and those of New York State, New York City, and Indiana, paying 5 percent.[83]

In 1857 other foreign securities were granted the privilege of official citation. Their increasing unofficial circulation in France called for a revision of the existing law for purposes of taxation and uniform protection. When quotation of foreign securities was "tolerated" at the Bourse, French legislators deemed it only fair to subject them to "taxes equivalent to those on French securities." Henceforth, they could not be quoted or negotiated without payment of these taxes. Since the law of 1857 did not subject foreign companies to the same restrictions as the French, the decree of May 2, 1858, partially corrected this discrimination. It imposed upon foreign railroad companies certain rules and regulations before their stocks and bonds could be quoted. This was really the French answer to costly recent experiences with American railroads.[84] The number of foreign stocks and bonds admitted at the Bourse indicated that foreigners took the regulatory laws in stride. They increased from 28 in 1830 to 109 in 1869.[85]

American securities were widely advertised. Among many other

81. R. E. Cameron, "French Foreign Investments, 1850-1880" (Ph.D. dissertation, University of Chicago, 1952), p. 27. French investments abroad were mostly made in negotiable securities.

82. Loeb, p. 239.

83. R. G. Lévy, "La fortune mobilière de la France à l'étranger," RDDM (March, 1897), p. 421; see also L. Guillaume, L'épargne française et les valeurs mobilières étrangères (Paris, 1907), p. 13.

84. Loeb, pp. 240-44; see also B. Paul-Dauphin, Émission et circulation des titres des sociétés étrangères en France (Paris, 1907), pp. 21-22.

85. M. Marion, Histoire financière de la France depuis 1715 (Paris, 1928), V, 348.

French newspapers, *La Semaine Financière* published New York Stock Exchange quotations quite regularly. Such bankers as Hottinger, Rothschild, Seligman, Van der Broek, or the American banking firm of Greene & Company in Paris were always in a position to furnish information about American securities. Even smaller brokers advertised that they bought and sold negotiable American papers.[86] Several railroad companies sent their own agents to Europe to promote the sale of their stocks and bonds. They did quite well until the financial disaster of 1857 caused many French investors to lose confidence in them. Even after this calamity the Galveston Railroad Company published full-page advertisements. It facilitated the sale of its bonds and the payment of dividends through 145 local agents, primarily French banking houses.[87]

The tax laws of France and the United States offered certain advantages to prospective French investors. Until 1863, government securities, whether French or foreign, were tax-exempt in France.[88] The laws of the United States were even more generous in this respect. They did not impose any tax upon any kind of securities held by foreigners residing abroad.[89] Other incentives induced French investments: the desire to share in the growth of American wealth, the expediency of taking out this kind of "personal insurance policy," or, as in the case of the House of Rothschild, to protect investments and commitments already made.

The New York Stock Exchange was then operated very much like the one in Paris, except that it enjoyed complete freedom from security regulations. As far as the French investor was concerned, the financial soundness of the American securities he bought depended largely on the reputation and reliability of his broker. The law did not protect him otherwise.[90] The time difference between Paris and New York added another element of risk. The New York Exchange opened after the Bourse closed its doors. As Professor Henri Sée observed: "New York can daily liquidate its transactions at terms unknown in Paris."[91] Inasmuch as Frenchmen were usually long-term

86. A. Vitu, *Guide financière* (Paris, 1864), p. 179. See also A. H. Cole, "Evolution of the Foreign Exchange Market of the United States," *Journal of Economic and Business History,* I (1929), 400.

87. *La Semaine Financière* (February 27, 1858), p. 141.

88. Cameron, p. 183.

89. See letter of Secretary of the Treasury Salmon P. Chase in *American Railroad Journal* (October 12, 1861), p. 176.

90. Forest to Guizot, New York, May 31, 1847. *CCC New York,* XIV.

91. H. Sée, *Histoire économique de la France* (Paris, 1942), II, 359.

holders of American stocks and bonds, this handicap could have been costly to them only during critical situations.

For these reasons, French capitalists took all possible precautions before they purchased American securities. Contrary to British buyers who often took great chances when they bought their American stocks in London, the French played it so safe that they seldom bought theirs in Paris. In any case, they arranged their purchases through reputable firms. Large investors usually made the most critical on the spot examination of the projects and enterprises in which they intended to invest. Others paid higher charges for buying American securities in London rather than placing their orders in Paris. They were interested in keeping the Paris Bourse ignorant of the existence of certain securities as well as of the amount they held of them. They hoped to increase the safety of their investments by hiding information about them.[92]

Among the owners of American securities were many members of the French nobility. Finance knew no ideological barriers. Aristocrats helped in effect to meet the capital needs of the American republic's enterprises. One of the real motivations for investing their savings, however, was to be prepared to flee with them in their pockets in case of a political upheaval. Their ranks included the Prince de Beauvan, the Marquis de Champagne, the Count de Narbonne, the Count de Beaumont, and a multitude of other nobles. It is also noteworthy to find among the creditors of America the editor Charles Panckoucke and the celebrity Paul Julien. Augustin Scribe, the dramatic author, drew from his American investments an income of $2,000 a year. Tocqueville inquired about his American stocks quite frequently. At one time he worried about the security of the railroad stocks he had acquired. It made him uneasy that from a distance he could not "pick the right moment" for his financial transactions in America.[93]

American bonds attracted French investors because they paid higher interest rates than were customary in Europe. The consul general of France at New York deplored the fact that at a time when the Second Republic found itself in difficulties, French capital invested in American bonds. In the summer of 1848, for instance, the New York agent of the House of Rothschild bought United States government bonds to the amount of $3,000,000. According to the consul general, the

92. R. C. McGrane, *Foreign Bondholders and American State Debts* (New York, 1935), p. 276; see also *Bankers' Magazine* (July, 1850), p. 95.

93. Tocqueville to Edward L. Childe, Cannes, December 4, 1858, in *Quelques correspondants de Mr. et Mrs. Childe et de Edward Lee Childe* (London, 1912).

drain on the metallic reserves of the United States just prior to the California gold discoveries threatened a financial crisis which the Rothschilds hoped to prevent in the interest of world-wide economic considerations.[94] Such transactions were not unusual in the financial world. When France experienced a scarcity of specie in 1848, many international bankers came to the rescue of its business institutions. Among them was the firm of Brown & Duncan of New York.[95]

American foreign indebtedness did not reach great proportions prior to the Civil War. Those Americans who had certain reservations about dependence on foreign capital saw their fears materialized when at the beginning of this war English and French investors practically dumped their American securities. However, these Europeans hurriedly returned as creditors when the prospects for profits and safety looked much brighter in the United States than in the tense Old World. In a letter to a leading Wall Street firm a French banker noted in 1871 that many "new investors find American bonds superior in safety to any securities equally lucrative to be had elsewhere."[96] This renewed interest in American securities was also indicated by the fact that the National Stock Board received then daily about 150 messages via the French wires.[97]

Enough references exist to permit a fairly close estimate of the aggregate foreign indebtedness of the United States. Various French and American scholars have attempted to calculate the approximate amount of French foreign holdings. It remains then to determine the percentage of French capital that found its way to the United States.

France developed its modern role as international creditor in the middle of the nineteenth century. But reliable and useful information regarding foreign investments in the French portfolio prior to 1870 is scarce. The American economist Cleona Lewis placed them at $500,000,000 for 1850.[98] The distinguished French scholar Léon Say calculated that they amounted to about $2,500,000,000 by 1869.[99]

94. Simounet to Bastide, New York, July 22 and August 30, 1848. *CCC New York,* XIV.

95. J. Capefigue, *Histoire des grandes opérations financières* (Paris, 1858), III, 316.

96. *Commercial and Financial Chronicle* (September 16, 1871), pp. 359-60.

97. J. K. Medberry, *Men and Mysteries of Wall Street* (Boston, 1870), pp. 195-96. *House Ex. Doc.,* 41 Cong., 2 sess., No. 27.

98. Cleona Lewis, *America's Stake in International Investments* (Washington, D. C., 1938), p. 473.

99. Léon Say, *Rapport sur le paiement de l'indemnité de guerre* (Paris, 1874), p. 70. Later estimates lend much credibility to this figure. See E. Théry, *Les valeurs mobilières en France* (Paris, 1897), pp. 140-41; E. Becqué *L'internationalisation des capitaux* (Montpellier, 1912), pp. 62-65; and H. D. White, *The French International Accounts 1880-1913* (Cambridge, Mass., 1933), pp. 94-95.

TABLE VII

ESTIMATES OF THE TOTAL FOREIGN INDEBTEDNESS OF THE UNITED STATES, 1837-1869

Year	Millions of Dollars	Source of Information
1837.........	150[a] 200[b]	a) *American Railroad Journal* (January 27, 1855), 55. b) *Ibid.* (Estimate of the Comptroller of the State of New York)
1838.........	130[a] 200[b]	a) *Bankers' Magazine* (March, 1856), 728. b) W. J. Shultz, *Financial Development of the United States* (New York, 1937), 211.
1843.........	225	Cleona Lewis, *America's Stake in International Investments* (Washington, D. C., 1938), 519.
1852.........	261	*Bankers' Magazine* (September, 1852), 252.
1853.........	230	*American Railroad Journal* (January 27, 1855), 55.
1854.........	184[a] 200[b]	a) R. C. McGrane, *Foreign Bondholders and American State Debts* (New York, 1935), 277. (Estimate of the Secretary of the Treasury) b) *Merchants' Magazine and Commercial Review* (October, 1868), 241-48.
1856.........	300	*Bankers' Magazine* (March, 1856), 728.
1857.........	400 (plus)	C. K. Hobson, *The Export of Capital* (London, 1914), 128. (This figure refers only to American railroad stocks in England.)
1861.........	400	*Merchants' Magazine and Commercial Review* (October, 1868), 241-48.
1866.........	600[a] 938[b]	a) *Ibid.*, p. 245 (Estimate of the Director of the Bureau of Statistics) b) (Estimate of the *Merchants' Magazine*)
1869.........	1,465[100]	H. R. Ex. Doc. no. 27, 41:2, 1869. (Report of the Special Commisioner of the Revenue)

By far the greatest share of American securities held abroad belonged to Englishmen.[101] The Dutch and Germans had also made substantial investments. An analysis of the geographic distribution of French investments in foreign government securities shows a strong inclination towards European countries. In 1857, this type of American securities occupied only sixth place in the French portfolio and constituted 4 percent of the total. In 1867, it had risen to 8 percent.[102]

100. Jay Cooke & Company estimated that of this amount one billion dollars constituted national securities; the rest were state, railroad, and miscellaneous papers.

101. L. H. Jenks, *The Migration of British Capital to 1875* (New York, 1927), p. 85; C. K. Hobson, *The Export of Capital* (London, 1914), pp. 133-34.

102. Cameron, p. 194. See also Herbert Feis, *Europe: The World's Banker, 1870-1914* (New Haven, Conn., 1930), p. 51.

If these percentage figures are a reasonable indication regarding the geographic distribution of all types of foreign securities, Frenchmen showed very limited interest in the financial opportunities of America. In the early 1850's they may have invested there about $20,000,000, and by 1869, between $150,000,000 and $200,000,000. Their purchases of American stocks and bonds represented between 8 and 12 percent of the total foreign indebtedness of the United States.

The emphasis of the French on caution[103] and their preference for investment in real estate make it unlikely that they were more enterprising with regard to direct business investments in the United States. The distance between the two countries magnified risks until they appeared to be a gamble beyond control. The repudiation in the 1840's of "illegally issued" state bonds and losses in the 1850's resulting from taking chances with California gold mines and American railroads explain the relative unattractiveness of the United States to French capitalists.[104]

Furthermore, although the consular convention of 1853 regulated property and inheritance questions in such a manner as to offer the greatest security to investors, Frenchmen contemplating direct investments in the United States could not afford to overlook the interpretation of the convention's provisions by American courts. In 1856, for instance, Chief Justice Roger B. Taney ruled that "the treaty does not claim for the United States the right of controlling the succession of real or personal property in a state."[105] French heirs could thus become ensnarled in the states' rights issue. Toward the end of the century changing concepts of American constitutional law were reflected in Justice Stephen J. Field's ruling that the consular convention granted Frenchmen the right to possess personal and real property independently of state law. Further clarification came in 1923, when the Supreme Court of California rejected the state's contention that the rights of non-resident French heirs were not meant to be covered by the convention of 1853. As long as these uncertainties existed, they too deterred potential investors.

103. Sée, p. 247; D. S. Landes, "French Entrepreneurship and Industrial Growth in the Nineteenth Century," *Journal of Economic History,* IX (1949), 48.

104. An official sent to Europe to negotiate a loan for the use of the United States reported in 1843: ". . . no [banking] house . . . dares venture to present an American loan to the British, Dutch, or French public." *House Ex. Doc.,* 27 Cong., 3 sess., No. 197. See also Henry Blumenthal, "The California Societies in France, 1849-1855," *Pacific Historical Review,* XXV (1956), pp. 251-60.

105. See R. Hayden, "The States' Rights Doctrine and the Treaty-Making Power," *AHR,* XX (1917), 582-85; and V. V. Meekison, "Treaty Provisions for the Inheritance of Personal Property," *American Journal of International Law,* XLIV (1950), 313-32.

The French obviously found trans-Atlantic trade safer and more profitable than investments. The trade relations between the two countries were significant enough to contribute to both prosperity and occasional economic setbacks. They were, of course, vitally important to those thousands whose livelihood was directly affected by them. Basically, the French economy depended much more on American raw materials and business orders than the United States needed the market and products of France. That the American republic should, therefore, be in a position to wield much potential influence over the domestic affairs of France was not a comforting thought to Napoleon III.

CHAPTER V

The Civil War and France
(1861-1865)

I

In spite of the frequently strained relations between France and the United States prior to the Civil War, it remained to be seen whether Napoleon III would take advantage of the crisis which shook the Federal republic to its foundations. As the tensions mounted in the 1850's, informed Frenchmen began to debate whether permanent disunion of the United States was possible and what impact it would have on the future of Europe, as well as of America. Sartiges, for instance, doubted whether separation could be brought about without an armed conflict.[1] Such a war, another French diplomat[2] contended, would produce profound international consequences regardless of its outcome. For should one side be victorious, the restraining balance between the sections would be destroyed, and one colossal power would make its weight felt in the world. Should it result in a permanent division, the general balance of the world would also be upset.

Other European observers of the American scene saw no advantages in an eventual secession of the South. In 1859 the publicist Julius Fröbel published his keen analysis of the power-political relationships between the United States and the various European countries.[3] In it he warned against the mistaken notion that a divided North America would automatically be a weakened one. In case of a definitive split, he argued, the ensuing competition between the North and the South would accelerate the economic and military development of both sections to such an extent that within the near future two

1. Sartiges to Walewski, Washington, D. C., March 2, 1858. *CPEU,* CXVIII.
2. Treilhard to Walewski, Washington, D. C., January 16, 1860. *CPEU,* CXXIII.
3. Julius Fröbel, *Amerika, Europa und die politischen Gesichtspunkte der Gegenwart* (Berlin, 1859), pp. 37-46.

powerful states would emerge. He concluded, therefore, that Europe's self-interest lay in the maintenance of the status quo.

Secession soon ceased to be a hypothetical question. When it came, President Lincoln's determination to preserve the Union at all cost excluded the possibility of peaceful separation. But until the fighting began, all doors were not as yet closed to reconciliation. France and Great Britain had an opportunity to contribute to it. For once secession became a reality, they had a legal right, and perhaps a moral duty, to react to it. Their official silence was likely to be interpreted as acquiescence in the birth of the new nation. A public declaration from them that the rebelling states would be left to their own fate might have given reconciliation a last chance. To induce Napoleon III to make such a statement, if he would have been at all agreeable to it, called for an American minister of unqualified loyalty to the Union. It was unfortunate for the Union that during the crucial months from Lincoln's election to the fall of Fort Sumter a loyal citizen of the State of Virginia represented it in France. In 1859 President Buchanan appointed Charles J. Faulkner to the important diplomatic post as United States minister to France. From the beginning, this appointment of the former Congressman from Virginia displeased those who remembered that in 1856 Faulkner was among the first to demand secession in case of a Republican victory. When the secession of Southern states actually began, the Virginian statesman lost little time resolving the conflict of his dual loyalty by informing Secretary of State Jeremiah S. Black: "I could not retain my position of trust and honor after my state shall have assumed towards the Federal Government the relation of a foreign and Independent Power."[4] Against the advice of his Southern friends, he requested his recall early in 1861. Under the circumstances, this was the only honorable course to take. Indeed, no evidence has been found to suggest that Faulkner violated his trust as envoy of the United States. His failures were those of omission.

Since Lincoln's election, for instance, it had been rumored that a Southern commission had obtained French assurances of military and naval aid in case of a war. Faulkner waited until the end of February of the next year before he inquired officially about this alleged promise. He had not pursued this matter immediately, he explained, because he thought the rumors were a "preposterous hoax

4. Faulkner to Black, Paris, January 14, 1861. *DDFDS*, XLIX. See also Donald R. McVeigh, "Charles James Faulkner in the Civil War," *West Virginia History*, XII (1951), 129-41; and the Washington *National Intelligencer*, June 8, 1861.

. . . utterly devoid of any plausible foundation."[5] That Édouard Thouvenel, the French Foreign Minister, denied ever having had a meeting with an agent from South Carolina did not, of course, exclude the possibility of some contact between Southern agents and other French officials.

It is evident from Faulkner's despatches to the State Department that at his numerous interviews with the Emperor and Thouvenel, the French statesmen did most of the talking. Napoleon showed an extraordinary interest in the election of 1860 and the fateful events which followed it. On several occasions he expressed his hope for a peaceful settlement of the controversy between the two American sections. In these conversations Faulkner deliberately avoided all allusions to the question of recognition of the seceding states.[6] But he also failed to mention that the Constitution authorized the use of force to maintain the integrity of the republic. Instead, practically on the eve of the war, he let the French government believe that the Lincoln administration would not resort to war.[7] In a letter to Secretary of State William H. Seward he expressed his conviction that no administration in Washington could be "so mad and reckless as to attempt the exercise of force against the seceding states."[8] Personally he believed that, if the Confederacy would ask for immediate recognition, France would not grant it.[9] What it would do in the future, of course, nobody could foretell.

Faulkner's recall became imperative. He took his final leave from the Emperor and Eugénie on May 12, 1861. Loyal Americans in Paris were to deplore that Washington took a long time to send a successor. They regarded it as a calamity that at this juncture the American legations in Paris and London were in the trust of men who did not vigorously take care of the interests of the Union.[10] The appointment of William L. Dayton, a former senator from New Jersey, to the French capital and of Charles Francis Adams to the Court of St. James's gave Secretary of State Seward the kind of assistance he

5. Faulkner to Cass, Paris, November 28 and December 6, 1860. *DDFDS*, XLVIII. Faulkner to Black, Paris, February 21, 1861. *DDFDS*, XLIX.

6. Faulkner to Seward, Paris, April 5, 1861. *DDFDS*, XLIX.

7. Seward to Dayton, Washington, D. C., July 6, 1861. *FIDS*, XXVI. In fairness to Faulkner it should be pointed out that the State Department had encouraged him to make this assumption.

8. Faulkner to Seward, Paris, April 5, 1861. *DDFDS*, XLIX.

9. Faulkner to Black, Paris, March 19, 1861. *DDFDS*, XLIX.

10. The Reverend Dr. McClintock, who made these comments in a letter to his friend George R. Crooks in New York, occupied a central position in the American colony in Paris. Crooks to Seward, New York, April 24, 1861. Seward Papers.

needed for the effective execution of the administration's foreign policy. The discreet and devoted Dayton[11] and the resourceful Consul General John Bigelow[12] henceforth served as an alert team at the French capital.

II

To grasp the tremendous responsibility of the Secretary of State it must be realized that the fate of the Union depended not only on the industrial and military superiority of the North, but also on the nonintervention of foreign powers. To prevent France and Britain from giving any effective aid and encouragement to the Confederacy was the main objective of Northern diplomacy. Seward pursued it with all the energy he could muster. In fact, his original aggressiveness, which in time gave way to patient diplomacy, made him a controversial figure at home and abroad. He undoubtedly complicated his task for at least the first two years of the war by delivering his sensational bombshell in the wake of Spanish troop movements to Santo Domingo. With reference to them, he submitted the extraordinary recommendation to President Lincoln (April 1, 1861) "to demand explanations from Spain and France, categorically, . . . and if not satisfactory . . . to convene Congress and declare war against them."[13] Édouard-Henry Mercier, the French minister at Washington, did not regard this as an April Fools' Day joke, as for all practical purposes Lincoln did. He wondered whether the Secretary of State was a reckless political gambler who, against all odds, would involve the United States in an international war as a means of averting a civil war.[14] Although Lincoln saved Seward and the Union from thus committing political suicide, the Secretary has been severely criticized for contemplating it.[15]

By itself, Seward's *Thoughts for the Consideration of the President* cast indeed great doubts on his political maturity, doubts which are out of character with the total record of his diplomatic accomplish-

11. On the occasion of Dayton's funeral services late in 1864, Bigelow eulogized him as one of his country's "most experienced statesmen . . . and distinguished diplomats." See copy of John Bigelow's remarks at the funeral services of the late William L. Dayton. Dayton Papers, Box 1. The French government appreciated Dayton's conciliatory spirit. Mercier to Thouvenel, Washington, D. C., September 9, 1862. *CPEU*, CXXVIII.

12. Margaret Clapp, *Forgotten Citizen: John Bigelow* (Boston, 1947). After Dayton's death Bigelow was appointed as his successor.

13. Roy P. Basler, ed., *The Collected Works of Abraham Lincoln* (New Brunswick, N. J., 1955), IV, 316-18.

14. Mercier to Thouvenel, Washington, D. C., May 23, 1861. *CPEU*, CXXIV.

15. T. K. Lothrop, *William Henry Seward* (New York, 1898), p. 278.

ments. It should not be taken for granted that the irresponsible idea of a diversionary war originated with Seward. Late in January of 1861 Mercier attended a dinner at Senator Douglas' residence at which Seward, Crittenden, and several other personalities were present. On that occasion general agreement was voiced that "a good war would have been the best way of prolonging the life of the Union."[16] The Secretary did not have to go much beyond this opinion to make the dramatic recommendation of April 1, for which, of course, he had to assume full responsibility.

Another contemporary development is likely to have had considerable bearing on the formulation of the *Thoughts*. Mercier's Southern leanings were no secret. On March 29, 1861, the French diplomat recommended to his government that it recognize the Confederacy as a possible means of discouraging the outbreak of the impending civil war.[17] Seward's diplomatic bombshell quite conceivably may have been designed primarily to caution those foreigners who were also playing with a dangerous idea, that of recognizing the Confederate government. It would make quite a difference whether he advanced his foreign war proposal as a policy objective or merely as a policy maneuver. The suspiciously demonstrative militancy of the secretary contrasted sharply with the sober restraint of the chief executive. As far as the conduct of American foreign policy was concerned, it was as true then as at any other time that the Secretary of State may propose policies, but the ultimate responsibility for decisions rests with the President. In the light of historical perspective it is noteworthy that Seward's militancy was primarily a reaction to the extreme position of those European statesmen who would not have hesitated to accept American disunion as a *fait accompli*. His war scare evidently had the effect of strengthening the hands of those abroad who were resigned to wait until the combatants themselves decided their controversy one way or another.

In other respects too Seward reacted to European dispositions and conditions. From the Union's point of view it was unfortunate that the first crucial year of the war coincided with a period of relative calm in Europe. Given time, the Secretary counted on intra-European complications to tie the hands of those governments which otherwise might be tempted to capitalize on the North's predicament. Troubles in Greece and Italy as well as complications growing out of the joint

16. Mercier to Thouvenel, Washington, D. C., February 1, 1861. *CPEU,* CXXIV. See also E. D. Adams, *Great Britain and the American Civil War* (New York, 1925), I, 124.

17. Mercier to Thouvenel, Washington, D. C., March 29, 1861. *CPEU,* CXXIV.

expedition England, France, and Spain sent to Mexico in 1861-62, the Polish insurrection of 1863, and the Austro-Prussian War against Denmark in 1864 were in a sense answers to his prayers. These developments compelled Napoleon III to relegate the American conflict to the background.[18]

Time played a major role in other regards as well. The Union needed time to mobilize its industrial and military capacities before it could either overwhelm or exhaust the South and, incidentally, use its might as a deterrent to potential interventionists.[19] Also, the legal basis for recognition of the South or for the refusal to recognize the blockade was apt to be weakened with the passing of time. For the longer that foreign powers waited to take these steps, the more they exposed themselves to the charge, in case of intervention, of violating legal principles they had heretofore respected. The longer they upheld these principles, the more, in effect, they contributed to the demoralization of the South which counted heavily on foreign support.

These considerations explain too why Seward's warnings were so energetic during the early phase of the war. In May of 1861, for instance, he cautioned the presumably friendly power of France: "Let her avoid giving countenance to treason!"[20] On another occasion he intimated that if the maritime powers alienated the Union, it might retaliate by embarrassing them in their future conflicts.[21] Taking still another approach, he conceded what few American statesmen in the nineteenth century admitted, that "the President recognizes, to a certain extent, the European idea of a balance of power."[22] One of the inevitable consequences of a divided United States, he asked the French government to reflect upon, would be the irrepressible temptation again to make "North America a theater for the ambition and cupidity of European nations."[23] The success of the South, he implied, would play into the hands of Britain. For an independent Confederacy would gravitate towards that European power which could provide the ships, the credit, and the marketing facilities without which it could not exist.

Napoleon III was too unpredictable to permit contemporaries to

---

18. Dayton to Seward, Paris, November 7, 1862, and February 23, 1863. *DDFDS*, (MF) XXXIV-55-56. See also Donaldson Jordan and Edwin J. Pratt, *Europe and the American Civil War* (Boston, 1931), p. 214.

19. Seward to Dayton, Washington, D. C., July 16, 1864. *FIDS*, XVII.

20. Seward to Mercier, Washington, D. C., May 23, 1861. *CPEU*, CXXIV.

21. Seward to Dayton, Washington, D. C., February 13, 1864. Confidential. *FIDS*, XVII.

22. Seward to Dayton, Washington, D. C., April 22, 1861. *FIDS*, XV.

23. *Ibid.*

estimate how much weight such an argument carried with him. He was capable of taking great chances in pursuit of objectives which tempted him. Seward was not sure whether the Emperor might not try to embarrass the Union regardless of political consequences, in order to discredit its republican system. Contemporary observers on both sides of the Atlantic were in remarkable agreement that the Civil War put republicanism as such on trial. European monarchists had always maintained that national sovereignty and domestic tranquility fared best under a monarchical system. The successful American experiment in self-government notwithstanding, they continued to adhere to the view that republics meant instability and, in the end, failure. Interpreting the breakup of the Federal republic as the breakdown of republican institutions, they claimed that history had once again demonstrated the validity of their arguments.[24]

These were not just theoretical considerations designed to instill renewed faith in monarchical principles. They had practical meaning. Seward was mindful of what he called "the antagonism in principle between the Imperial system [of France] and our Republican one."[25] Specifically, he observed: "When we remember that . . . the security of the constitutional republican system in other countries . . . has been everywhere thought dependent on its success here, it is not to be wondered at if we think that whatever wrong it [France] commits against us in the crisis through which we are passing, is a wrong suffered by us in the cause of freedom and humanity with which we identify republican institutions."[26] In spite of the republican character of the South, the Secretary of State feared that Napoleon might direct his anti-republicanism against the North. He deemed it expedient, therefore, to allay the Emperor's long-standing apprehensions regarding American propaganda by instructing Dayton to assure imperial France that "the United States are not an international agitator, but devoted to the interests of peace and order throughout he world."[27] This assurance notwithstanding, the Lincoln administration continued to count on the sustained support of those French sympathizers who identified their own chances for political emancipation with its success in America.

It is an irony of history that the United States, whom foreign critics

24. Lewis Einstein, *Napoleon III and American Diplomacy at the Outbreak of the Civil War* (London, 1905), p. 6.

25. Seward to Dayton, Washington, D. C., February 19, 1864. Confidential. *FIDS*, XVII.

26. Seward to Dayton, Washington, D. C., June 3, 1862. *FIDS*, XVI.

27. Seward to Dayton, Washington, D. C., August 23, 1862. *FIDS*, XVI.

often accused of being a disturber of the social order of the West, now claimed to be really conservative. On the other hand, the presumably law-abiding and tradition-upholding monarchists of France lent at least their moral support to the insurrectionists of the South.[28] To compound this irony, Napoleon maneuvered to plant a monarchy in Mexico at a time when the United States reiterated its policy not to extend its political system to Europe by any active efforts. Those Frenchmen, moreover, who invoked the principle of nationality to justify the recognition of an independent South expediently violated it in Mexico.

III

Not since the Revolutionary War had the Union stood in greater need of France's friendship than during this tragic trial. Lincoln and Seward worried and wondered: how reliable would France prove to be? When the President proclaimed the blockade of Confederate ports (April 19, 1861), he unintentionally elevated the domestic up-heaval into a war between two belligerent parties. Foreign powers acted in conformity with international law when henceforth they recognized the belligerency of the Confederacy.[29] The haste with which the European powers extended this recognition of belligerency greatly disturbed the Lincoln administration. On June 10, 1861, one month after Britain had done so, Napoleon issued a proclamation of neutrality in which he referred to the Confederacy's assertion of independence.[30]

 That France and Great Britain proclaimed their "strict neutrality" so promptly was no coincidence. They had previously come to an ex-press understanding to coordinate all their policies with respect to the conflict in the United States. By the time Lord Russell apprized Wash-ington of this understanding, the Lincoln administration had already been informed about it by its legation at St. Petersburg. Indeed, it also knew of another fact which Russell had preferred not to communicate: London and Paris had requested other European governments to follow their lead on the subject of eventual recognition of Southern independence.[31] The two maritime powers were not necessarily motivated by unfriendliness towards the Union when they made their

28. Henri Moreau, *La politique française en Amérique, 1861-1864* (Paris, 1864), p. 9.

29. F. Prévost and P. Pecquet, *Le blocus américain—droit des neutres* (Paris, 1862), pp. 11-12.

30. *Moniteur*, June 10, 1861. See also *Annuaire diplomatique de l'empire français* (Paris, 1862), pp. 158-59.

31. Seward to Dayton, Washington, D. C., June 17, 1861. *FIDS*, XVI.

agreement. According to Dayton, they were afraid and jealous of each other. Neither power wanted the other to gain advantages from independent intervention in American affairs.[32] Both entertained the hope, furthermore, that their close cooperation might impress President Lincoln with the necessity of making some concessions for the sake of peace.[33]

An important practical application of this entente occurred on June 15, 1861. On that date the British and French ambassadors gave Seward advance notice of their governments' decision to recognize the belligerent status of the South. He refused to receive this communication on procedural and substantive grounds. He bluntly informed the two diplomats that the Federal government would continue to discuss all questions with each power separately. He also let it be known that he preferred to deal with London and Paris directly and that he would be obliged if the envoys would just inform him about the views of their respective governments. As to the substance of the notice, the Secretary told Mercier that he could not consent to France's taking it upon herself to decide a question involving the sovereignty of the United States. He insisted that "the United States are one whole undivided nation, especially as far as foreign nations are concerned."[34] Seward would never admit that the insurgents were entitled to belligerent rights and he challenged the legal existence of a Southern flag.[35] But his many demands for the withdrawal of such recognition were in vain. Foreign Minister Thouvenel thought that the Secretary of State attached an undue importance to it and that its withdrawal would have no practical effect on the continuation of the war.[36] His successor, Édouard Drouyn de Lhuys, took the same position until the end of the conflict.

Under these circumstances, the French government expected both belligerents to honor those two principles of maritime law which protected enemy goods under neutral flags and neutral goods under enemy flags, except contraband of war.[37] In turn, France promised, despite the inconvenience caused by the blockade, to respect it "so long as it would be maintained in accordance with the law of na-

32. Dayton to Seward, Paris, July 13, 1861. Confidential. *DDFDS*, (MF) XXXIV-53.

33. Flahaut to Thouvenel, London, August 6, 1861. Papiers Thouvenel, VIII.

34. Seward to Dayton, Washington, D. C., June 17, 1861. *FIDS*, XVI. See also E. A. Pollard, *The First Year of the War* (Richmond, Va., 1862), p. 87.

35. Seward to Dayton, Washington, D. C., July 1, 1861. *FIDS*, XVI.

36. Dayton to Seward, Paris, March 31, 1862. *DDFDS*, (MF) XXXIV-54.

37. Thouvenel to Mercier, Paris, May 11, 1861. *FNTDS*, XVIII.

tions."[38]   Nevertheless, although the British and French admirals judged the blockade as not ineffective enough to warrant a protest,[39] Napoleon vainly asked the British government in October of 1861 to join him in breaking it. The needs of the French economy seemed to justify such an action.[40] The administration in Washington was not insensitive to France's impatient appeals for the modification or termination of the blockade. Seward repeatedly promised to accommodate the French at an early date. [He felt greatly relieved, therefore, when in the spring of 1862 he could advise the French government of the reopening of New Orleans.[41] If hereafter cotton was still unavailable, Southern obstructions could be blamed for it instead of Northern restrictions.]

By this time the strategic ramifications of the not wholly effective blockade began to give the Emperor some concern. He hardly needed the prompting of John Slidell, the Southern diplomatic agent in France, to realize that perhaps Britain respected the existing blockade in order to establish a precedent for the future.[42] In any future war between France and England, the English might prevent all neutral commerce with an ineffectively blockaded France and justify it on the ground that the Emperor had submitted to a loose interpretation of the Fourth Article of the Declaration of Paris at the time of the American Civil War. Persuasive as this argument sounded, Napoleon felt that he could not afford to interpose in America without the cooperation of Great Britain.[43] This was a cardinal point of his Civil War diplomacy. Since he considered a concerted intervention on the part of London, Paris, and St. Petersburg as holding out the greatest promise of success, French policies with respect to the American conflict became greatly dependent on the attitudes of England and Russia.

The *Trent* affair subjected Anglo-French cooperation to an unexpected test. This British mail steamer was on its way to Europe when, on November 8, 1861, a Northern captain stopped it and re-

38. Motley to Seward, Paris, October 18, 1861. Seward Papers.

39. James D. Richardson, *A Compilation of the Messages and Papers of the Confederacy* (Nashville, Tenn., 1906), II, 107.

40. Henry W. Temple, "William H. Seward," in Bemis, ed., *The American Secretaries of State*, VII, 82-83.

41. Seward to Dayton, Washington, D. C., January 2 and May 10, 1862. *FIDS*, XVI. The Lincoln administration had previously agreed to permit British and French warships to touch at Southern ports from time to time. Mercier to Admiral Reynaud, Washington, October 6, 1861. *CPEU*, CXXV.

42. Slidell to Hunter, Paris, February 21, 1862. *CDS*, Letter Book, I, pt. 1.

43. John Bigelow, *France and the Confederate Navy* (New York, 1888), p. 127.

moved from it John Slidell and James M. Mason, the Confederacy's designated ministers to France and Britain. This dramatic episode threatened to plunge Britain and the United States into a war. For as soon as the news of this incident broke, London and Paris jumped to the unwarranted conclusion that Captain Charles Wilkes had acted on orders from Washington. Had this been the case, then the United States might possibly have been guilty of violating the rights of neutrals.

Britain's demand for the release of the prisoners and for explanations disavowing the action found France's immediate approval.[44] After careful reflection the French government decided that it could not remain silent in a matter involving the security of neutrals. Thouvenel recognized that it had never been definitely determined whether persons could be treated as contraband of war. Nevertheless, he deplored vexatious practices on the high seas against which the United States had always protested in the past.[45] To the gratification of Britain, but unsolicited by it,[46] he urged the Federal government to to comply with London's demands.

For several weeks the danger of an Anglo-American war appeared so great that Dayton officially inquired about the likely attitude of France in the event of its explosion. The reply he received led him to conclude that France should not be taken for granted. Economic and political considerations pointed towards its neutrality, but its moral force was certain to be with Britain.[47] It was even rumored in London that France would join England as an ally, provided it would be given a "free swing in taking Syria."[48]

As far as Russia and Prussia were concerned, they reacted with mixed feelings to the prospect of an Anglo-American conflict. St. Petersburg preferred that France stay out of it and exercised its influence in that direction. Prince Gortchakov raised the suggestive question in a conversation with the French ambassador: "After having destroyed the Black Sea fleet, do you want to contribute to the destruction of American sea power?"[49] The Prussians denounced the

44. Flahaut to Thouvenel, London, November 30, 1861. Papiers Thouvenel, VIII. See also E. D. Adams, I, 203-43.

45. Thouvenel to Mercier, Paris, December 3, 1861. *CPEU*, CXXV.

46. V. Wellesley and R. Sencourt, *Conversations with Napoleon III* (London, 1934), p. 204.

47. Dayton to Seward, Paris, December 6, 1861. *DDFDS*, (MF) XXIV-54. This opinion was shared by the French public. A. de Gasparin, *Une parole de paix—sur le différend entre l'Angleterre et les États-Unis* (Paris, 1862), p. 17.

48. James Leslie, Jr., to Seward, London, December 4, 1861. Seward Papers.

49. Montebello to Thouvenel, St. Petersburg, December 27, 1861. *CP Russie*, CCXXV.

seizure of the Southern commissioners as a violation of international law.[50] Still, their interest lay in a diplomatic adjustment of the incident, lest Britain's preoccupation with America give Napoleon a free hand in pursuing his plans against Germany.[51] In spite of Napoleon's statement that such a war would be a calamity for Europe, they feared—as did also British officials—that he might help to engineer it without participating in it.[52]

Seward's skillful disposition of the crisis put a quick end to these rumors and speculations. Washington's satisfaction of Britain's demands not only restored its international prestige, but also vindicated the liberal maritime principles it had always championed.[53] Perhaps one of the most valuable by-products of this episode was that it incidentally revealed the positions of various powers with respect to American affairs. Seward's hopes were raised that conflicting interests of the European governments would block their effective intervention on behalf of the South.

IV

Throughout the Civil War the Secretary of State labored tirelessly to dissuade the European governments from any hasty intervention. Time and again he urged them to dismiss the notion that the Union would agree to its dissolution, either peacefully or by force. Whatever the sacrifices, it would fight to the finish. In his judgment, the greatest contribution to an early peace that London and Paris could make would be for Queen Victoria or Napoleon III to declare: "If the life of this unnatural insurrection hangs on an expectation of our favor, let it die."[54] When threats of secession filled the air around election time in 1860, the propriety of such a declaration might have been open to question. But that it was not clearly made in the following months, and even years, was deplored by the North. Whatever retrospective opinions may be worth, Judah P. Benjamin, the Confederate

---

50. *Berliner National Zeitung,* December 31, 1861.

51. Ralph Lutz, *Die Beziehungen zwischen Deutschland und den Vereinigten während des Sezessionskrieges* (Heidelberg, 1911), p. 67. Consult also the editorial "Die Trent Angelegenheit," in *Preussische Jahrbücher* (Berlin, 1861), VIII, 635. Bigelow wrote from Paris: "The idea is prevalent here that a war between England and America would occupy the British navy to such an extent as to enable France to occupy the Rhine, which is the dream of all imperialists." Bigelow to Seward, Paris, December 5, 1861. Seward Papers.

52. *Berliner National Zeitung,* December 3, 1861. See also Henry R. C. Wellesley, *Secrets of the Second Empire* (New York, 1929), p. 224; and Émile Ollivier, *L'empire libéral* (Paris, 1900), V, 269.

53. *Le Temps,* January 11, 1862.

54. Seward to Dayton, Washington, D. C., May 5 and June 3, 1862. *FIDS,* XVI.

Secretary of State, later implicitly admitted that such an unequivocal statement prior to the outbreak of the war would have caused the leadership of the South to reconsider its fateful decision.[55]

The Lincoln administration explored every possible avenue to induce France at least to abstain from any unfriendly action. It was well known that Napoleon III and Empress Eugénie had displayed more than a casual interest in the anti-Catholic propaganda of the Know-Nothing movement.[56] Fearing that French Catholics might now show their resentment against Northern Protestants in particular, the President and Seward asked Archbishop John Hughes of New York to go to Europe on a counterpropaganda mission. His assignment was "to promote healthful opinions concerning the great cause of the Union."[57] Sensitive about his own position, Dayton resented the special mission of this Catholic dignitary so much that he was anything but cooperative in facilitating his activities in Paris.[58] Archbishop Hughes, for instance, was compelled to rely on his own initiative and contacts to arrange an audience with the Emperor. Their Majesties received him on December 24, 1861. The length of the interview, one hour and ten minutes, would indicate that the distinguished prelate from New York was a welcome visitor at the Tuileries.[59] His presence in Paris at the time of the *Trent* crisis enhanced the significance of his visit. Appealing to the Emperor's ambition to be the moderator of the world, he asked Napoleon to use his good offices for the peaceful adjustment of the Anglo-American controversy. Above all, of course, he pleaded for nonintervention in the Civil War. In the course of his conversation he also refuted erroneous or exaggerated stories about the plight of American Catholics. Before the interview ended, the Empress broached the question of Cuba on which she was naturally sensitive. Archbishop Hughes rendered perhaps his greatest service when he used this opportunity to point out that Southerners had always schemed to seize the island and that the Confederate States rather than the Union would threaten its inde-

55. Mercier to Thouvenel, Washington, D. C., April 28, 1862. *CPEU,* CXXVII.

56. Faulkner to Cass, Paris, October 8, 1860. *DDFDS,* XLVIII.

57. Victor F. O'Daniel, "Archbishop John Hughes—American Envoy to France, 1861," *Catholic Historical Review,* III (1917), 336-39.

58. R. M. Andrews, "Archbishop Hughes and the Civil War" (Ph.D. dissertation, University of Chicago, 1935), p. 7.

59. Hughes to Seward, Paris, December 27, 1861. Hughes Papers. For a discussion of this meeting, see also John R. Hassard, *Life of the Most Reverend John Hughes* (New York, 1866), pp. 463-68; and G. McGuire, "The Mission of Archbishop Hughes to Europe" (Master's thesis, Columbia University, 1946), pp. 20-22.

pendence. By planting this suspicion in the minds of the imperial rulers, he could not but hurt the Confederate cause.

The Irish-born dignitary from New York made an effort to meet as many influential Frenchmen as possible. He saw the Foreign Minister and dined with the Archbishop of Paris and the Cardinals of the Empire. He talked with several of the bishops from the districts which suffered from the interruption of trade with the United States and actually went to Lyons where the economic distress was great.[60] Everywhere he pleaded for an understanding of the Union's struggle against slavery. On the proper occasions he expressed the view that the future of Catholicism in North America looked more hopeful in the North than in the South, a view which the French historian Henri Moreau later reiterated in his Civil War study.[61]

Undoubtedly the Lincoln administration acted wisely when it sent the Archbishop as a good-will ambassador to Europe.[62] When the Confederacy belatedly recognized the wisdom of influencing Catholic opinion in Europe, it appointed in the spring of 1864 Bishop Patrick N. Lynch of Charleston as Commissioner to the States of the Church.[63] While in Paris, the Bishop conversed with many of the same personalities Archbishop Hughes had previously tried to influence. But by then it was too late to accomplish much.

It took both belligerents some time before they realized that propaganda campaigns abroad must supplement the military and diplomatic endeavors which absorbed their energies and resources. Gradually, they paid increasing attention to this problem. The North entrusted the task of influencing public opinion in France to John Bigelow,[64] the co-owner and managing editor of the New York Evening Post. The South was less fortunate in the choice of Edwin De Leon,[65] a

60. Hughes to Seward, Paris, December 12, 1861, and February 6, 1862. Hughes Papers. Hughes to Seward, Paris, January 29, 1862. Seward Papers.

61. Moreau, pp. 35-36. See also Abbé Baroux, Lettre à J. Denève (Orléans, 1863), p. 66.

62. O'Daniel, pp. 336-39. O'Daniel's enthusiastic appraisal of Hughes' contribution to the diplomacy of the Civil War goes beyond the legitimate conclusions evidence permits.

63. Leo Francis Stock, "Catholic Participation in the Diplomacy of the Southern Confederacy," Catholic Historical Review, XVI (1930), 17.

64. Clapp, pp. 155 ff.; see also B. Willson, America's Ambassadors to France (New York, 1928), pp. 263-89; and Poultney Bigelow, "John Bigelow of Ulster County and His Relations with William H. Seward," Ulster County Historical Society Proceedings (1932), p. 34.

65. F. L. Owsley, King Cotton Diplomacy (Chicago, 1931), pp. 167-86; Edwin De Leon, Thirty Years of My Life on Three Continents (London, 1890). For critical comments on Confederate propaganda see Paul Pecquet Du Bellet, The Diplomacy of the Confederate Cabinet of Richmond and Its Agents Abroad (New York, 1865).

friend of Jefferson Davis. In addition, other officials and a host of private individuals disseminated their ideas about the issues of the war by way of conversation or correspondence. The big job was to reach the great mass of the French people through the medium of the press. This involved peculiar problems which the belligerent agents understood better than their governments at home.

While English journalists enjoyed the reputation of writing, if not from conviction, at least not against it, many of their French colleagues were suspected of being less scrupulous. For a fee they would sell their journalistic talents or open their papers to editorials which would add enthusiasm to conviction. Soon after his arrival in Paris William L. Dayton asked, therefore, for authorization to distribute "a little money judiciously . . . to compensate the press for its extra service."[66] Slidell later accused the political director of the French press of suppressing articles and intelligence favorable to the South and of imposing the insertion of those of the opposite tendency. He was convinced that this official received a "fee" for this "service" and that this money, coming from Dayton's contingent fund, was used to cover his considerable gambling losses.[67] For that matter, in addition to the $30,000 which De Leon spent for Confederate propaganda,[68] Southern agents reportedly placed 500,000 bales of cotton at the disposal of politicians and of the press to further their interests with the French government.[69]

To charge the entire French press with intellectual prostitution because some influential Frenchmen may have lacked integrity would obviously be improper. Opinions regarding the trans-Atlantic upheaval rested to a large extent on political and moral considerations of long standing. The liberal and republican-orientated papers pleaded the cause of the Union. The semi-official, conservative, and clerical papers, widely supported by the court, high finance, army circles, and the followers of the ultra-conservative Catholic philosopher Joseph de Maîstre, championed the cause of the secessionists. Even the official *Moniteur* found it difficult to be strictly neutral and manifested its veiled partiality by giving prominence to Northern defeats and

---

De Leon's usefulness ended in 1863. He did not get along with Slidell and his ineptness even exceeded his immodesty.

66. Dayton to Seward, Paris, May 22, 1861. *DDFDS*, (MF) XXXIV-52.

67. Slidell to Benjamin, Paris, April 7, 1864. *CDS*, Letter Book, I, Pt. 2.

68. Clapp, p. 169; see also W. Reed West, *Contemporary French Opinion on the American Civil War* (Baltimore, 1924), p. 106.

69. Dayton to Seward, Paris, September 9, 1862. Strictly confidential. *DDFDS*, (MF) XXXIV-55.

Southern successes, or by omitting to print such an important news item as Lincoln's Emancipation Proclamation.[70] It has been estimated that the French press as a whole was about evenly divided in its leanings towards the belligerents.[71] A flood of tendentious pamphlets and occasional comments in the National Assembly also served to inform Frenchmen who followed the events in America.

As Southerners defended the right of secession on constitutional grounds, those in France who sided with them invoked the principle of nationalities to justify it. They urged their government to take the initiative in acknowledging the independence of the Confederacy and not to permit Britain to be the first to recognize the unalterable fact of separation. The extremists among them saw in a divided America a blessing for Europe and a necessity for world peace. In view of its habitual disregard for the law of nations, they asserted, a reconstituted Union would continue to endanger the security of Europe's possessions in the Western Hemisphere.[72] They also feared that the conquest of the Confederacy by the North, an industrial rival of France, would intensify its world-wide competition. As far as this group was concerned, these political and economic aspects eclipsed the importance of the slavery issue. The plight of the Negro in Washington, Boston, or New York, it charged, did not entitle the North to pose as the moral guardian of the dignity of all men.

Many other Frenchmen thoroughly disagreed with this position. They condemned the scourge of slavery and those who would perpetuate this institution. Among them were the workers and liberals of various shades. Although many French workers suffered as the result of the war in America, their sympathies were with the North. Much as they desired the restoration of peace, they understood as well as British laborers that the support of free labor anywhere was in the interest of free labor everywhere. The cause of the Union was also defended by the Liberal Catholic Party in France. Its leader, Charles de Montalembert, appealed to Catholics to rally to the slavery-fighting North. Perhaps equally important was the declaration early in 1862

70. B. Willson, *John Slidell and the Confederates in Paris, 1862-1865* (New York, 1932), pp. 47-48; Stephen McQueen Huntley, *Les rapports de la France et la Confédération pendant la guerre de sécession* (Toulouse, 1932), pp. 152-53.

71. Jordan and Pratt, p. 221.

72. On French pro-Southern attitudes see Émile Nouette-Delorme, *Les États-Unis et l'Europe* (Paris, 1863), pp. 6-16; François G. Barrillon, *Politique de la France et de l'humanité dans le conflit américain* (Paris, 1861), pp. 39-40; É. Belliot des Minières, *La question américaine* (Paris, 1862), p. 25; A. P. Grandguillot, *La reconnaissance du sud* (Paris, 1862), p. 29; Marc de Haut, *La crise américaine* (Paris, 1862), p. 90; and Jordan and Pratt, pp. 219-21.

by several French bishops that it would "not be objectionable" to pray for the emancipation of the slaves in America. Many French liberals were in fact disappointed when Lincoln's Emancipation Proclamation, in order not to offend the border states, did not set all slaves free. Furthermore, to the despair of the Confederate agents, most of the articulate intelligentsia of France, who exercised an influence far beyond their numerical strength, "leagued themselves with ignorance and radicalism . . . to paralyze the wise intentions of the Emperor."[73] Such prominent Frenchmen as Alexis de Tocqueville and Victor Hugo, the scholar Jean-Jacques Ampère and the geographer Élisée Reclus, the publicists Agénor-Étienne de Gasparin and Eugène Pelletan, and the historians Henri Martin and Henri Moreau spoke up on behalf of the North. The cause of the Union produced the political miracle of gathering in its camp men of such divergent views as the conservative monarchist Guizot, the Liberal Thiers, the Liberal Catholic Montalembert, the Socialist Louis Blanc, Prince Napoleon, and the Orleanist princes.

Prince Napoleon visited the United States in August, 1861.[74] The Lincoln administration welcomed the opportunity of meeting the Emperor's cousin. His firsthand acquaintance with Northern policies and personalities was expected to exercise a sobering influence upon Napoleon III. In September, 1861, the Orleanist princes went to Washington. Originally, the Prince de Joinville and his two nephews, the Count de Paris and the Duke de Chartres, had not come to the the United States for the purpose of serving in the Union army.[75] However, after their arrival they decided to offer their services to gain the most realistic kind of military experience. Assigned to the staff of General McClellan, they performed their duties with courage and distinction. Welcome as were the friendly manifestations of the Orleanist princes and many of their supporters in France, they embarrassed the relations between the Federal government and Napoleon III. From the Emperor's point of view, the publicity and

73. Hotze to Benjamin, London, September 26, 1863. *CDS*, Henry Hotze Letter Book. On the subject of French pro-Union support, see Jordan and Pratt, pp. 228-29, 240-41; West, 10-14, 85, 152; S. Bernstein, *Essays in Political and Intellectual History* (New York, 1955), pp. 121-33; Pierre Belperron, *La guerre de sécession, 1861-1865* (Paris, 1947), pp. 301-2; W. C. Teichmann, *Englands und Frankreichs Stellung zum Bürgerkriege in den Vereinigten Staaten von Amerika, 1861-1865* (München, 1885), pp. 26-27; Louis M. Sears, "A Neglected Critic of Our Civil War," *Mississippi Valley Historical Review*, I (1915), 533.

74. Prince Napoleon, "Voyage aux États-Unis," *Revue de Paris* (Sept. 15, 1933), pp. 241-72 and (Oct. 1, 1933), pp. 549-87.

75. Ella Lonn, *Foreigners in the Union Army and Navy* (Baton Rouge, 1951), pp. 278-79.

training the three noblemen received in the United States came close to being offensive to him.

Those Frenchmen who rallied to the defense of the Union deplored its dismemberment as detrimental to the best interests of France and as a blow to the cause of liberty. Since it was not unusual for Frenchmen to judge foreign political questions in the light of internal political considerations, some favored the North simply because Napoleon, whom they despised, showed partiality for the secessionists. Also, finding it difficult or too risky openly to attack Napoleon's domestic policies, French liberals resorted to the indirect method of criticizing the Emperor's regime by extolling the virtues of democracy in their discussions of the American Civil War. For this purpose they deemed it convenient to identify the North with individual rights and representative government, and the South with slavery and aristocracy.

One of the most eloquent French defenders of the Union's cause was the distinguished jurist and historian Édouard Laboulaye, whose mature analysis of the ramifications of the war merits special attention.[76] He invited his compatriots to understand that Lincoln performed the patriotic duty of defending the integrity of his country. Would not Frenchmen regard it as their sacred obligation to fight, he asked, if one or another province of France should revolt and insist on separation? Moreover, would France in such a case admit the right of Germany or Great Britain to propose a mode of stopping the fight which, in effect, would strengthen the rebels' position? Laboulaye then raised certain questions which struck at the center of the American problem, one far more complex than appeared on the surface. An independent Confederacy, he argued, would compel the truncated Union to maintain large armed forces in order to protect its long frontier. Quite aside from the fact that nonmilitarism and nonintervention had in his opinion been the secret of America's prodigious success, he found the prospect of Northern militarism anything but reassuring to Europe. It disturbed him even more to foresee the likelihood that, as the only European power capable of granting maritime protection to an independent South, England would seize the monopoly of cotton. If that should happen, the triumph of the South would in the last analysis be a triumph for Great Britain. With a rare grasp of the issues involved, Laboulaye challenged the premises of those French circles who played with the idea

76. Édouard Laboulaye, *Upon Whom Rests the Guilt of the War?* (New York, 1863).

of aiding the South. As he saw it, they invoked the name of humanity to end the fratricide, but ignored Southern slavery; they invoked economic advantages that France would supposedly gain from Southern independence, but ignored superior benefits Britain would derive from it; and they invoked power-political interests that would presumably be served by weakening the United States, but ignored the still valid opinion of Napoleon I that the security of France depended on co-operation with a formidable America as a counterweight to Britain's preponderance on the seas.[77]

V

French public opinion with respect to the American war was thus divided. Napoleon III, who is said to have paid much attention to public sentiment, found himself, therefore, in the dilemma of alienating part of the French or American people, no matter what he did. The indecision, if not two-sidedness, which he displayed also reflected the differences of opinion among his closest advisers.

Thouvenel, his Foreign Minister during the first two years of the Civil War, counseled, as consistently as it was possible, a policy of strict neutrality. From the very start of the conflict he was determined not to prejudge its ultimate outcome, nor to take any position with respect to the justice of the Southern grievances or Northern justifications of the resort to force. His approach was basically a legalistic one. After Lincoln's proclamation of the blockade, international law permitted France's recognition of the belligerency of both sides. Beyond this step Thouvenel would not—and did not—go, in spite of tremendous pressures on the part of his intervention-minded compatriots.[78] Obviously, he could not have long resisted these pressures without strong and compelling arguments based on the realities of the situation. By the summer of 1862 he admitted reluctantly that he too no longer believed in the possibility of the Union's re-establishment.[79] Had the military state of affairs warranted it, he would have been prepared to recognize the South. The condition which he deemed absolutely essential for recognition was the winning of the war, not

77. For similar views see Moreau, p. 55, and Eugène Véron, "Dissolution de l'union américaine, ses causes et ses conséquences," *Revue nationale et étrangère* (February, 1861), pp. 321-45.

78. Thouvenel to Mercier, Paris, April 29, May 11 and 16, 1861. *CPEU,* CXXIV. See also Richard Korolewicz-Carlton, "Napoleon III, Thouvenel et la guerre de sécession" (Ph.D. dissertation, Université de Paris, 1951), pp. 195-98; and Lynn M. Case, *French Opinion on the United States and Mexico, 1860-1867* (New York, 1936), p. 245.

79. Slidell to Benjamin, Paris, July 25, 1862. *CDS,* Letter Book, I, Pt. 1.

just of battles. As long as this was not clearly established, he continued to discourage the Southern commissioners whom he treated as private individuals on the rare occasions he granted them an interview.

Thouvenel adhered to the British alliance and disapproved of any major move in American affairs except in concert with Britain. This stand was in part dictated by his fear that premature recognition of the South involved the risk of war with the North. To assume this burden, in addition to involvements in China, Italy, and Mexico, would be "truly too much."[80]   Also, financial factors made another expensive expedition to America most inadvisable. In principle, Thouvenel wished to localize these troubles, not to inflate them. He concentrated, therefore, on efforts to diminish the economic effects of the Civil War on his country and on defending the rights of neutrals. Nothing would have pleased him more than to contribute to an early peace by persuading the Lincoln administration to accept the good offices of France. Proposals of this kind, however, were taboo in Washington.

When Napoleon replaced Thouvenel in October of 1862, the American envoy to France deplored that ". . . we lose a friend at an important time."[81]   The political considerations which motivated the French monarch to appoint Drouyn de Lhuys as Thouvenel's successor involved, among others, the Italian and American problems.[82]   Napoleon wanted a foreign minister who would be willing to support his policies without mental reservations. As far as American affairs were concerned, this meant that he expected Drouyn de Lhuys to go along with his determination to intervene in the Civil War. Drouyn de Lhuys was indeed prepared to rationalize that French attempts to mediate were "above all inspired by the friendship which animates the Imperial Government toward the United States."[83]   He wished to see the war ended by foreign mediation or by direct negotiation between the belligerents. But he was careful not to drive matters to a breaking point between France and the United States. Once in office, he realized that the failure of the South to win decisive victories, the unwillingness of Britain and Russia to intervene in the war, and the growing complications in Europe made prudence in American affairs even more imperative during the last two years of the war than during its initial phase. He did not really depart, therefore, from the

80. L. Thouvenel, *Le secret de l'empereur* (Paris, 1889), II, 414 ff.
81. Dayton to Seward, Paris, October 17, 1862. *DDFDS,* (MF) XXXIV-55.
82. Korolewicz-Carlton, p. 187.
83. Drouyn de Lhuys to Mercier, January 9, 1863. *CPEU,* CXXIX.

neutrality position which Thouvenel had defended. The two French foreign ministers differed only in degree regarding the Civil War policy of France. In a real sense, though, Napoleon was his own foreign minister. During Drouyn de Lhuys's term of office the Emperor initiated a number of moves which, had they been successful, would have hurt the North. While Drouyn de Lhuys acquiesced in them, he interpreted their failure as a warning to France to move with caution.

Unlike the heads of the French Foreign Office, the French envoy to the United States, Édouard H. Mercier, could not resist the temptation of playing a dramatic part in the diplomacy of the Civil War years. As a believer in the virtues of monarchism and somewhat concerned over the all too rapid pace of America's growth, he permitted his personal prejudices to color his official judgments. His friendly associations with the political leaders of the South prior to the war and his reserved attitude toward Secretary of State Seward rendered his mission during the war less satisfactory than his intellectual capacity warranted.

Mercier was bewildered by Seward's "arrogance vis-à-vis the European powers."[84] He was not quite sure whether the Secretary behaved that way because he wanted to flatter the vanity of the American people or because he was a power-drunk parvenu. In any case, in order not to complicate matters, he and the British ambassador decided after the diversionary war threat for the time being to avoid all conversation with the Secretary of State. He consequently did not follow Thouvenel's instructions of April 29, 1861, to use the earliest opportunity to tell Seward—without intimating the offer of good offices—that France would be only too happy to prove its friendly dispositions towards the United States. Instead, Mercier merely talked with Seward's son, who was the Under Secretary of State. Mercier anticipated that a full-fledged war would hurt the mercantile interests of his country. Yet he made no major last minute attempt to prevent it by exhausting all diplomatic approaches. Such an effort would most likely have been doomed to failure because Seward treated both secession and the impending war to suppress it as strictly domestic affairs. However, the international repercussions of such a domestic war were a legitimate concern which imposed upon diplomats the

84. Mercier to Thouvenel, Washington, D. C., May 23, 1861. *CPEU,* CXXIV. More than a year later he wrote: "I don't understand the role Seward is playing. To save the Union, he once said, he would introduce slavery into New England. He is not bothered by scruples." Mercier to Thouvenel, Washington, D. C., September 23, 1862. Papiers Thouvenel, XIII.

obligation of exploring all possibilities as to how their countries could contribute to the maintenance of peace without violating the sovereign sphere of the United States. This Mercier failed to do.[85] By his own admission, he continued to maintain the greatest reserve toward Seward in the belief that the Secretary of State preferred this kind of relationship. Seward, indeed, regarded Mercier as "one of the most impudent men in history."[86]

In contrast, Mercier's early contacts with Southern Senators had been so close that in December of 1860 Slidell and Benjamin took him into confidence about their future plans. They envisioned a great confederacy under Southern stewardship which would include all the states of the Union except New England. Their blueprint provided for New England to be joined with Canada as a British possession. Fantastic as this scheme was, Mercier wrote to Thouvenel: "It is not impossible to obtain this result."[87] From the moment of Lincoln's election until his promotion in 1864 to the ambassadorial post at Madrid, Mercier asserted time and again that the re-establishment of the Union was impossible. Seward's verbal optimism to the contrary he dismissed as that of a false prophet.[88]

He took the initiative in several proposals which, for all practical purposes, favored the cause of the Confederacy. He repeatedly recommended that France and Great Britain either recognize the Confederacy or otherwise "provoke a peaceful settlement" of the war at the earliest possible moment.[89] While he hoped that his government would initiate such a move, he stressed the advisability of joint action. In March of 1861 Mercier suggested to his Foreign Minister speedy, but not premature, recognition as a means of stopping the impending war before its eruption would cause great damage to the trans-Atlantic trade.[90] It is significant that he did not suggest the alternative approach of warning the South not to expect aid from France. Later in the year he urged intervention to stop the bloody conflict before the violent emancipation of the slaves would lead to a most tragic

85. Korolewicz-Carlton, p. 27.

86. F. W. Seward, *Reminiscences of a War-Time Statesman and Diplomat, 1830-1915* (N. Y., 1916), p. 425; see also Mercier to Drouyn de Lhuys, Washington, D. C., January 27, 1863. *CPEU,* CXXIX.

87. Mercier to Thouvenel, Washington, D. C., December 17, 1860. *CPEU,* CXXIII.

88. Mercier to Thouvenel, Washington, D. C., May 6, 1861. *CPEU,* CXXIV. Senator Sumner is reported to have snapped his finger at the French envoy for holding the view that "division of the Union is inevitable." E. T. Welles, *The Diary of Gideon Welles* (Boston, 1911), I, 494-95.

89. Mercier to Thouvenel, Washington, D. C., October 10, 1861. *CPEU,* CXXV.

90. Mercier to Thouvenel, Washington, D. C., March 29, 1861. *CPEU,* CXXIV.

slave insurrection.[91] When Paris remained neutral, he conceded that
it would be best to wait for the proper psychological moment, which
depended on the military developments, before extending recognition.[92]

In his search for a compromise peace Mercier produced quite a
sensation by suddenly arranging a trip to Richmond in April of 1862.
The circumstances surrounding this extraordinary mission are not
quite clear. The French Foreign Minister had neither authorized it
nor was he afterwards satisfied that its timing had been well chosen.[93]
Evidence to prove the tempting speculation that Napoleon had secretly
ordered this visit is not available.[94] The Confederate Secretary of
State suspected that Seward had requested Mercier to find out whether
any possible terms would induce the South to return to the Union.[95]
But in a message to the Senate Lincoln denied that the French envoy
had ever been induced or authorized by his administration "to make
any representations of any kind or on any subject to the so-called
authorities at Richmond."[96] On his part, Mercier also denied the in-
timation of his British colleague, Lord Lyons, that the trip was premeditated. His own version that it was the outgrowth of a spon-
taneous comment is at least plausible. In the course of a conversation
he casually mentioned to Seward that he labored under the handicap
of not having a firsthand impression of affairs at Richmond. To his
surprise, the Secretary was willing to grant him permission to go to
the Confederate capital. While immediately seizing this opportunity,
Mercier reserved the right, though, to consult with his British colleague
before making a final decision. He evidently sensed that Seward was
so agreeable in this instance because he hoped to sow mistrust between
the ambassadors. If this was one of the ulterior motives behind the
Secretary's surprising cooperation, his authorization of the trip also
was a show of confidence the leaders at Richmond could hardly mis-
interpret. Lincoln notwithstanding, according to the French envoy,
Seward extended through him an invitation to all the Southern Senators to visit the North and judge for themselves the hopelessness of
their fight.[97]

91. Mercier to Thouvenel, Washington, D. C., October 8, 1861. *CPEU,* CXXV.
92. Mercier to Thouvenel, Washington, D. C., July 1, 1862. *CPEU,* CXXVIII.
93. Sanford to Seward, Paris, May 13, 1862. Private. Seward Papers. See also
E. D. Adams, I, 280-88.
94. Slidell did not exclude this possibility. Slidell to Benjamin, Paris, May 15,
1862. *CDS,* Letter Book, I, Pt. 1.
95. Benjamin to Slidell, Richmond, July 19, 1862. *CDS,* Letter Book.
96. Basler, ed., *Works of Abraham Lincoln,* VI, 99.
97. Mercier to Thouvenel, Washington, D. C., April 13, 1862. *CPEU,* CXXVII.

Startled as the Confederate government was when Mercier inquired whether he would be welcome as a private visitor, it granted his request. He left for Richmond on April 13, 1862. Although he did not see Jefferson Davis, he talked with many leading figures, some of whom leaned toward moderation and reunion. His most important talks, of course, were with Secretary of State Judah Benjamin.[98] Mercier gained the overwhelming impression from them that, in spite of many deprivations, the Confederates were determined to carry on the struggle until the North had either exterminated them or agreed to separation. In the course of these discussions the French statesman proposed his favorite compromise of an agreement based on political separation but economic union. In view of the historic sectional differences on tariff policies, it is difficult to understand how Mercier could imagine that such an American *Zollverein* would be practicable. When Judah Benjamin turned down the idea of a confederation of the divided nation, he saved the French diplomat from a great embarrassment. For the mere making of such a proposal amounted to a violation of his country's neutrality which he really took pains to stress in Richmond as well as in Washington.

Upon his return, the French minister communicated his experiences to President Lincoln and the Secretary of State who listened with apparent interest and satisfaction. Mercier's account to the Quai d'Orsay produced an important reaction. After studying the envoy's report Thouvenel concluded from it that France should not modify its policy as long as uncertainty prevailed in America.[99] The trip had an unexpected effect on Mercier himself. It gradually dawned on him that without a large merchant marine France would not profit very much from the Confederacy's free trade offer. He began to see, moreover, that an impoverished South, precariously at peace with its Northern neighbor, would not have the money to pay for French imports. Since "one makes good business only with the rich,"[100] he stressed from now on France's interest in a strong and prosperous North American customer. This did not mean, however, that he changed his original opinion about the impossibility of the restoration of the pre-war Union. Thouvenel studied Mercier's despatches, but did not follow the envoy's often unrealistic and inconsistent recommendations. It was the Emperor who found them suggestive enough to play with them.

98. For a summary of Mercier's conversation with the Confederate Secretary of State, see Mercier to Thouvenel, Washington, D. C., April 28 and May 26, 1862. *CPEU,* CXXVII.

99. Thouvenel to Mercier, Paris, May 15, 1862. *CPEU,* CXXVII.

100. Mercier to Thouvenel, Washington, D. C., May 6, 1862. *CPEU,* CXXVII.

VI

Between 1861 and 1864 many rumors circulated about Napoleon's impending intervention in the American conflict. That he remained neutral throughout the war does not by itself prove the groundlessness of these rumors, nor does it ipso facto exonerate the Emperor from charges of indecision and duplicity. What was his American policy during these years? For public opinion may at best influence foreign policy; it does not determine it. Napoleon would take public opinion and the advice of his ministers into account, but he regarded the making of the final policy decision as his own responsibility and prerogative.

In January of 1861 he conveyed to Faulkner his sincere regrets about the misfortune which had fallen upon the United States.[101] About the same time, however, he remarked to Lord Cowley, the British ambassador: "England will never find a more favorable occasion to abate the pride of the Americans."[102] Five months later, he confided to Cowley that "he could not forget the overbearing insolence of the United States government in its days of prosperity"[103] and that he hoped Great Britain would join him in siding with the South. Her Majesty's ambassador lost no time in disillusioning the Emperor. But it required more than the British envoy's contrary opinion to change Napoleon's mind. He persisted in raising the issue of joint intervention periodically. In this, Napoleon was not just motivated by personal prejudices against the United States and its people or by his ambition to go down in history as the moderator of the great national movements of his time. He was exposed to increasing public pressures to do something about the economic crisis in France which the blockade of Southern ports appeared to have aggravated.[104] The political implications of this situation at home worried the Emperor and account to some extent for his anxiety to restore normal trans-Atlantic trade relations.

To be effective in this respect he needed and sought Britain's full cooperation. But it was not forthcoming. It is interesting to observe in retrospect how wrong American public opinion had been in assuming that greedy John Bull would spearhead the foreign drive to destroy the Union. The South also discovered that in the last analysis Napoleon's influence on the British Cabinet was not what it had

101. Faulkner to Cass, Paris, January 2, 1861. *DDFDS*, (MF) XXXIV-51.
102. Wellesley and Sencourt, *Conversations with Napoleon III*, p. 192.
103. *Ibid.*, p. 198.
104. Case, pp. 256-58.

supposed it to be. As early as March 1862 Slidell warned that unless England took the initiative in European intervention, the Confederacy would be left to work out its own salvation.[105] Thouvenel had evidently arrived at a similar estimate and deliberately tried to avoid giving the impression that France was impatiently forcing the march of events in America.[106]

As was to be expected from a realistic point of view, England consulted its own interests in the American question. The impact of the Civil War on its economy never reached proportions which might have forced action. The sentiments of British labor, moreover, were entirely with the North. Aside from the slavery issue and Lincoln's Emancipation Proclamation, Britain's course of inaction was also influenced by the fear that the Northern peace party might be weakened by foreign interference. In the English press concern was expressed that intervention would in the long run compel the United States "to remain a great military and naval power, which is not for the interest of England, nor for the peace of the world."[107]

When in October of 1861 Napoleon invited the British government to join him in an effort to end the war, or at least its undesirable effects, he learnt to his regret that Palmerston preferred to "lie on his oars."[108] Also the manner in which the *Trent* episode was adjusted indicated that London had really no intention of becoming deeply involved in the contest across the Atlantic. Still, in the spring of 1862 the Emperor made another attempt, this time an indirect one, to explore the chances of organizing an Anglo-French intervention. Toward this end he held on April 11, 1862, informal conversations with William S. Lindsay, a member of the British Parliament. On that occasion Napoleon III declared his readiness to despatch a formidable fleet to the mouth of the Mississippi for the purpose of lifting the blockade, provided that England would send an equal force.[109] On April 13 and 18 Napoleon held two more interviews with his British consultant. Since Lord Cowley's reaction to the contemplated project was negative, Lindsay made a hurried trip to London between these two dates in order to ascertain the British government's reaction. But Lord Russell refused to receive him because he insisted that communications from a foreign power should be handled through

105. Slidell to Hunter, Paris, March 26, 1862. *CDS*, Letter Book, I, Pt. 1.
106. Thouvenel to Mercier, Paris, January 16, 1862. *CPEU*, CXXVI.
107. This comment of the London *Daily News* was reprinted in the Washington *National Intelligencer*, June 26, 1862.
108. Jordan and Pratt, p. 205.
109. Slidell to Benjamin, Paris, April 14, 1862. *CDS*, Letter Book, I, Pt. 1.

the regular diplomatic channels.[110] This turn of events embarrassed Napoleon even more than an unfavorable response to a direct overture would have done.

Lindsay's mission, however, was not an entirely futile one. Before returning to Paris, he had managed to talk with the leader of the Tories, Benjamin Disraeli, who told him that if France would take the initiative in ending the state of affairs produced by the war, a large majority of Parliament would support it. In that case, the Conservative statesman believed, Lord Russell would reluctantly give in, in order to avoid a change of ministry. This optimistic outlook could not easily be reconciled with Disraeli's claim that he had reason to believe a secret understanding existed between Russell and Seward, according to which England would respect the blockade and withhold recognition from the Confederacy.[111] Napoleon, to whom Lindsay confided these comments, immediately recognized the ominous implications of this alleged understanding. For in view of the source from which it came, the question of the accuracy of this kind of information was of secondary importance.

By July the Emperor tried again to determine unofficially whether Palmerston still preferred to lie on his oars. Thouvenel, who then visited London, discovered no fundamental policy change on the part of the British Cabinet.[112] The time of diplomatic decisions depended largely on the military situation in America.[113] The Southern victory in the Second Battle of Bull Run (August 29-30, 1862) brought the Confederates as close to triumph as they ever came. Recognition by France and Great Britain was then within their reach, for the statesmen of Britain were finally ready to consider it. A special Cabinet meeting to discuss this issue was scheduled for October 23. However, when this day arrived, the tide of Southern military fortunes had receded, and the majority of the Cabinet informally decided that watchful waiting still was the wisest policy.[114]

110. Korolewicz-Carlton, pp. 150-51.

111. Slidell to Benjamin, Paris, April 18, 1862. *CDS*, Letter Book, I, Pt. 1. See also E. D. Adams, I, 295.

112. Spencer Walpole, *The History of Twenty-Five Years* (London, 1904), II, 55. See also Flahaut to Thouvenel, London, July 23, 1862. Private. Papiers Thouvenel, VIII.

113. In a private letter to Count Agénor-Étienne de Gasparin, dated August 4, 1862, Lincoln expressed his dissatisfaction with Europe's reactions to the fighting in America. He considered it as unreasonable "that a series of successes . . . should help us so little, while a single half-defeat should hurt us so much." Basler, ed., *Works of Abraham Lincoln*, V, 355-56.

114. John Russell, *The Later Correspondence of Lord John Russell, 1840-1878* (London, 1925), II, 319; E. D. Adams, II, 38-71; Charles F. Adams, *The Crisis of*

In the knowledge that Queen Victoria and King Leopold of Belgium were seeing eye to eye with him,[115] and believing that the military impasse in America would not soon be broken, Napoleon initiated a major mediation offensive in the fall of 1862. He approached Britain and Russia to concert with him in a move to induce the belligerents to agree to an armistice of six months.[116] These three powers were to serve merely as the vehicle that would bring the North and the South to the conference table. No pressures or threats were to be employed to force the calling of such a conference. Nor was the rejection of the good offices to entail dire consequences.[117]

As this latest diplomatic offensive gained momentum, it temporarily produced an atmosphere of suspense. Expectations were high in Paris and Richmond. Anxiety prevailed in Washington. These sentiments were, of course, reversed when London and St. Petersburg declined to follow the Emperor's lead. The British government feared that Washington's rejection of the proposition would prevent its renewal at a more opportune time.[118] And in spite of the fact that in view of the South's military successes Lord Russell had only recently favored peaceful intervention in the Civil War, he was basically of the opinion that pacification must come from within and could not be imposed by any power or combination of powers.[119]

Russia was looking after its own interests, not those of the United States, when it frustrated Napoleon's mediation attempt. The French ambassador at St. Petersburg described Prince Gortchakov as "willing to associate himself with success, but as unwilling to run the risk of reversal."[120] The Prince also did not conceal Russia's ambition of desiring, at the proper moment, to assume the role of the sole mediator in the American war.[121] Nor did he foreclose the possibility of ratify-

Foreign Intervention in the War of Secession, September-November, 1862 (Boston, 1914), p. 20; and Robert Owen Jones, "British Pseudo-Neutrality during the American Civil War" (Master's thesis, Georgetown University, 1952), pp. 112-16.

115. Korolewicz-Carlton, p. 191.

116. Thouvenel to Mercier, Paris, October 30, 1862. Confidential. *CPEU,* CXXVIII.

117. Dayton to Seward, Paris, November 6 and 12, 1862. *DDFDS* (MF) XXXIV-55; see also Thomas W. Evans to Seward, Paris, November 18, 1862. Seward Papers.

118. Russell to Cowley, London, November 13, 1862. *CP Angleterre,* DCCXXII. Indicative of Palmerston's attitude toward Napoleon III was his letter to Lord Russell, dated November 2, 1862: "As the Emperor is so anxious to put a stop to bloodshed, he might try his hand . . . by putting down the stream of ruffians which rolls out from that never failing fountain at Rome." Russell, *The Later Correspondence,* p. 333.

119. *National Intelligencer* (Washington, D. C.), December 30, 1862.

120. Montebello to Drouyn de Lhuys, St. Petersburg, November 10, 1862. *CP Russie,* CCXXIX.

121. Montebello to Drouyn de Lhuys, St. Petersburg, November 9, 1862. *CP Russie,* CCXXIX.

ing any change that should occur on the American scene.[122] The Russians played their cards during the Civil War so adroitly that they satisfied both belligerents and succeeded in embarrassing and confounding their own European rivals at the same time.[123] In principle, they wished to preserve the Union intact. The interests of the two countries did not clash and the cotton crisis was not felt by them. Cotton supplies from Bokhara and the Caucasus were sufficient to take care of domestic needs. Indeed, the Russians actually sold some raw cotton to English manufacturers.[124] Equally important were the positive aspects of Russo-American relations which had been greatly strengthened since the Crimean War. Russia looked upon the United States as a most useful counterweight to the maritime powers of Europe.[125] Gortchakov even went so far as to tell the French ambassador: "In case of European complications, America is an ally of Russia without the necessity of an alliance."[126] Whether this optimism was justified or not, London and Paris could not ignore the possibility of a Russo-American entente.

The arrival of the Russian squadrons in New York and San Francisco in October of 1863 intensified speculations that such an entente was in the making. Mercier, for instance, did not accept the explanation of his Russian colleague, Baron de Stoeckl, that those ships had been sent to the American ports to keep them, in case of a war over Poland, out of the range of Anglo-French guns. This argument did not hold with respect to the ships which had arrived directly from Kronstadt. Had they remained there, they simply might not have been able to get out of the Baltic. It was widely supposed, therefore, that St. Petersburg intended these vessels as a nucleus of a Russo-American maritime combination.[127] In the event of the rupture between the United States and France or Britain, Russia expected the Federal republic to cast off its isolationism and to establish a unified front with it against a common enemy. The Lincoln administration had done nothing to justify such far reaching assumptions. It had,

122. Gortchakov to Oubril, St. Petersburg, October 27, 1862. *CP Russie*, CCXXIX.

123. Richmond *Dispatch*, February 8, 1864.

124. Fournier to Thouvenel, St. Petersburg, July 29, 1862. *CP Russie*, CCXXVIII. See also Taylor to Dayton, St. Petersburg, November 17, 1862. Confidential. Dayton Papers, Box 2.

125. J. R. Robertson, *A Kentuckian at the Court of the Tsars* (Berea, Ky., 1935), p. 80; see also A. A. Woldman, *Lincoln and the Russians* (Cleveland, 1952), p. 85.

126. Fournier to Thouvenel, St. Petersburg, July 29, 1862. *CP Russie*, CCXXVIII.

127. Mercier to Drouyn de Lhuys, Washington, D. C., October 6, 1863. *CPEU*, CXXX. This view both confirms and supplements Professor Golder's thesis. See F. A. Golder, "The Russian Fleet and the Civil War," *AHR*, XX (1915), 802-3.

in fact, recently reiterated its traditional policy of nonintervention when it declined the invitation of France, Great Britain, and Austria to participate at the conference on Poland.[128]   As a country that insisted on Europe's nonintervention, the Union could hardly have acted otherwise.   But by declining the invitation, it also pleased St. Petersburg.   More than that, these developments brought out an identity of interest which evidently led the Russians to conclude that Anglo-French threats of intervention in the Polish and Southern rebellions could and should be countered with Russo-American threats of retaliation.

The Union's position with respect to foreign intervention in any form had been made crystal clear at the beginning of the war.   On February 28, 1863, a concurrent resolution of Congress restated the position which Seward had all along impressed upon the statesmen of the Old World: any proposal of outside interference in the rebellion would be regarded as an unfriendly act.[129]   Congress as well as the Lincoln administration deplored the very consideration of such suggestions because they helped to sustain the hopes and morale of the Confederacy.

This was an altogether touchy matter, the seriousness of which Mercier tried to minimize by suggesting that under disappointing circumstances the North might welcome mediation.   Seward immediately took this hint at the major military victory which the South was prophesying for the fall of 1862, exactly the time at which Napoleon launched his vain appeals to Britain and Russia.   The Secretary of State realized that there were various types of intervention, and he tried to disabuse the French of the effectiveness of them all.   If the South should register a decisive military victory, he argued, then the war would come to an end without foreign intervention.   But as long as the Northern situation was not hopeless, "intervention could never make it so."[130]   For mere recognition of the Confederacy would not only fail to end the war, it would enlarge its scope by transforming it from a domestic to an international conflict.   Even military intervention, Seward warned, would be "ineffectual unless attended by permanent armies . . . committed to maintain slavery."[131]   Is this, he asked, to be the climax of the world's progress in the nineteenth century?   Men like Édouard Laboulaye in France and Richard

128. Seward to Dayton, Washington, D. C., May 11, 1863. *FIDS*, XVI.
129. *Senate Misc. Doc.*, 37 Cong., 3 sess., No. 38.   This resolution was communicated to foreign governments.
130. Seward to Dayton, Washington, D. C., September 8, 1862. *FIDS*, XVI.
131. Seward to Dayton, Washington, D. C., October 20, 1862. *FIDS*, XVI.

Cobden in England were fully aware that military intervention would be so costly that "it would be cheaper to feed the laboring classes, who are now starving in consequence of the American crisis, on game and champagne."[132] Seward's apprehension of foreign interference never ceased. But after the summer of 1863 he became increasingly confident that this danger was receding due to Europe's own preoccupations and the growing strength of the Union. Consequently, he instructed Dayton not to manifest any anxiety concerning fresh rumors of French intervention, and in case of Napoleon's flagrant violation of his pledged neutrality, to leave France.[133]

Warned by the North, turned down by Britain and Russia, afraid of the risks of going it alone, and undecided what to do, the Emperor played the diplomatic game of holding both belligerents in suspense. He alternated professions of friendship for the Union with those for the Confederacy, and official declarations of strict neutrality with unofficial promises of partiality to the South. Surrounded by such influential sympathizers of the Confederate cause as his ministers Jean de Persigny, Eugène Rouher, and Achille Fould, and such prominent defenders of neutrality, if not of the Union's cause, as Thouvenel, Drouyn de Lhuys, and Prince Napoleon, the Emperor evidently decided to steer a middle course. For he also faced a divided press and public and felt the need of at least appeasing the uneasy feelings of those Frenchmen whose income depended largely on trade with the United States.

He continued, therefore, to search for ways and means which would contribute to the early end of the war. An opening for another peace maneuver presented itself early in 1863. The Confederates needed a breathing spell. According to the French consul at Richmond,[134] they were now willing to make concessions if the North would agree to discussions between their respective representatives, perhaps assisted by the diplomatic agents of foreign powers. Benjamin was still opposed to a tariff union between the North and the South, but he had come to feel that a uniform moderate tariff for both sections might serve as an attractive basis for an all around compromise. The French government was so impressed with this idea that, once again, it stood ready to bring the belligerents together for direct conversations. It hoped that this might, if necessary, lead to a peaceful separation.[135]

132. Laboulaye, p. 9.
133. Seward to Dayton, Washington, D. C., July 8, 1863. *FIDS*, XVI.
134. Paul to Mercier, Richmond, November 23, 1862. *CPEU*, CXXVIII.
135. Drouyn de Lhuys to Mercier, Paris, January 9, 1863. *CPEU*, CXXIX.

In view of Seward's plain talk on this subject, it was a foregone conclusion that France had exposed itself to another diplomatic rebuff, which certainly did not enhance its prestige or its relations with the United States.

It is perhaps even more incomprehensible why Napoleon also antagonized the British government by by-passing it for a second time when he permitted the Roebuck episode to take place. On June 22, 1863, John A. Roebuck and William S. Lindsay visited the Emperor at Fontainebleau. These two members of Parliament wanted Napoleon again to attempt to obtain an agreement with the British jointly to recognize the Confederacy. After an interview, which lasted two and one half hours, they saw Slidell and related to him what had been discussed in exactly the way Roebuck later stated it before Parliament.[136] According to this version, Napoleon authorized his English visitors to tell the House of Commons that, contrary to rumors circulated in London, he would follow England's lead should it decide to extend recognition. This procedure caused considerable embarrassment. It was anything but diminished by the Emperor's subsequent denial of having authorized Roebuck to deliver a personal message to Parliament. The British government wondered whether the French monarch had two ambassadors in England, one to express his views through proper channels, and the other to express them in Parliament. Above all else, who was to be believed, Napoleon or Roebuck? The question of veracity aroused a great deal of doubt about Napoleon's sincerity. It drew public attention in England from the issue of intervention and substituted for it the question of the dignity of Parliament which had allegedly been abused. Emphasizing the importance of this incident, Henry Adams commented: "Roebuck has done us more good than all our friends."[137] The great mistake of the central figures in this affair was of a procedural nature. As far as substantive policy was concerned, the instructions to the French ambassador at London confirmed the accuracy of the declaration that the Emperor would follow Palmerston in any move designed to bring peace to America.[138]

In addition to these diplomatic machinations, Napoleon also became involved in secret schemes to equip the Confederacy with a navy. His neutrality proclamation of June 10, 1861, forbade French-

---

136. Virginia Mason, *The Public Life and Diplomatic Correspondence of James M. Mason* (Roanoke, Va., 1903), pp. 419-25. See also E. D. Adams, II, 167-77.

137. W. Charles Ford (ed.), *A Cycle of Adams Letters, 1861-1865* (New York, 1925), II, 43.

138. *Le Moniteur Universel,* July 5, 1863.

men to arm and equip vessels of war for either belligerent. This practically eliminated France as a country where ships for the Confederate navy could be procured. In violation of this proclamation, however, Napoleon intimated to Slidell that a Confederate ship construction program could be secretly launched in French dry docks.[139] He alluded to such an arrangement on October 28, 1862. The date is significant. For it coincided with his major mediation offensive which, in the light of this secret naval scheme, assumes an outright sinister character. Once the imperial signal was given, the Ministers of Foreign Affairs and of Commerce closed their eyes to the illegal arrangements between the Confederate agents and Arman, the leading shipbuilder in France and member of the Chamber of Deputies. Their original contract called for four corvettes of 1500 tons, which were to be equipped with fourteen six-inch guns.[140] The Minister of the Navy and Colonies approved this contract because Arman had officially declared that these ships were destined to navigate the China Seas.

John Bigelow's alertness helped to uncover this underhanded maneuver. The 15,000 francs he paid his informant were a sound investment, considering the damage these ships and subsequently ordered ironclads could have done to the North.[141] As soon as the secret leaked in September of 1863, Dayton and Seward protested vigorously against this flagrant violation of neutrality. Although the Confederates were for a short time left to believe that they might yet receive the ships, Northern vigilance made this very unlikely. For that matter, official orders nullified the original plans and by June 9, 1864, Arman advised the Confederate agent that the ships in question had been otherwise disposed of.[142] If Napoleon thought that these vessels might, under favorable conditions, decide the outcome of the conflict, or at least protract the war until Maximilian was firmly established in Mexico, this turn of events destroyed his calculations.[143] In this scheme, his deception, first of the North and then of the South, reached a demonstrable low.

The considerate treatment of Confederate ships in French ports was another controversial matter about which the Lincoln adminis-

139. Slidell to Benjamin, Paris, October 28, 1862. *CDS,* Letter Book, I, Pt. 1.

140. H. H. Todd, "The Building of the Confederate . . . Navy in Europe" (Ph.D. dissertation, Vanderbilt University, 1940), pp. 17-23; see also S. B. Thompson, *Confederate Purchasing Operations Abroad* (Chapel Hill, N. C., 1935), pp. 38-39.

141. Willson, *Ambassadors,* p. 265.

142. James D. Bulloch, *The Secret Service of the Confederate States in Europe* (New York, 1884), II, 41.

143. Bigelow, *Confederate Navy,* p. 195.

tration complained. France recognized the right of the South to own men-of-war under the Confederate flag, and it permitted such ships as the *Alabama, Florida, Georgia,* and *Rappahannock* to take supplies of coal and to repair damages in its ports.[144] It denied strongly, however, that it also allowed them to recruit new crews or to receive armaments of war; and it refused to be held accountable for injuries these ships might cause to Federal commerce.[145]

Aside from the danger of a possible collusion between French authorities and rebel ship captains, Northerners worried also about the French war vessels and ironclads which carried a suspiciously large number of soldiers to Mexico. What was their real purpose? Were they to be used in a demonstration against Texas and Louisiana?[146] Ever since December of 1860 it had been seriously suggested that France might have to establish a protectorate over Louisiana to enforce that clause of the Treaty of 1803 which guaranteed to the descendants of French colonists the enjoyment of their property.[147] Napoleon's schemes in Mexico lent some credence to conjectures that he intended to solidify his Mexican exploits by adding to them Louisiana, Texas, and Arizona. Dayton was in a position to transmit, on December 31, 1863, intelligence to Washington, according to which leading secessionists in Paris, including Slidell, actually considered the transfer of Texas to France in exchange for recognition.[148] The government at Richmond would not identify itself with such an act of desperation. Refusing to be a party to such a nefarious transaction, it had previously expelled the consular agents of France at Galveston and Richmond because they had participated in an intrigue to bring Texas under French protection.[149] In Paris, Drouyn de Lhuys categorically denied any negotiation regarding the cession of Texas. "France," he declared, "would not take Texas as a gift, even if it were accompanied with a handsome bribe besides."[150]

From the point of view of the Union, Napoleon's intervention in Mexico was potentially more dangerous than any of his other un-

144. Bulloch, II, 282; Clapp, pp. 200-17.

145. Dayton to Seward, Paris, February 11, 1864. *DDFDS,* (MF) XXXIV-57. It is noteworthy that the United States did not institute "Alabama Claims" against France because, as Senator Sumner explained, few blockade runners came from French shores. Faverney to La Valette, Washington, D. C., June 1, 1869. *CPEU,* CXLV.

146. Motley to Dayton, Vienna, October 29, 1862. Dayton Papers, Box 2.

147. *La Presse,* December 4, 1860.

148. Dayton to Seward, Paris, December 31, 1863. *DDFDS,* (MF) XXXIV-57.

149. Benjamin to Slidell, Richmond, October 17, 1862. *CDS,* Letter Book. See also Richmond *Daily Dispatch,* January 23, 1863.

150. Dayton to Seward, Paris, March 11, 1864. *DDFDS,* (MF) XXXIV-57.

friendly acts. It confronted the Lincoln administration with a delicate and perilous situation, for it could not assume that the leader of a great power would risk undertaking such an imperialistic enterprise without being determined to bring it to a successful conclusion. By any realistic standard, not just the immediate success but ultimately the permanence of his Mexican adventure depended on the fate of the Union. A reconstituted United States could hardly have been expected to resign itself to this challenge of the Monroe Doctrine, as a divided and weakened one might possibly have been compelled to do. Many contemporary observers would, therefore, not have been surprised had Napoleon put forward "the spurious government of Mexico to take the initiative in recognition [of the South]" and then "support the act on the part of France."[151] The Emperor timed his Mexican scheme to coincide with the internal struggle in the United States which practically eliminated the danger of effective interference. He continued to coordinate his policies regarding Mexico and the American Civil War by constantly proposing measures which, in effect, would all have benefited the Confederacy, such as his pleas for peace, recognition, mediation, lifting of the blockade, or his secret navy deal. Similarly, as irritating complications abated his enthusiasm for the Mexican experiment, his interest in the Confederacy diminished.[152] And finally, it should be noted that the Emperor did not go all out in pursuing his objectives in regard either to Mexico or to the Confederacy. Playing with both, he attained neither. The reasons for the failure of his Mexican adventure will be discussed in the next chapter. Not the least important among the factors which contributed to the frustration of Napoleon's Civil War policy was Britain's reaction to his Mexican policy. The British government, without whose cooperation the Emperor would not intervene in the Civil War, declined to accept his suggestions for intervention because, among other reasons, it suspected that they were really designed to further French ambitions in Mexico.[153] London had no intention of helping Napoleon III make a success of his Mexican empire scheme.

VII

Mounting economic difficulties also influenced Napoleon's Civil War diplomacy. He was haunted by the fear that the cotton famine

151. *Illinois State Journal* (Springfield), August 3, 1863.

152. *National Intelligencer* (Washington, D. C.), August 12, 1862. According to the Paris correspondent of this paper, "the French have had a sickener of intervention in the Mexican affair."

153. E. D. Adams, I, 260-62.

would produce disastrous consequences, once existing stocks were exhausted. Several hundred thousand Frenchmen depended for their livelihood on Southern cotton and the American market. The reports of the attorney generals[154] and the alarming number of petitions for relief which reached Paris from the provinces indicated a politically unsafe degree of distress. In the spring of 1862 Thouvenel made an incognito inspection tour of several manufacturing districts which convinced him that the gravity of the situation would sooner or later compel France at least to reopen its accustomed channels of trade and commerce.[155] The Emperor's mediation projects in the second half of 1862 were in part prompted by this concern for the plight of his people.

How sound was the contention that the French cotton industry suffered immeasurable damage because it was cut off from its principal source of supply? A study of the pertinent evidence shows that in 1860 and 1861 French manufacturers had imported extraordinarily large amounts of American cotton. At the time of the proclamation of the blockade French warehouses were, moreover, filled with enough cotton cloth to meet demands for at least another year.[156] And the future was not so bleak as it appeared, because France managed to import considerable quantities of raw cotton from India, Brazil, Algeria, and other places.[157]

If concern over a cotton shortage was justifiable in 1862, Table VIII shows that it was less warranted in subsequent years. It was important, though, that contemporaries, facing an uncertain future, believed that the prospect of diminishing cotton supplies would hurt them financially.

The original contention that the textile crisis in France was the result of the Civil War also falls under the weight of other facts. The Cobden Treaty of 1860, for instance, provided for a very moderate tariff on British cotton goods entering France after October 1861.

154. For extracts from these reports consult Case, *French Opinion on the United States and Mexico*. See also A. L. Dunham, "The Development of the Cotton Industry in France and the Anglo-French Treaty of Commerce of 1860," *Economic History Review*, I (1928), 294; and W. O. Henderson, "The Cotton Famine on the Continent, 1861-1865," *Economic History Review*, IV (1933), 199.

155. Dayton to Seward, Paris, April 22, 1862. *DDFDS*, (MF) XXXIV-54.

156. A. L. Dunham, *The Anglo-French Treaty of Commerce of 1860* (Ann Arbor, 1930), pp. 192-94; see also Henderson, p. 196; and A. Thiers, *Discours parlementaires* (Paris, 1881), XI, 584.

157. Earl S. Pomeroy, "French Substitutes for American Cotton, 1861-1865," *Journal of Southern History*, IX (1943), 555-60. The French, however, preferred the superior quality of American cotton. The purchase of Oriental cotton, moreover, caused an unwelcome drain on their silver reserves.

TABLE VIII. Import of Raw Cotton into France, 1859-1865
(Expressed in bales).

1859—432,631
1860—684,594
1861—624,600
1862—271,570
1863—381,539
1864—450,880
1865—509,805

Source: A. L. Dunham, "The Development of the Cotton Industry . . . ,"
Economic History Review, I, 291.

When this date arrived, British manufacturers shipped some of their surplus stocks to this newly opened continental market. Although, in anticipation of this competition, French industrialists had made costly improvements in their mills,[158] the arrival of the British goods at this particular time had a depressing effect on their business. Thus, even if the Civil War had not broken out in 1861, many French cotton manufacturers admitted they would have been faced with the same calamitous problems.

Seward was aware of this state of affairs. Henry S. Sanford, the extremely well-informed American minister at Brussels, had sent him a very detailed report about the cotton problem in France.[159] Armed with introductions from Rouher, the powerful Minister of Commerce and Public Works, Sanford visited the principal manufacturers in Rouen and neighboring towns in the fall of 1862. There he found that the smaller mills had closed down, and the large number of handlooms were generally stopped, while large and better equipped establishments continued to work from half to full time. In his opinion, the cotton operators in Normandy could have met English competition as successfully as the manufacturers at Lille and Mühlhausen, had they used modern machinery instead of handlooms.[160] He was also convinced that the textile crisis has been caused by an overproduction of previous years rather than by a want of cotton.

Most large manufacturers profited from the interruption of American cotton supplies. They had bought large stocks at low prices and used them to fill reasonably-priced orders. In this respect they acted more in the interest of the public than their British counterparts who speculated with the raw material. While French chambers of com-

158. A. L. Dunham, "Government Aid to Industry in the French Economic Reforms of 1860," *Economic Journal* (1927), pp. 300-306.

159. Sanford to Seward, Paris, November 4, 1862. Private. Seward Papers.

160. Sanford to Seward, Paris, April 24, 1863. Seward Papers.

merce urged their government to intervene in America, these large manufacturers told Sanford that peace or a sudden opening of the cotton ports would be a disaster. Such a turn of events, they maintained, would not bring immediate relief because the French market was glutted with goods which could only be absorbed in time.

The French government did not do much to stimulate the activities of the small cotton manufacturers or to ameliorate the suffering of the unemployed operators.[161] It may have been politically convenient, therefore, to blame their deplorable conditions on the American Civil War. While the plight of the French cotton industry could not really be attributed to this conflict, the war undoubtedly had a detrimental effect on the French economy as a whole. Americans had long been accustomed to draw on the credit balances of their cotton exports to pay for their general imports from France. The suspension of the cotton exports created, therefore, serious financial complications in both countries.[162] Also, many French enterprises were hit hard by the impact of the contest across the Atlantic because the emergency compelled the North to curtail its imports very extensively. Several industries and communities whose prosperity rested primarily on normal relations with the United States suffered much. Among them were the silk industry of Lyons, the lace producers of Mirecourt, the hat makers of Bordeaux, the china manufacturers of Limoges, and a multitude of other French specialties. The losses and misfortunes of people engaged in these trades were real enough. It was small consolation to them that the linen, hemp, and wool industries prospered during this emergency or that French business as a whole was able to compensate for the temporary loss of the American market by increasing its trade volume with Great Britain.[163] These facts, though, deprived the French government of the rationalization that its intervention in America was a matter of the most vital urgency. Seward had never believed that the economic consequences of the Civil War were really so serious as to justify French intervention. In any case, he suggested, France could shorten the war and its effects simply by depriving the Confederates of the illusion of eventual recognition.

161. A. Legoyt, "De la crise cotonnière," *Journal des économistes* (March, 1863), p. 438.

162. Case, pp. 6-23; see also Bigelow to Seward, Paris, October 25, 1861. Seward Papers.

163. Jordan and Pratt, p. 214. *The World* (New York) of February 2, 1863, published the relatively optimistic economic reports of the French government.

VIII

From the beginning of this conflict the South had counted on Europe's assistance in one form or another. It seemed reasonable to expect that the Old World would welcome the opportunity of checking the dynamic industrial and commercial rival in North America whose high tariff policies were as objectionable as impolitic. It seemed reasonable to assume, moreover, that France and Great Britain could not afford to tolerate the disruptive effects of a long war in America.[164] That the industrial powers of Europe suffered and survived these consequences for four years, of course, proved the foreign political assumptions of the South to have been fallacious.

Convinced of the righteousness of their cause, the leaders of the secession gambled at incredible odds with the fate of their movement and of the people who supported it. They took the risk that secession might mean war, that war might mean emancipation of the slaves, and that they might have to fight this war alone. Maturity is measured by a sober evaluation of the consequences of one's actions. And mature statesmanship operates within the framework of realistic estimates of the worst as well as of the most hopeful possibilities. Foreign assistance could not have been taken for granted. It was tragically naïve to think that the maritime powers would lightly risk conferring international respectability on a rebellion whose lasting success remained yet to be demonstrated.

An inquiry into the Confederacy's foreign policy shows an appalling unpreparedness in this respect. The Jefferson Davis administration was slow in developing what might possibly be called a foreign policy. During the short term of office of Secretary of State Robert Toombs little more was done than to send three commissioners to Europe in April of 1861 to determine the chances of recognition. Realizing that the European powers were in no hurry to accept the Confederacy as a new member of the family of nations, these agents deemed it inexpedient to press the issue of recognition as one of utmost urgency, lest they betray a lack of confidence in their own cause.[165]

Upon Toombs' resignation on July 24, 1861, Robert Hunter of Virginia assumed the secretaryship for the next six months. In his

164. Clement Eaton, *A History of the Southern Confederacy* (New York, 1954), p. 62. See also, Owsley, p. 24.

165. W. L. Yancey and A. Dudley Mann to Toombs, London, May 21, 1861. U. S. Navy Department, *Official Records of the Union and Confederate Navies in the War of Rebellion* (Washington, D. C., 1922), Ser. 2, III, 215-16. See also Richardson, *Papers of the Confederacy,* pp. 40-42, 54, 99.

instructions to John Slidell, the envoy extraordinary and minister plenipotentiary to France, he developed the principles which henceforth were to guide the foreign relations of the South.[166] According to them, the leaders at Richmond wanted Europe to understand that the Southern states were not rebellious provinces, but states defending their constitutional right of self-government and capable of discharging international obligations. They sought no material aid or assistance, no defensive or offensive alliances. They desired only recognition of their independent status. In exchange, they offered France a low tariff, advantageous terms for cotton and tobacco supplies, as well as cheap coal, iron, and naval stores. They also ventured to hope that France would be interested in establishing a balance of power in North America which would contribute to the repose of neighboring nations. By April of 1862 the Confederate Senate, furthermore, authorized President Jefferson Davis to hold out attractive terms to France, Great Britain, and Spain if they would be willing to negotiate treaties of amity and commerce. However, besides recognition, this bargain would also have required shipments of arms and munitions to the Confederacy and a declaration that the blockade was illegal.[167]

With the exception of winning recognition of its belligerency and negotiating the Erlanger loan, the South failed to achieve any of its foreign political objectives. Obviously, the failure of its diplomacy cannot be attributed to it alone. Without a decisive military victory for the South, the issue of recognition depended on the European governments, and they were accustomed to relate American questions to the usually complex world situation as it affected each of them.

After the initial period of "sanguine expectations," the Southern press gradually played down the importance of recognition by first rationalizing that it was not a necessity and then declaring it a matter of the most perfect indifference.[168] By April of 1862 the Richmond *Dispatch* directed its wrath at the "far-sighted malignity" of Britain under whose leadership, it asserted, Europe aimed at the exhaustion and destruction of both belligerents. Little stock was henceforth put into the recurring rumors of French assistance. For it was well understood that, as long as Paris and London distrusted each other,

166. Hunter to Slidell, Richmond, September 23, 1861. U. S. Navy Department, *Official Records*, pp. 265-73. See also Henry H. Simms, *Life of Robert M. T. Hunter* (Richmond, Va., 1935), pp. 189-90; and Eaton, p. 65.

167. *Journal of the Congress of the Confederate States of America, 1861-1865* (Washington, D. C., 1904), XXVI, 192-93.

168. Richmond *Daily Dispatch*, June 17 and July 23, 1861.

Napoleon III could not be counted upon to give concrete form to his good will toward the South.[169]

Inasmuch as their survival depended upon foreign aid and assistance, the Confederates opened themselves to the charge that they did not exhaust all means of inducing France and Great Britain to take an active interest in them. They were so concerned with their rights as a nation, the legality of the blockade, and their recognition as an independent state that they did not take timely action to create the practical conditions which might have greatly enhanced their chances of success. France and Great Britain, it is well to remember, never ruled out their recognition. If they withheld it from a South still struggling for victory, they guarded themselves against the implications of encouraging secession. They also knew, of course, that only victory makes a glorious struggle for independence out of a rebellion.

The Confederates realized too late that the primary objective of their foreign policy should, therefore, have been to get the implements necessary for victory rather than recognition which would have followed it. It was the irony of Southern diplomacy that it relied on "King Cotton" as the indispensable ruler of Europe, but neglected to exploit his potentialities as the ruler of the Confederate States of America. Had he been President of the Confederacy, former Secretary of State Toombs asserted, for instance, he would at once have mortgaged its cotton crops as a collateral for loans large enough to . make French and English creditors vitally interested in a Southern victory.[170] Several military and political leaders of the South, among them Alexander H. Stephens, Judah P. Benjamin, and Joseph E. Johnston, had actually recommended shipping as many staples to Europe as could get through the blockade and converting them into funds for the purchase of supplies.[171] Instead of complaining about the paper blockade, the Confederates might thus have taken advantage of it, particularly during the first year of the war.[172] It took the North some time before it fully organized its naval patrols. Moreover, fearing a lengthy American war, Europe would have been eager to build up its cotton reserves beyond immediate needs.

169. *Ibid.*, December 2, 1862. See also James M. Callahan, *The Diplomatic History of the Southern Confederacy* (Baltimore, 1901), p. 273; and Carl Sandburg, *Abraham Lincoln—The War Years* (New York, 1939), III, 607.

170. Pleasant A. Stovall, *Robert Toombs* (New York, 1892), pp. 234-35.

171. E. M. Coulter, *The Confederate States of America* (Baton Rouge, La., 1950), p. 166.

172. Pecquet Du Bellet, pp. 90-91.

In the summer of 1861 the Marquis de Lafressange proposed to deliver 90,000 muskets and to advance considerable credits to the Confederacy upon the cotton in its possession. When, to his surprise, this offer was turned down, he concluded that the "Confederates are not serious men! They are far below the circumstances in which their country is situated."[173] The course of events vindicated the contemporary critics of the Davis administration. Failure to mobilize at once for a life and death struggle did turn out to be fatal. One can sympathize with President Davis' hesitation to mortgage the future of the Confederacy and to sacrifice its sons in an immediate all-out war effort. But once it had seceded, the South had risked so much that it had little choice but to risk all.

It would be erroneous to conclude from these comments that the Confederacy altogether ignored the power of cotton as an instrument of diplomacy. Originally, however, it used it in a negative way. The Southerners intended to provoke France and Great Britain into challenging the blockade by withholding cotton. They feared that, if they supplied these countries with their staples, they would destroy the Europeans' incentive to intervene. Precious time was lost experimenting with this unproductive strategy of exerting pressure abroad by making raw materials unavailable. By adopting it, the South not only overestimated its economic bargaining power, it also acted as if it possessed an exclusive monopoly of cotton and tobacco which, of course, it did not. Worst of all, this strategy had the practical effect of supplementing the very blockade it was designed to lift.

It was not until the middle of 1862, after the North had taken control of New Orleans, that this policy was changed. From then on the South stepped up its offers to supply France with all the cotton it needed, provided that French ships would carry European supplies to Confederate ports.[174] To induce Napoleon to break the blockade, and thus to become involved in the war, it held out such enticing bait as tariff-free admission of French goods, a subsidy of 100,000 bales of cotton, and a secret treaty granting France for some years to come an exclusive monopoly of its entire cotton production.[175] Tempting as these propositions were, their acceptance entailed a risk the Emperor hesitated to assume. In August, 1863, Secretary of State Judah Benjamin made still another suggestion. He offered to sell ten million dollars' worth of cotton directly to the French government at the

173. *Ibid.*
174. Benjamin to Slidell, Richmond, April 8, 1862. *CDS,* Letter Book.
175. De Leon, pp. 67-69; see also Burton J. Hendrick, *Statesmen of the Lost Cause* (Boston, 1939), p. 312.

phenomenally low price of eight to ten cents per pound. If France preferred it, he would even have been agreeable to holding the cotton in Southern warehouses until the end of the war.[176] Nothing came of this either. For that matter, Secretary of the Treasury Christopher G. Memminger objected to the unorthodox method of projecting the Confederate government into business, which these propositions would have made inevitable.[177]

The value of cotton as a means of strengthening the financial position of the Confederacy was clearly demonstrated in 1863 by the successful negotiation of the Erlanger loan of $15,000,000.[178] In this instance the French firm of Erlanger & Company agreed to sell 7 percent Confederate bonds which it acquired at the attractive discount of 23 percent, in addition to other benefits. These bonds were backed by forty-five million dollars' worth of cotton stored in Southern warehouses. The Erlangers and the government at Richmond profited from this transaction before the collapse of the Confederacy resulted in the worthlessness of the bonds as far as individual French investors were concerned.

Early in 1865, when it was already in its death struggle, the Davis administration finally planned to mobilize all its resources to finance and sustain its war effort. One of the projects it contemplated in cooperation with European financiers was the establishment of a Franco-Confederate Bank. The sale of huge cotton shipments to Europe, it was confidently expected, would provide this institution with a solid capital foundation. The armies of Generals Grant, Sheridan, and Sherman prevented the execution of this plan. If the leaders of the South had shown this kind of initiative during the first crucial year of the war, they would at least not have had reason to reproach themselves for having dethroned "King Cotton."

Without decisive military victories at home, the resourcefulness and zeal of the Confederate commissioners in Europe was of little avail. In contrast to James M. Mason in England, Slidell managed to circulate freely in the most influential circles in France. Inasmuch as his introduction to Thouvenel had been anything but flattering, this accomplishment reflected as much on his personality as on the political morality of the France of Napoleon III. Mercier and Sartiges, the two French experts on the United States, had warned the Quai

176. R. D. Meade, *Judah P. Benjamin, Confederate Statesman* (New York, 1943), pp. 294-95.

177. Coulter, pp. 166-67.

178. For detailed information on this transaction, see Thompson, pp. 60-71; and C. K. Hobson, *The Export of Capital* (London, 1914), p. 132.

d'Orsay that Slidell was an unscrupulous and dangerous individual. Sartiges described him as a man who "hides behind his friendly and respectable front the soul and spirit of the most evil men of the worst days of our revolutionary tribunals."[179]   No wonder that Thouvenel and Drouyn de Lhuys kept their distance from the Southern diplomat. Slidell readily overcame this handicap by cultivating a friendship with Persigny, the confidential adviser of the Emperor, who apparently was heart and soul with the Confederacy.[180]   Other powers about the throne also listened sympathetically to the commissioner's arguments. Slidell's charming wife, moreover, endeared herself to the influential Empress. Eugénie's active role in Napoleon's Mexican empire scheme disposed her now more than ever to favor a policy that would weaken the North. That Mrs. Slidell kept this important channel of communication open was, of course, very helpful to her husband.

In the long run, however, Napoleon taught Richmond's agent the lesson that sympathies do not necessarily control the policies of nations. In the end, the South was as little interested in the Emperor's explanations why he alone could not help it as in his admission that it had been a mistake to respect the blockade in the first place.[181] Since the spring of 1862 the Southern commissioners in Europe had in fact become increasingly pessimistic about the diplomatic chances of the South. For once the Civil War passed into a chronic phase, the original alarm at the possible injuries the war might inflict upon Europe subsided. The American conflict, moreover, passed from the spotlight as tensions mounted in Europe. Garibaldi's march on Rome, the uprising of the Poles, the defeat of Denmark, and the rise of Prussia kept the Old World in suspense. The hope of intervention on behalf of the South gradually faded away.

Under these circumstances, the Confederate Congress had debated since the fall of 1862 the advisability of recalling the commissioners.[182] No action, however, was taken on a resolution to that effect. Nor did Judah Benjamin feel that the Confederate Congress was on sound legal grounds when it called for the withdrawal of recognition from those foreign consuls who were originally accredited to the United States. In any case, it would be impolitic to expel them as long as

179. Sartiges to Thouvenel, The Hague, October 28, 1861.   Papiers Thouvenel, XVII.
180. Einstein, *Napoleon III and American Diplomacy*, pp. 18-22.
181. Bigelow, *Confederate Navy*, p. 118.
182. *Journal of the Congress of the Confederate States*, XXIX, 421-22, 464-67.

they observed an attitude of neutrality, as the consular agents of France by and large did. However, when it accidentally came to his attention that the French Baron de Saint André had assumed consular functions at Charleston after the establishment of the Confederacy and that he had done so without applying for an exequatur at Richmond, Benjamin would not tolerate this offense to the sovereign Confederate States.[183]

Gradually, the Davis administration came to the conclusion that Napoleon was a man whose friendly assurances could not be trusted. In a letter to Slidell (June 23, 1864) Benjamin charged the Emperor with bad faith, deception, and broken promises.[184] A few months later he presented a bill of particulars in which he condemned France as an unfriendly power.[185] He accused it of respecting a paper blockade, of closing its ports to Confederate prizes of war, of inducing Emperor Maximilian to seek favors from the North by avoiding intercourse with the Confederacy, and of altogether entertaining the closest amicable relations with the enemy. Embittered and exasperated, Benjamin asked: "What is the policy and what are the purposes of the Western powers in relation to this contest?"[186] The South, he claimed, was at least entitled to a frank exposition of the terms and conditions under which they would concede its independence. No sacrifice, he pledged, would be too great, "save that of honor." Although they had been under the impression that Napoleon was not particularly concerned with the slavery question, [187] early in 1865 the Southerners even considered the possibility of emancipating the slaves in exchange for recognition.[188] But this concession came too late to save the people of the South from their great tragedy.

183. By and large the consular agents of France in the Confederate cities observed an attitude of neutrality. They and their colleagues in the North saw to it that French nationals would either be exempted or released from compulsory military service in the armies of the belligerents. M. L. Bonham, Jr., "The French Consuls in the Confederate States," *Studies in Southern History and Politics* (New York, 1914), p. 104. French volunteers were permitted to serve in both armies. See Lonn, *Foreigners in the Confederacy*, pp. 53, 97, 102, 112; see also Lonn, *Foreigners in the Union Army and Navy*, pp. 126-29.

184. Benjamin to Slidell, Richmond, June 23, 1864. *CDS*, Letter Book. See also J. G. Randall, *The Civil War and Reconstruction* (Boston, 1953), pp. 656-57.

185. Richardson, *Papers of the Confederacy*, II, 674-78: Benjamin to Slidell, Richmond, September 20, 1864. See also the message of Jefferson Davis to Confederate Congress (November 7, 1864), *ibid.*, I, 485.

186. Benjamin to Slidell, Richmond, December 27, 1864. *CDS*, Letter Book.

187. Napoleon was opposed to slavery. Thomas W. Evans, *Memoirs* (New York, 1905), p. 121.

188. Callahan, *Diplomatic History*, pp. 245-65.

IX

As the fate of the Confederacy was about to be sealed, apprehension gripped the financial and political world of France. People whose pocketbooks were certain to suffer from expected price drops and other financial losses became panicky. Politicians who worried about the future policies of the victorious United States were said to have prayed: "God grant the war may be yet a little prolonged."[189] The conscience of leading French statesmen was less troubled when the news of General Robert E. Lee's surrender reached Paris. In spite of all that had been said and done or attempted during the trying four years, Drouyn de Lhuys and Rouher did not hesitate to assert that there never existed any doubt about France's strict neutrality or its exclusive recognition of the entire United States.

Looking toward the future, quite aside from the Mexican problem, Napoleon himself was anxious to restore the ancient friendship with the American republic. His sorrow and profound indignation on the occasion of Lincoln's assassination, the impressive disbanding of the American armies, and the withdrawal of French troops from Mexico in 1867 were the kind of gestures which warranted an optimistic outlook for the future relations of the two countries.

Still, the war had left deep scars. France had irritated both the North and South; and by doing so it had further deepened the American people's distrust of European governments. As President of the Confederacy, Jefferson Davis was charitable enough to attribute "Europe's callousness to the injustice and inhumanity" which his people had suffered to lack of interest in the fate of republics.[190] As we have seen, the policies of France—and of the other powers— were much more complex than would justify such an oversimplification. Psychologically it was understandable that the South felt particularly let down by Napoleon to whom it had looked for substantial support.[191] Ex-President Davis' deliberate personal slight to the French Emperor during his tour through Europe expressed the lingering bitterness of the defeated and abandoned South.

While, in retrospect, the North had reason to be grateful for Napoleon's abstention from intervention, it too could not easily forget his nerve-wracking unreliability when the fate of the Union hung in

189. Bigelow to Seward, Paris, March 9, 1865. Private. Seward Papers.

190. Richardson, *Papers of the Confederacy*, I, 485.

191. On March 14, 1865, Palmerston told Mason: "If France desired to do an act in concert with England, in which the latter was not disposed to unite, her failure to do the act singly was her own affair." U. S. Navy Department, *Official Records*, III, 1272-76.

the balance. He helped to preserve the Union for reasons of expediency, not principle or friendship. He abstained from throwing his weight into the Southern side of the scale because of the uncertain international ramifications of such a move. Thouvenel and Drouyn de Lhuys restrained the Emperor from committing a major blunder by evidently convincing him that risking a war with the United States would dangerously weaken his position at home and in Europe.[192]

192. Lewis Einstein, "Napoléon III et les préliminaires diplomatiques de la guerre civile aux États-Unis," *Revue de l'histoire diplomatique* (1905), pp. 345-47.

CHAPTER VI

The Maximilian Affair

AFTER YEARS OF CLOSE ASSOCIATION with the Emperor, Foreign Minister Drouyn de Lhuys once remarked: "Napoleon III has immense ambitions and limited faculties. He always wants to undertake the extraordinary and pursues in fact the extravagant."[1] The merits of this comment were particularly well illustrated by the Maximilian affair.

Before the Civil War, the Buchanan administration had let it be known that it would vigorously oppose any armed intervention of the European powers designed to control the political destinies of Mexico.[2] Obviously, the United States did not want a strong rival along its frontiers who, incidentally, might also be in a position to decide Cuba's fate. The spectacle in 1861 of both Mexico and the United States being torn internally convinced the French Emperor that the time was opportune to promote French interests in the Western Hemisphere in a spectacular fashion.

Encouraged to believe that the Mexicans would rather see the French flag hoisted next to their own than the Stars and Stripes, the French government embarked on its ill-fated adventure. Originally France, Great Britain, and Spain agreed in the London Convention of October 30, 1861, to send a joint expedition to Mexico for the express and limited purpose of redressing specific grievances.[3] The parties pledged themselves not to seek special advantages in Mexico. Although, at Britain's recommendation, the United States was invited to join this intervention, it declined to do so. Lincoln looked upon this armed expedition with such deep concern that in order to prevent it, his administration would have been disposed to advance the funds necessary to satisfy Mexico's creditors.[4]

1. Maurice Paléologue, *Les entretiens de l'Impératrice Eugénie* (Paris, 1928), p. 109.
2. Mercier to Thouvenel, Washington, D. C., September 15, 1860. *CPEU,* CXXIII.
3. Thouvenel to Mercier, Paris, October 30, 1861. *CPEU,* CXXV.
4. Seward to Dayton, Washington, D. C., September 24, 1861. *FIDS,* XVI. Mercier to Thouvenel, Washington, D. C., October 14, 1861. *CPEU,* CXXV. For an en-

The failure of this attempted dollar diplomacy turned out to be more costly to France than to the two other powers. When early inter-allied dissensions left the French alone to deal with the Mexicans, Napoleon discovered that the republican government of President Juarez constituted a more formidable obstacle to his plans than he had anticipated.

Britain had never intended to regard the expedition as a major operation. Lord Russell made it no secret that he considered this kind of interference in American affairs as fraught with far-reaching consequences. Through Lord Cowley, the British ambassador in Paris, he let the French know that "there was a sort of understanding that so long as European powers did not interfere in America, the United States might abstain from European alliances."[5] He feared that if a combination of European powers organized a government in Mexico, Washington would henceforth feel justified in taking an active part in the wars and politics of Europe. Since London's representative in Mexico, Sir Charles Wyke, believed that President Juarez could establish order and insure honest collection of duties, there was little excuse for becoming a party to the Convention of 1861 and even less for later recognizing Maximilian's government.[6] At best, London could rationalize its Mexican policy during these years as having been dictated by the desire to check the extent of French influence in that part of the world. It is also conceivable that Palmerston indulged Napoleon's plans in Mexico because he foresaw the snares in which the French Emperor would become entangled.

The Spanish had certain reservations about the intervention. General Juan Prim appraised the situation correctly when he reported that, contrary to the claims of a minority, the great mass of the Mexican people were not devoted to monarchical institutions.[7] In view of the hopelessness of imposing an alien system upon the Mexicans, Prim was powerful enough to shift Spain's forces from Mexico to Santo Domingo. A conflict of dynastic interests also influenced this decision. If a throne were to be erected in Mexico, Madrid wanted it to be occupied by one of its princes and not by an Austrian, as the French proposed for reasons of political expediency.[8]

lightening discussion of this question see Dexter Perkins, *The Monroe Doctrine, 1826-1867* (Baltimore, 1933), pp. 422 ff.

5. Russell to Cowley, Foreign Office, September 27, 1861. *CP Mexique*, LV. Copy.

6. Wyke to Russell, Vera Cruz, February 23, 1862. *CP Mexique*, LVIII.

7. Prim to Napoleon III, Orizaba, March 17, 1862, in E. Lefèvre, *Documents officiels recueillis dans la secrétairerie privée de Maximilien* (Bruxelles, 1869), I, 299 ff.

8. According to Dayton, "France is looking for the means of affording an equiva-

The French Emperor deceived nobody with his declarations that he envisioned no conquest of any part of Mexico for his country or for his family.[9] As far back as the early 1840's, when Louis Napoleon served his prison term at Ham for his second unsuccessful attempt to overthrow the government of Louis Philippe, he began to dream of a great empire in Central America. It might be to a French empire what India had been to Great Britain. It would bring immortal fame to him, glory and riches to France. When Emperor Napoleon III embarked upon his Mexican enterprise, he was guided by the mental blueprints of the prisoner of Ham. His letter to General Élie Forey, the commander of the expeditionary force of some 36,000 troops, revealed the multiple objectives of his scheme.[10] The collection of claims and the protection of French nationals were only secondary to the containment of the dominating influences of the United States in the Gulf region. According to the more than frank interpretation of *La France*, sometimes called the unofficial mouthpiece of the Empress, the expedition put the Americans on notice: "You shall go no further."[11] Positively, it sought to strengthen the Latin race, Catholicism, monarchical institutions, and French commercial relations. Among other prominent personalities, Empress Eugénie and Finance Minister Achille Fould eliminated any doubt about the priority of these ulterior motives.[12] The proclamation of a monarchy by a selected group of Mexicans and the subsequent invitation to the Archduke of Austria to head it implemented the original French design.

Under these circumstances, the role Napoleon's half-brother, the Duke de Morny, played in the launching of this adventure was subordinate. As the result of a deal with the Swiss-born banker

---

lent to Austria for what the Dynasty of Napoleon means, at a convenient season, to take from her." Dayton to Seward, Paris, February 18, 1862. *DDFDS*, (MF) XXXIV-54. Bigelow suggests that Napoleon chose Maximilian to appease the Church and Austria. John Bigelow, *Retrospections of an Active Life* (New York, 1909-13), II, 254. See also M. Paléologue, *The Tragic Empress* (New York, 1928), pp. 92-93.

9. Dayton to Seward, Paris, March 24, 1863. *DDFDS*, (MF) XXXIV-56.

10. The full text of this letter of July 3, 1862, has been published in Vine Wright Kingsley, *French Intervention in America* (New York, 1863), p. 21.

11. *La France*, September 9, 1862. See also Frank Edward Lally, *French Opposition to the Mexican Policy of the Second Empire* (Baltimore, 1931), pp. 56-57.

12. Fould to Napoleon III, Paris, August 14, 1866, in *Papiers et correspondance de la famille impériale* (Paris, 1870), pp. 73-77. For Eugénie's influence in this affair, see P. Gaulot, *L'expédition du Mexique, 1861-1867* (Paris, 1906), pp. 19 ff.; F. Loliée, *The Life of an Empress* (London, 1908), p. 230; M. Paléologue, *Tragic Empress*, pp. 90 ff.; and Robert Sencourt, *The Life of the Empress Eugénie* (New York, 1931), pp. 162-67.

Jean-Baptiste Jecker, Morny had made considerable investments in Mexico.[13] When in 1860 President Juarez discontinued payments on Mexican bonds, he provoked some powerful Frenchmen, including Morny. Faced with the prospect of substantial losses, these French investors expected their government to protect their interests. It could, therefore, be taken for granted that this group would be among the strongest advocates for the dispatch of an expeditionary force. The primary objective of the French expedition to Mexico, though, was the realization of Napoleon's dream of empire.

Empress Eugénie more than encouraged her husband to go ahead with the realization of his empire plans. In spite of the ultimate failure of the Mexican enterprise, she courageously admitted in later years that it was she who in 1861 induced the Emperor to make the final decision. For several years Eugénie had given some thought to the Mexican project. José Hidalgo, a Spanish diplomat and an old friend of her family, convinced her in 1857 of the lasting merits of the establishment of a Latin and Catholic monarchy in Mexico. In the fall of 1861 she met Hidalgo again at Biarritz. In view of the deplorable conditions in Mexico and the preoccupation of the United States with its internal conflict, they agreed that the time was opportune for action that would bring stability to Mexico and block the future advance of Protestantism and republicanism in America. From that time on Eugénie maneuvered behind the scene until the Mexican adventure was launched.

The United States did not deny the right of France to make war against Mexico much as it would have liked to see an early end of the invasion. But it strenuously objected to any permanent occupation of Mexico with the aim of establishing a monarchical government in violation of the sovereign rights of the Mexican people. Such a course could only lead to fatal animosities.[14] Washington was not alone in holding the view that the continuance of free institutions throughout America was essential to the safety and progress of the New World. Other American governments urged Seward to organize a Pan-American alliance to drive the French from Mexico. In September of 1862 President Ramón Castilla of Peru published a manifesto in which

13. The details of these financial matters have been discussed by E. de Kératry, *La créance Jecker—les indemnités françaises et les emprunts mexicains* (Paris, 1868). See also G. Bratianu, *Napoléon III et les nationalités* (Paris, 1934), p. 21; and Octave Aubry, *The Second Empire* (New York, 1940), p. 290.

14. Seward repeatedly instructed Dayton to convey these views to the French government. Seward to Dayton, Washington, D. C., June 21, 1862; September 21, 1863; September 26, 1864. *FIDS, XVI.*

he expressed his resentment against the destruction of a sister republic. Weak as they were, the republics of Latin America saw their own existence menaced if France were permitted to get away with its imperialistic policy in Mexico.[15]

The United States never recognized the government of Maximilian. Nevertheless, as long as the Civil War necessitated it, the Lincoln administration held out to it the vague hope of recognition if it would not enter into negotiations with the Confederate States.[16] Since the Archduke fully understood that his political survival depended in a considerable measure on the future attitude of Washington, he was extremely careful not to foreclose American recognition by antagonizing the North. It is conceivable that Napoleon's Civil War policy was in the last analysis also determined by this consideration. Seward's diplomatic instructions, however, made it quite plain that as long as it was in his power, he would deliberately refuse to take cognizance of Maximilian's existence. Already before the end of the war he insisted that the diplomatic officials of the United States must not even associate with any of the so-called emperor's agents. This nonrecognition was carried so far that when Maximilian sent a special messenger to President Andrew Johnson to deliver a letter of condolence following Lincoln's assassination, the letter was not accepted.[17] The President also studiously avoided any mention of Maximilian in his first annual message to the Congress. As far as the United States was concerned, President Juarez headed the legitimate government of Mexico.[18]

Under these circumstances the already tenuous Mexican throne

15. F. Nolte, *L'Europe militaire et diplomatique au dix-neuvième siècle* (Paris, 1884), III, 364. See also J. F. Rippy, *The United States and Mexico* (New York, 1931), p. 260; and N. L. Ferris, "The Relations of the United States with South America during the American Civil War," *Hispanic American Historical Review*, XXI (1941), 65, 75.

16. Slidell to Benjamin, Paris, March 16, 1864, in *Official Records of the Union and Confederate Navies*, III, 1063-65. Also the American minister in Vienna had received reports to the effect that Lincoln was amiable to Maximilian. Motley to Seward, Vienna, March 21, 1864. Private and confidential. Seward Papers. See also K. A. Hanna, "The Role of the South in the French Intervention in Mexico," *Journal of Southern History*, XX (1954), 14.

17. Montholon to Drouyn de Lhuys, Washington, D. C., July 18 and December 11, 1865. *CPEU*, CXXXIV and CXXXV. See also H. M. Hyde, *Mexican Empire: The History of Maximilian and Carlota of Mexico* (London, 1946), pp. 157-58.

18. Seward's instructions to Campbell, the American minister to Mexico, and his conversations with the French envoy in Washington left no doubt that the United States regarded Juarez as the legitimate executive of Mexico. Memorandum of a conversation between Seward and Berthemy, Washington, D. C., January 17, 1867 *CPEU*, CXXXVIII.

received a fatal blow when on October 18, 1865, Drouyn de Lhuys offered to withdraw French troops in exchange for American recognition of Maximilian. Seward concluded from this offer that it would not have been made if France had been willing to fight for its puppet. From Maximilian's point of view this diplomatic maneuver was not only inadequate, but it also foreshadowed Napoleon's ultimate desertion. Writing to his mother, he bitterly denounced "the Old World cowards who tremble before North America."[19] To secure his recognition, he relied, therefore, increasingly on his own propaganda and attempts to bribe American politicians and newspapers.[20]

Drouyn de Lhuys's withdrawal offer amounted to an admission of Seward's repeated charge that the French troops were not in Mexico merely to settle legitimate grievances. This diplomatic *faux pas* further weakened the French claim that they had not been sent there to make monarchical proselytes, but only to get financial satisfaction. Seward did not object to the temporary presence of French soldiers in Mexico for purposes recognized in international law, but to their employment as political instruments for the purpose of making Maximilian's position secure. He could not, therefore, accept Drouyn de Lhuys's proposition.

Frenchmen debated the wisdom of the Mexican expedition. Those favoring it as an essential prerequisite for the universally beneficial regeneration of Mexico were also optimistic about America's eventual acquiescence in the developments south of the border. On the other hand, opposition to the undertaking became more vociferous as complications mounted. Scattered early warnings about incalculable consequences which might result from it grew by 1866 to a general clamor to end the "gigantic blunder." Not only in Paris, but in the provinces as well, people demanded the early return of the troops. Such political leaders as Antoine Pierre Berryer, Jules Favre, Louis Garnier-Pagès, and Louis A. Thiers vigorously attacked the policy which "confounded reason." These critics opposed even the attempt to reduce Mexico to a vassal state because it was certain to antagonize the United States and to make France suspect throughout the Western Hemisphere. They expected neither an enhancement of the glory of France nor the revitalization of the Latin race to come out of this financially unsound adventure.[21] History also vindicated the judg-

19. Egon Caesar Corti, *Die Tragödie eines Kaisers* (Wien, 1949), p. 250.

20. Robert W. Frazer, "Maximilian's Propaganda Activities in the United States, 1865-1866," *Hispanic American Historical Review*, XXIV (1944), 4-29.

21. For comments on French opinion, see Case, p. 349; Lally, pp. 30-32; René Arnaud, *La Deuxième République et le Second Empire* (Paris, 1929), p. 226;

ment of the French ambassador to the Court of St. James's, Count Flahaut, who vainly cautioned his government on May 18, 1862, that "the overthrow of Juarez . . . means a heavy burden without compensation."[22]

As long as Southerners saw in Maximilian's government an instrument that was potentially capable of being a key to their recognition by foreign powers, they were not inclined to discard it. Once this hope became baseless, they joined the rest of the American people in a unified condemnation of French encroachments on the Western Hemisphere. The North had all along only disagreed on the method of handling the French challenge. Some endorsed the course charted by the Secretary of State which aimed at the withdrawal of the foreign troops through diplomatic negotiations. Certainly, as long as the Civil War lasted, France was not to be provoked into military intervention against the Union. Others regretted that the Senate Foreign Relations Committee buried the resolution (January 11, 1864) of Senator James A. McDougall of California, which called for a declaration of war against France if its troops were not withdrawn within a stipulated—but reasonable—time.[23] The Chicago *Tribune* and the New York *Herald* reflected the mood of many Americans who were mentally prepared for such a war to take place soon after the restoration of the Union.[24] Supporters of firm action were particularly annoyed by what they called Seward's dilly-dallying soft policy after the Civil War. In the summer of 1865 press attacks against the foreign occupation of Mexico became so violent that the French minister visited James Gordon Bennett, the editor of the New York *Herald,* at his country home to assure him that this occupation was not intended to last forever.[25] Gradually the American press came around to Seward's view that a pacific solution of the problem was both feasible and preferable.

Jules Favre, *Discours parlementaires* (Paris, 1881), II, 167 ff.; A. Thiers, *Discours parlementaires* (Paris, 1881), XI, 240 ff. For a journalistic defense of the expedition, consult *La France,* November 18 and 19, 1865, and *Le Constitutionel,* January 7, 1866. On the opposing side, see *Le Temps,* September 3, 1863.

22. Flahaut to Thouvenel, London, May 18, 1862. Papiers Thouvenel, VIII.

23. *Sen. Res.,* 38 Cong., 1 sess., No. 13. (January 11, 1864). The Lincoln administration had reason to be pleased with Senator Sumner's "judicious" handling of this belligerent proposition. Edward L. Pierce, *Memoirs and Letters of Charles Sumner* (Boston, 1893), IV, 118.

24. Francis Xavier Gerrity, "American Editorial Opinion of the French Intervention in Mexico, 1861-1867" (Ph.D. dissertation, Georgetown University, 1952), pp. 92-97, 334-35. See also Gazley, pp. 297-301.

25. Montholon to Drouyn de Lhuys, Washington, D. C., August 8, 1865. *CPEU,* CXXXV.

From the beginning of this episode Napoleon's official explanation for the presence of French troops in Mexico left the door open for their eventual withdrawal. Presumably they constituted only a "police force" to establish order, not an army to conquer.[26] According to the Convention of Miramar (April 10, 1864) the number of French soldiers in Mexico was to be gradually reduced to 20,000 by 1867. Although France pledged itself in the secret supplement to this convention that its "assistance shall never fail the new Empire,"[27] the unqualified use of the term "assistance" could be broadly interpreted. It could mean moral, diplomatic, and financial as well as military assistance.

Once the American Union had been re-established, relations with the United States again weighed more heavily in the international scales of France than those with Mexico. Seward's tactic of applying ever-growing pressures to force France into a diplomatic retreat frankly alarmed Paris. What was the meaning, it wondered, of the Secretary's insinuation to the Prussian envoy that the Mexican question was moving from the hands of the governments to those of the peoples?[28] During this crucial time in European history the possibility of a war with the United States disturbed French statesmen. To reinsure himself against such an eventuality, Napoleon proposed an alliance to Britain (November 30, 1865) by which the two countries would come to each other's assistance in case of aggression by the United States against either of them. Lord Cowley correctly anticipated the negative reply of his government to such a suggestion. On December 4 Lord Clarendon turned it down on the ground that Britain would gain nothing from such an arrangement. If the United States seized Canada, he doubted very much that Napoleon would be in the position to send an adequate army to help save this British possession. Such an alliance would, therefore, not only be inoperative, but might provoke the injury it would be designed to cure.[29]

Although neither France nor the United States wanted a war, the Mexican question was explosive enough that they might drift into one. It is a matter of record that, when Lincoln permitted the politically experienced Francis P. Blair to meet Jefferson Davis on January 12, 1865, they discussed the possibility of a united military effort against

26. Willson, *Ambassadors to France*, pp. 284-85.
27. Corti, *Tragödie*, p. 107.
28. Montholon to Drouyn de Lhuys, Washington, D. C., November 20, 1865. CPEU, CXXXV.
29. F. A. Wellesley, ed., *Secrets of the Second Empire* (New York, 1929), p. 290.

Napoleon's puppet.[30] General Grant's readiness for a march into Mexico and the surreptitious transfer of arms to the forces of Juarez caused Marshal Bazaine to concentrate his forces so that he could repel an American attack if it should take place.[31] Some French observers considered President Andrew Johnson quite capable of precipitating it in order to silence his domestic opposition.[32] Actually, Seward and the French minister in Washington worked hard to head off such a conflict.[33] Typical of the Secretary's basically peaceful intentions was his success in persuading General John M. Schofield to go to Paris to talk the French out of Mexico rather than to fight them in Mexico. Although Schofield, a known advocate of military intervention in Mexico, never got his "legs under Napoleon's mahogany," his presence in the French capital (he arrived in December, 1865) furthered Seward's war of nerves.[34] For this was the real meaning of Schofield's mission. Prior to it Seward had made a series of veiled diplomatic threats.[35] Bigelow, too, saw no harm in conveying to his foreign colleagues the impression that his government's forbearance with Napoleon's Mexican policy was nearing a critical stage.[36]

The Secretary of State was determined to negotiate the early removal of French troops and to insist on the complete disappearance of the European inspired and controlled monarchical regime of Mexico. That not all the credit for such a final settlement is due to him alone detracts nothing from the patient perseverance and skillfulness with which he handled this delicate problem. Several factors played into his hands. Among them were the difficulties French troops encountered in Mexico, the failure of Maximilian to make himself acceptable to the Mexican people, and the growing political ferment in

30. Coulter, The Confederate States, pp. 551-52.

31. On September 1, 1865, General Grant recommended to President Johnson "that notice be given the French that foreign troops must be withdrawn from the continent." Perkins, p. 496. Some French officers, too, would not have minded "une belle et bonne guerre" with the United States. Taxile Delord, Histoire du Second Empire (Paris, 1869), IV, 273; Nolte, III, 402-3.

32. Berthemy to Moustier, Washington, D. C., January 14 and March 6, 1867. CPEU, CXXXVIII.

33. Montholon was a very unenthusiastic defender of Maximilian's interests. E. C. Corti, Maximilian and Charlotte of Mexico (New York, 1928), p. 618; Frazer, pp. 6, 28.

34. For Schofield's own report, see John M. Schofield, Forty-Six Years in the Army (New York, 1897), pp. 384-93.

35. These developments have been well described by Perkins, pp. 489-502. The French were particularly upset when in November of 1865 the United States nominated a minister to the Republic of Mexico. Montholon to Drouyn de Lhuys, Washington, D. C., November 20, 1865. CPEU, CXXXV.

36. Bigelow to Seward, Paris, November 21, 1865. Bigelow Papers.

Europe. Under these circumstances it became increasingly apparent to Napoleon that he alone could not deal firmly with the Mexican and American opposition. He could temporarily disregard his own domestic opposition to this adventure, but when his key ministers—Fould, Rouher, and Drouyn de Lhuys—urged him to extricate himself from this debacle the Emperor clearly had to choose the lesser evil. Even his greatly disappointed wife courageously agreed that the venture has been a costly mistake.[37]

Confronted with a difficult situation in Mexico, the Emperor made an agonizing reappraisal. By the end of 1865 the cost of the expedition had already exceeded the original claim against Mexico, and there was little hope for an early domestic peace in this troubled land. The unexpected restoration of the Union and the drift toward a major crisis in Europe also contributed to Napoleon's decision to abandon his ill-conceived adventure. Hoping to avoid a war with the United States, he issued his evacuation order as early as January 15, 1866.[38] It did not come as a surprise to Marshal Bazaine, for Napoleon and Drouyn de Lhuys had previously advised him that "several reasons, unnecessary to enumerate, call for the end of our occupation."[39] The Foreign Minister had also sent confidential instructions to alert Maximilian to the impending turn of events.[40]

There can be no doubt that the dramatic developments in Mexico in 1866 and 1867 were accelerated by the Austro-Prussian struggle for supremacy in German affairs.[41] As the outcome of this rivalry was certain to affect the continental balance of power, French authorities recognized that they could not afford to have 110,000 soldiers outside of Europe. The astute American minister at Brussels, Henry S. Sanford, reported on November 10, 1865, that "it is very evident that the Emperor's policy now is to concentrate his strength . . . in view

37. M. Fleury, Memoirs of the Empress Eugénie (New York, 1920), II, 121; Robert Schnerb, Rouher et le Second Empire (Paris, 1949), pp. 180-81; Lally, pp. 148-50. The House of Rothschild, too, had little faith in the Mexican Empire. Sanford to Seward, Brussels, August 1, 1865. Seward Papers.

38. Paul Gaulot, L'Empire de Maximilien (Paris, 1890), pp. 321-22; H. Murray Campbell, The French Intervention and the Empire of Maximilian, 1862-1867 (Mexico City, 1951), p. 24.

39. Gaulot, p. 322; Ch. Blanchot, L'intervention française au Mexique (Paris, 1911), III, 79.

40. Drouyn de Lhuys to Dano, Paris, November 28, 1865. CP Mexique, LXIV.

41. Claude A. Duniway, "Reasons for the Withdrawal of France from Mexico," American Historical Association Reports, I (1902), 315-28; Albrecht zu Stolberg-Wernigerode, Bismarck und die Verständigungspolitik, 1864-66 (Berlin, 1929), pp. 81-82; Aubry, p. 401; and Gaulot, pp. 326 ff.

of the contingencies in European politics."[42] The French Foreign Minister frankly admitted in January of 1867 that "in view of the future, the Emperor's government desired to concert its policy with that of the United States."[43]

It must be realized, moreover, that Otto von Bismarck played an important role in the Franco-American conflict over Mexico. He followed the Franco-American crisis late in 1865 with more than an ordinary interest. He was concerned that its sudden liquidation might dispose France to interfere with his Austrian policy. He also did not want the United States to push the French Emperor to the point of humiliation, lest Napoleon might seek to recover the prestige he lost in the New World by troubling the Old.[44] The Prussian statesman preferred to see France either faced with the threat of an American war or actually engaged in it. At the same time he wished to give the appearance of being well disposed towards both countries.[45] His Machiavellian instructions to Count Robert von der Goltz, the Prussian ambassador in Paris, made it plain that his transcending interest in the Mexican question was to exploit it so as to minimize French intervention in case of a conflict with Austria.[46] The outbreak of such a conflict was merely a matter of time. For Bismarck had long been convinced that the unification of Germany would be impossible as long as Austria was in a position to dominate German affairs. He prepared well for the showdown with Austria, both diplomatically and militarily. By the time the dispute over Holstein led to the Austro-Prussian War in June, 1866, the Iron Chancellor had done his best to isolate Austria. He could count upon Great Britain's abstention from interference in primarily continental affairs. Russia was not only on friendly terms with Prussia to which it was grateful for its cooperation at the time of the Polish uprising (1863), but it also had not forgotten Austria's occupation of Wallachia and Moldavia during the Crimean War. Italy's grievances against Austria were of long standing. Still, to assure himself of Italy's aid, Bismarck promised it Venetia. And

42. Sanford to Seward, Paris, November 10, 1865. Seward Papers. The Prussian military attaché in Paris also reported that French authorities were fully aware of the handicap created by the stationing of 30,000 soldiers in Mexico and 80,000 in Algeria. Stolberg-Wernigerode, pp. 82-83.

43. Moustier to Dano, Paris, January 15, 1867. *CP Mexique*, LXIX.

44. The Prussian ambassador in Paris conveyed this view to Bigelow in the course of a long conversation on January 4, 1866. Bigelow to Seward, Paris, January 5, 1866. Confidential. Seward Papers. See also Sanford to Seward, Brussels, February 2, 1866. Seward Papers.

45. Instructions to Count von der Goltz, Berlin, December 18, 1865. Otto von Bismarck, *Die Gesammelten Werke* (Berlin, 1928), V, 340-42.

46. Instructions to Count von der Goltz, Berlin, January 5, 1866. *Ibid.*, V, 350-51.

as far as France was concerned, he tried to cultivate an atmosphere that would make Napoleon hesitate before turning against Prussia. Toward that end he vaguely intimated to the Emperor that Prussia would raise no objections to the territorial expansion of France. It is important to keep these European developments in mind because they had a profound influence on the French course in Mexico. The growing European tensions preoccupied the ailing Emperor. On March 12, 1866, Austria warned him that in case of its defeat the rest of Europe would not escape the consequences of such a disaster. It pleaded for his support, at least his moral support, so as to induce Italy to remain neutral in case of an Austro-Prussian war.[47] But underestimating the military capacities of Prussia, Napoleon expected either an Austrian victory or a drawn-out war which would enable him to take full advantage of the situation at a time of his choosing. The Prussians' quick victory over the Austrians after seven weeks of fighting deprived Napoleon of timely intervention and, of course, of the opportunity of making the hoped-for territorial gains. What was even worse, a mighty Prussia, capable of accomplishing the unification of Germany, constituted a considerable threat to France. Bismarck's insistence on moderate peace terms for Austria, moreover, did not augur well for the future of Franco-Prussian relations. In view of these developments the French government became convinced of the wisdom of liquidating the costly Mexican adventure as soon as possible and of restoring normal relations with the United States. As the impending Austro-Prussian War was one of the important factors leading to Napoleon's decision to evacuate his troops from Mexico, the completion of this evacuation ahead of schedule was in the last analysis brought about by the major power-political shifts in Europe.

The role of James Watson Webb in the negotiations leading to the troop evacuation has long been a matter of controversy. General Webb's personal acquaintance with the French Emperor can be traced to Louis Napoleon's exile in the United States. He renewed this contact on July 27, 1861. President Lincoln had recently appointed him as minister to Brazil, and he decided to go to Rio de Janeiro via France. Napoleon received him at Fontainebleau and discussed with him, among other questions, the problems arising from the blockade of Southern ports.[48] The two continued to correspond. In the course

47. Chester Wells Clark, *Franz Joseph and Bismarck before 1866* (Cambridge, Mass., 1934), pp. 404-5.

48. Webb to Seward, June, 1863. Webb Papers. See also Blanchard Jerrold, *The Life of Napoleon III* (London, 1882), IV, 342-46.

of this correspondence Webb warned the Emperor of the danger of war with the United States if he persisted in pursuing his empire scheme in Mexico. In his reply of May 23, 1863, the French monarch assured Webb that he entertained no ambitious plans with respect to Mexico and that he would withdraw his troops as soon as he could do so honorably. It is very likely that the contents of this letter, which Webb forwarded to the Secretary of State who in turn showed it to the President, caused the Lincoln administration to exercise more restraint than it otherwise might have felt justified to adopt even during the war years.[49]

In 1865 he returned home via France. When, late in 1865, Napoleon learned of the General's presence in Europe, he sent him a cordial invitation to come to St. Cloud. The Emperor liked secret diplomacy, and just at this time he wanted to talk with an American diplomat whom he could entrust with a verbal message for President Johnson. Thus neither Bigelow nor his own Foreign Minister would for the time being know what he had said. The Emperor expressly insisted on this secrecy when he "breakfasted" with Webb for two hours and five minutes on the morning of November 10.[50] According to Webb's memorandum about this meeting,[51] it was he who once more asked the Emperor to agree in principle to the evacuation. Napoleon was willing to do this, but he hesitated to go into details when Webb raised the question of setting a definite time for the withdrawal. He rejected the idea of even a partial withdrawal in six months because he felt the need for enough time to make the necessary physical and psychological preparations for such a reversal of policy. In the end Napoleon declared his readiness to withdraw his troops from Mexico over a period of the next two years. If such an arrangement would be acceptable to the President, he promised to announce it through the *Moniteur* in April of 1866. The question of Maximilian's recognition by Washington was also discussed. It appears that both statesmen believed in the practical wisdom of leaving to the Mexican people the

49. This letter, now part of the Yale collection of Webb Papers, was so treasured by Seward that he "found" it only after several requests for its return. A translated copy of it is among the Seward Papers at the University of Rochester Library. On October 22, 1863, Webb reported to Seward about another letter in which Napoleon wrote: "The Mexican affair torments me. All I desire is to see the country prosperous, so that I can withdraw my troops." Seward Papers.

50. Webb advised Seward of this "most satisfactory meeting" in an unofficial note, dated Paris, November 13, 1865. Seward Papers. That Napoleon showed an inclination to disregard regular diplomatic channels was previously illustrated by his conversations with Lindsay and Roebuck in the course of the Civil War.

51. The Webb Papers contain this detailed memorandum.

ultimate choice of their system of government. Webb arrived in New York on December 5 and repaired immediately to Washington. On the evening of the following day Seward asked him to inform Napoleon of the President's cordial approbation of the proposed solution of this diplomatic problem.[52]

By the time the Secretary of State warned France to consider the consequences which might result from European attempts to overthrow republican institutions in America (December 6, 1865),[53] Seward knew that in the Emperor's mind the decision to evacuate the troops had already been made. Also the subsequent inquiry regarding the date of their withdrawal was primarily designed to expedite the final exodus, aside from appeasing those domestic critics of the Secretary who wanted him to get tough with France. The tone of Seward's diplomatic notes to France became more energetic in proportion to the determination of the French to retire from Mexico.

While Seward's diplomatic correspondence between December 6, 1865, and April of 1866 concealed his knowledge of these proceedings behind the scene, that of Bigelow and others revealed complete unfamiliarity with them. Bigelow appraised the situation correctly, however, when he continued to plead for a delicate handling of the problem so that the Emperor could leave Mexico with a minimum loss of face.[54] He was so confident that a satisfactory settlement of this issue could be worked out that he took the liberty of suggesting to Drouyn de Lhuys (December 21, 1865) that it would have a salutary effect if Napoleon would in his own time and way name a period when his flag would be withdrawn from Mexico.[55]

If vanity drove Webb to exaggerate his contribution to the settlement of this episode, it may also explain Seward's silence regarding it.[56] Even if Webb's claims were fully justified, it would, nevertheless,

52. On March 15, 1869, Berthemy sent a lengthy article of the New York *Times* regarding these confidential negotiations to Foreign Minister La Valette. *CPEU*, CXIV. Also the London *Daily News* of April 1, 1869, found the evidence about Webb's relations with Napoleon strong enough to acknowledge his contribution to the French decision to evacuate their troops from Mexico. It should be noted, however, that all this information originated with Webb. It is not clear whether and how Napoleon was advised of the Lincoln administration's reaction to his evacuation plan. Webb himself touched on this question in a letter to Seward, dated New York, April 24, 1866: "As the Emperor's messages and propositions were verbal, should they not receive a verbal reply by the same person?" Seward Papers. See also Richard Blaine McCormack, "James Watson Webb and French Withdrawal from Mexico," *Hispanic American Historical Review*, XXXI (1951), 274-86.
53. Seward to Montholon, Washington, D. C., December 6, 1865. *CPEU*, CXXXV.
54. Margaret Clapp, *Forgotten Citizen: John Bigelow*, pp. 244-46.
55. Bigelow to Seward, Paris, December 21, 1865. Confidential. Seward Papers.
56. In a memorandum, dated February 24, 1868, Webb complained about "Seward's

be historically unsound to credit him alone with an accomplishment which many conditions and officials made possible. In the last analysis Napoleon yielded to many pressures. The fear of war with the United States, which the Secretary of State had carefully fostered, and the gathering storm on the European horizon moved him to reverse his Mexican policy. Webb happened to be hardly more than the unofficial messenger of what the Emperor evidently wished to appear as his voluntary decision.

Actually, France and the United States had not reached a formal and binding agreement with respect to the evacuation problem. France had merely given a virtual promise to recall its troops. American apprehensions were not fully dispelled until the last French soldier was on his way home. But when the *Moniteur* announced on April 5, 1866, that the evacuation would be completed by November 1867, Seward went out of his way to do nothing that would impede the execution of this "voluntary" withdrawal.[57]

Before this affair was completely disposed of, new complications gave cause to renewed uneasiness. Rumors circulated to the effect that Vienna now played with the idea of substituting Austrian troops for the retiring French. Seward immediately warned the Austrians to abstain from such a dangerous course and authorized Motley, if necessary, to ask for his passports.[58] This unduly stern attitude surprised the American minister to Austria almost as much as the Austrian government. For during these early spring days of 1866, just a few weeks before the outbreak of the Austro-Prussian War, Vienna was not looking for trouble with the United States. It needed no advice from Washington—or Paris—to exercise prudence in American affairs.[59]

The French made a final diplomatic attempt to keep faith with the Mexican Emperor. They persisted in maintaining that the evacua-

---

deliberate determination from the first not to give me credit for settling this Mexican affair." Webb Papers. See also Lawrence Hill, *Diplomatic Relations between the United States and Brazil* (Durham, N. C., 1932), pp. 174-76.

57. Montholon to Drouyn de Lhuys, Washington, D. C., May 1, 1866. *CPEU,* CXXXVI. See also Paul Henry, *Napoléon III et les peuples* (Paris, 1943), pp. 80-81. Congress published official correspondence and newspaper editorials with reference to the French evacuation of Mexico in *House Ex. Doc.,* 39 Cong., 1 sess., No. 93 (April 23, 1866).

58. Gramont to Drouyn de Lhuys, Vienna, May 9, 1866. *CP Autriche,* CDXCI.

59. Lynch, *John L. Motley,* p. 89. Vienna was all along unhappy about this affair. Motley wrote to his mother on September 22, 1863: "That a Prince of the House of Hapsburg should become the satrap of the Bonaparte dynasty . . . is most galling to all classes of Austrians." George W. Curtis, ed., *The Correspondence of John Lothrop Motley* (New York, 1889), II, 238.

tion of their troops did not mean withdrawal of Maximilian's legitimacy.[60] The Secretary of State was satisfied to let this question be decided by the Mexican people. If after the departure of the French forces the Mexicans still wanted a monarchy, Seward pledged that the United States would not destroy it. There was no doubt in his mind, however, that the republic would not have been overthrown without forcible French intervention and that it would be restored once foreigners did not interfere with the judgment of the Mexican people.[61]

The final chapter of this episode proved Seward to be tragically right. Maximilian's throne began to crumble as soon as the last French troops left Mexico in the spring of 1867. Unfortunately, he did not abdicate in time to escape the vengeance of republican Mexicans in spite of appeals for mercy which several governments sent to President Juarez. In response to requests from Austria, Belgium, England, and France to intercede for Maximilian, Seward sent on June 1, 1867, telegraphic instructions to Lewis D. Campbell, the United States minister to republican Mexico. He ordered him to see President Juarez at once and to "urge clemency to Maximilian and other prisoners of war."[62] However, Campbell, who found it more convenient to establish his legation headquarters in New Orleans rather than close to the "moving" residence of the Mexican President, did not carry out this order, thus practically forcing Seward to ask for the minister's resignation on June 15. Campbell claimed that sickness and private business affairs delayed his departure for Mexico. In a letter to the Secretary of State he also confessed that he did not understand the Johnson administration's concern about "the safety of a fallen emperor whose unhallowed ambition led him to bid defiance to a principle long cherished in the hearts of the American people."[63] Under these circumstances, Seward appealed on June 15 directly to the Mexican minister in Washington, thus further attesting to the sincerity with which he pursued his diplomatic mission of mercy. Although Campbell caused his government a great deal of moral embarrassment, it is doubtful, as the French envoy to Mexico suggested to his Foreign Minister,[64] that anyone could have saved Maximilian from his ultimate tragedy.

Whether Napoleon embarked on this imperialistic scheme to chal-

60. Drouyn de Lhuys to Montholon, Paris, June 7, 1866. *CPEU*, CXXXVII.
61. Seward stood by this position which he had previously taken. Montholon to Drouyn de Lhuys, Washington, D. C., February 12, 1866. *CPEU*, CXXXVI.
62. *House Ex. Doc.*, 40 Cong., 1st sess., No. 30, p. 70.
63. *Ibid.*, p. 75. See also *Senate Ex. Doc.*, 40 Cong., 1st sess., No. 20, pp. 17-22.
64. Dano to Moustier, Mexico, July 29, 1867. *CP Mexique*, LXIX.

lenge the predominance of the United States in the Western Hemisphere, as the *Revue contemporaine*[65] asserted, or to restore the prestige he had lost because of his policy in Italy,[66] or simply for the officially announced purposes, his failure in Mexico caused him more than embarrassment. It constituted a major foreign political blunder. The full responsibility for it did not rest with the Emperor alone. Napoleon had been misinformed about the state of affairs in Mexico. Jean-Pierre Dubois de Saligny, his ambassador, and the spokesmen for the Mexican monarchists had misled him by describing the people as being eager for the establishment of a monarchy and a French protectorate. Mercier, his minister in Washington, had advised him that the United States would resign itself to an evil it could not prevent. Eugène Rouher, one of the most influential statesmen of the Second Empire, and other top advisers of the Emperor counted on the consolidation of the enterprise before Washington would be in a position to act decisively. In this respect the political leaders of France miscalculated badly. The United States was indeed temporarily preoccupied, but the French gamble in Mexico was destined to create more than temporary complications with North America.[67] What assurance did they have that even a well-prepared and energetically executed military intervention would have gone unchallenged by the Union whose military machine happened to be in high gear?

Napoleon's American empire dream weakened the position of France on both sides of the Atlantic. It dissipated her manpower and money at a time when French leadership on the continent called for their concentration, and it provoked an ancient friend. Napoleon III hoped that his withdrawal from Mexico would be convincing evidence to Washington that he "was not disposed to repudiate the great design of Napoleon I regarding the United States."[68] But it was now too late for him to revert to the Napoleonic idea of a "Great America." Speaking before the National Assembly (December 9, 1867), Louis Garnier-Pagès prophesied realistically that, because of the deep animosities Napoleon's policies aroused in America, "in a moment of peril you will find the Americans against us."[69]

65. October, 1862.

66. Teichmann, pp. 27-28; Lynch, pp. 85-86.

67. E. de Kératry, *L'élevation et le chute de l'Empereur Maximilien* (Paris, 1867), p. xviii.

68. Drouyn de Lhuys to Montholon, Paris, January 9, 1866. *CPEU,* CXXXVI. Paris now declared that it "would be completely indifferent to a United States protectorate or military occupation of Mexico." Moustier to Berthemy, Paris, September 11, 1868. *CPEU,* CXLIII.

69. L. A. Garnier-Pagès, *Discours sur la politique extérieure* (Versailles, 1868), p. 12.

CHAPTER VII

The United States and the Franco-Prussian War (1870-1871)

I

WHEN PRESIDENT ULYSSES S. GRANT appointed Elihu B. Washburne as minister to France, he meant to bestow a favor upon an old friend. Although Washburne, who had gained considerable political experience in Congress, had never been "initiated in the mysteries of diplomacy,"[1] he accepted the honor in the hope that a change of atmosphere might restore his health. The appointment to the beautiful capital of France promised to be more pleasure than work.

In the absence of any major issue he concentrated his efforts as head of the American legation in Paris on the negotiation of postal and telegraphic conventions. His correspondence in June of 1870 dealt with these projects and the long continued drouth which threatened to destroy the French hay crop.[2] To avoid the summer heat, he left Paris on the afternoon of July 2. He went to the Bohemian resort place of Carlsbad where he hoped to relax for six to seven weeks. Upon arrival at this "remote and inaccessible place"[3] he was made "somewhat uneasy"[4] by alarming news of a Franco-Prussian crisis. But believing that no really serious development was likely to take place, he did not deem it necessary to interrupt his vacation. He remained out of close touch with world happenings until July 15. The war news of that day left him no choice but to return to the French capital. After fifty-two hours of continuous travel by diligence

1. G. Hunt, *Israel, Elihu, and Cadwallader Washburn* (New York, 1925), p. 251.
2. Washburne to Fish, Paris, June 13 and 17, 1870. *DDFDS*, (MF) XXXIV-T-70.
3. *Ibid.*, July 19, 1870; see also Francis X. Gannon, "A Study of Elihu Benjamin Washburne: American Minister to France during the Franco-Prussian War and the Commune" (Ph.D. dissertation, Georgetown University, 1950), p. 69.
4. E. B. Washburne, *Recollections of a Minister to France, 1869-1877* (New York, 1887), I, 31.

and train he arrived in Paris just one day before France delivered its declaration of war to Prussia.

A relatively short crisis preceded this fateful turn of events. On July 3 the news reached Paris that Prince Leopold of Hohenzollern-Sigmaringen was a candidate for the Spanish throne.[5] It caused tremendous excitement. The French felt greatly provoked by this contemplated extension of Prussia's influence. Foreign Minister Antoine de Gramont immediately demanded the withdrawal of the Hodenzollern candidacy and issued the warning that otherwise "France would know how to do its duty in defense of its interests and honor."[6] Feverish diplomatic activities led to the renunciation of Leopold's candidacy on July 12.[7] The apparent cause of the tension seemed thus to have been removed.

However, during the next seventy-two hours Napoleon III and Otto von Bismarck pursued policies which, unwittingly or by design, destroyed the prospects of peace. The Emperor's demand for a Prussian promise never again to permit such a candidacy offended the national pride of the Germans. If Napoleon did not intend it as a reflection on the good faith of the Prussians, Bismarck chose to interpret it as a deliberate humiliation. He conveyed the impression that the Prussian answer to this demand was King William's refusal to have any further discussions with the French ambassador, Vincent Benedetti. If this studious insult was designed to goad France into a declaration of war, the Prussian count succeeded brilliantly.

The sequence of events immediately preceding the outbreak of hostilities does not fully explain the origin of this war. Even inquiries into its underlying causes have failed to establish unanimity of opinion among historians. Although France started the war in a technical sense, several considerations point toward Bismarck as its subtle engineer. His Austrian policy demonstrated that he would not hesitate to fight a war for the sake of Germany's unification. If he wanted peace, why did he secretly engineer the controversial Hohenzollern candidacy?[8] And why did he edit the Ems telegram so as to provoke the French?[9] It might, of course, be asked with

---

5. R. H. Lord, *The Origins of the War of 1870* (Cambridge, Mass., 1924), p. 26. See also the scholarly article by Willard A. Smith, "Napoleon III and the Spanish Revolution of 1868," in *Journal of Modern History*, XXV (1953), 211-33.

6. Jerrold, IV, 459.

7. Lord, pp. 26-80; Case, *War and Diplomacy*, p. 251.

8. Lord, pp. 22 ff.; Case, *War and Diplomacy*, pp. 244-45.

9. Lord, pp. 81-106. French historians hold Prussia responsible for the war. Consult A. Sorel, *Histoire diplomatique de la guerre franco-allemande* (Paris, 1875); and H. Welschinger, *La guerre de 1870—causes et responsabilités* (Paris, 1910).

equal justice: Why did Napoleon press the Prussians for future guaranties? Moreover, did he really fall into Bismarck's skillfully laid diplomatic trap or had he been waiting for an opportunity to crush the rising power of Prussia-Germany?[10]

The first American reactions to the tense situation in Europe were unfavorable to Napoleon. Wickham Hoffman, the chargé d'affaires of the United States legation at Paris, traced the crisis to jealous rivalry: "Since Bismarck has appeared prominently upon the scene, the Emperor's star has paled and his policy has been thwarted."[11] Other American diplomats thought that Napoleon was running great risks when he demanded assurances for the future of Hohenzollern-Spanish relations.[12] They and the New York *Times*,[13] which found it hard to understand "why France should needlessly complicate existing difficulties," evidently failed to see that a German-Spanish combination might be a serious threat to the security of France. George Bancroft, who represented the United States in Berlin, was greatly impressed by Prussia's military preparedness. He ventured to predict that Napoleon and his political supporters would soon find out that they had underestimated it.[14] He took it, nevertheless, for granted that this conflict constituted just another attempt on the part of France to hold Germany down.

The sudden crisis in Europe caught Washington by surprise. Events moved faster than the diplomatic despatches which commented on them. Secretary of State Hamilton Fish realized the gravity of the situation on July 12. On that day the Prussian envoy, Baron von Gerolt, read to him a confidential message which Bismarck had requested to be sent to the legation at Washington. It ominously inquired whether in case of war with France the United States would supply Germany with the means of maritime defense.[15] Fish promptly discussed this note with the President. Grant was astonished. Up to that moment he "had no idea that such a war was even threatening."[16]

10. A distinguished German historian saw in the war another manifestation of France's historic drive towards the Rhine. Hermann Oncken, *Napoleon III and the Rhine* (New York, 1928), pp. 188-94.

11. Hoffman to Fish, Paris, July 8, 1870. *DDFDS*, (MF) XXXIV-T-70. According to Bigelow, the French resented the fact that "the growing power of Germany was putting France's cherished supremacy in peril." Bigelow, *Retrospections*, IV, 416.

12. Sanford to Fish, London, July 11, 1870. Private. Fish Papers, LXX. Bancroft to Fish, Berlin, July 16, 1870. *DDGDS*, (MF) XLIV-16.

13. July 10, 1870.

14. Bancroft to Fish, Berlin, July 12 and 16, 1870. *DDGDS*, (MF) XLIV-16.

15. Hamilton Fish's Diary, July 12, 1870. Fish Papers. See also, Lord, pp. 197, 236.

16. Quoted in James Grant Wilson, ed., *General Grant's Letters to a Friend, 1861-1880* (New York, 1897), p. 68.

However, if it should break out, he told the Secretary of State, the United States would remain neutral and permit both belligerents to obtain maritime means.

On July 14 the American chargé d'affaires Wickham Hoffman cabled from Paris: "Chances this evening strong for war."[17] That the outbreak of hostilities was imminent could also be gathered from the fact that on the next day the Prussian ambassador in Paris asked Hoffman whether his country would consent to be entrusted with the care of Prussia's interests in France.[18] Since both the State Department and the Quai d'Orsay agreed to such an arrangement, other German states made the same request after the war had begun.[19]

Inasmuch as France entrusted Britain with the protection of its subjects in Germany, diplomats began to speculate why Bismarck, too, did not ask London to take care of Prussian interests in France. Actually, Lord Loftus, the British ambassador in Berlin, had gone to Bismarck to offer this friendly service. Instead of accepting it, the Prussian statesman complained about the impropriety of Britain first making such an arrangement with Prussia's enemy.[20] Since this argument was very unconvincing, Bismarck's reason for turning to the United States remained open to question. Was he afraid that he might be compelled to fight an Anglo-French combination in case his Blitzkrieg did not work out according to plans? Or was this merely another of his flattering gestures towards the United States, for the people and resources of which he showed genuine respect? Thinking in terms of a future war and trying to reinsure himself against its uncertainties, Bismarck impressed upon von der Goltz, the Prussian ambassador to France, as far back as January 5, 1866: "We must place the highest value on very good relations with the United States."[21] Observing this cultivation of German-American ties, Lord Loftus surmised in a confidential report to the Foreign Office: "Bismarck's repeated flirtations with America seem to indicate that he is planning to enlist American naval aid in case of the outbreak of a war."[22] Berlin's inquiry of July 12, 1870, attested to the soundness of this comment.[23]

17. Hoffman to Fish, Paris, July 14, 1870. *DDFDS*, (MF) XXXIV-T-70.

18. Wickham Hoffman, *Camp, Court, and Siege* (New York, 1877), pp. 136-40.

19. Several American governments also asked Washburne to take their citizens under his protection. Hunt, p. 255.

20. Veit Valentin, *Bismarcks Reichsgründung im Urteil englischer Diplomaten* (Amsterdam, 1937), pp. 425-26.

21. Quoted in Stolberg-Wernigerode, *Bismarck und die Verständigungspolitik*, p. 74.

22. Quoted in Valentin, p. 396. The report is dated Berlin, March 13, 1869.

23. To emphasize the importance he attached to the United States, Bismarck saw

Confident that he had the situation under control, Napoleon was satisfied with America's neutrality. But his government became increasingly anxious because the Secretary of State had given only verbal assurances to that effect.[24] According to the New York *Times* of August 4, 1870, the President was uncertain whether or not to proclaim neutrality. It was not until August 22, or a little over one month after the beginning of the war, that President Grant issued his neutrality proclamation.

In accordance with international law, the laws of the United States permitted private industry to sell arms and ammunitions to both warring parties. This satisfied neither the Germans nor the French who had hoped for a benevolent neutrality in their respective favor.[25] As a maritime power, France was actually in a better position to take advantage of the American laws than Germany. Congress could have interdicted the sale of contraband. But it was not in session during the critical months of this conflict, and President Grant did not decide to call a special session. More than 400,000 rifles and a sizable amount of ammunition had been sold and shipped to France before the President suspended sales from the large surplus stocks of the Federal arsenals.[26] The French interpreted this action as an attempt to appease annoyed Germany.[27] Grant's second neutrality proclamation[28] produced a similar reaction in Paris because it had the effect of preventing French cruisers from operating in the waters off the American coast. Although it greatly restricted the use of American port facili-

---

to it that his important instructions and diplomatic circulars during the war were also sent to Washington. Otto zu Stolberg-Wernigerode, *Germany and the United States of America during the Era of Bismarck* (Philadelphia, 1937), p. 117.

24. J. C. B. Davis to Fish, Washington, D. C., August 5, 1870. Fish Papers, LXXI. The mysterious suicide of the French envoy right after the outbreak of the war also caused anxiety in France. Parisians unjustly suspected that the United States was somehow responsible for it. See Othon Guerlac, "Le suicide de Prévost-Paradol à Washington et l'opinion américaine," *Revue de littérature comparée*, VIII (1928), 112; and Allan Nevins, *Hamilton Fish* (New York, 1936), p. 402.

25. Lord, p. 236; see also the decoded telegram from Gramont to Prévost-Paradol, Paris, July 18, 1870. *CPEU*, CXLVII. It read: "We are confident that the United States will observe strict neutrality and that it will take steps to prevent the exportation of arms and the sale of ships to Prussia or the Northern Confederation."

26. After the war Congress investigated these arms sales. *Senate Report*, 42 Cong., 2 sess., No. 183. The French consulate in New York received many offers from American business firms, promising prompt delivery of great quantities of arms, ammunitions, provisions, uniforms, etc. Place to Favre, New York, September 20, 1870. *CCC New York*, XXXI. See also Nevins, pp. 403-4.

27. Treilhard to Favre, Washington, D. C., January 27, 1871. *CPEU*, CXLVIII.

28. For the text of Grant's two proclamations see Richardson, *Messages*, VI, 4040-45. The United States advised both belligerents that it expected its rights as a neutral to be scrupulously respected.

ties by the ships of either belligerent, France charged that it placed its superior navy at a greater disadvantage than that of Germany. The French were, furthermore, resentful that United States marshals removed eighty-six passengers from the *Lafayette* because they were supposed to have enrolled in their army, while several Germans, among them medical doctors, managed to join the Prussian forces via England.[29] Instances of this kind occurred in violation of the express warning American authorities had issued. That the United States meant to enforce its neutrality was evidenced by the fact that it promptly informed the French envoy about rumors in San Francisco of a contemplated German filibustering expedition to Tahiti.[30]

The Germans did not regard American shipments to France as important. Bismarck thought that they would prolong the war, but dismissed them as typifying a mercantile spirit.[31] It was widely expected that the United States would benefit economically from the war. One French scholar even charged that it had enriched itself at the cost of France.[32] But the foreign trade statistics belie these charges and expectations. American exports to France fell off sharply during the war.[33] Moreover, the blockade of the Baltic and North Seas temporarily interrupted commerce with that region and contributed to a decline of the German-American trade as well.[34] The uncertainties created by this short war also had a detrimental effect on the sales of United States government bonds and the values of Federal obligations in Europe.[35] If anything, mercantile and financial considerations led Americans to favor an early termination of the conflict.

II

While the Grant administration pursued a policy of neutrality, the American people were not neutral in thought. Instead of judging the issues of the war on their merits, high officials, the press, and the public at large permitted themselves to be swayed by long-standing

29. Berthemy to Favre, Washington, D. C., September 27, 1870. *CPEU,* CXLVII.

30. Berthemy to Gramont, Washington, D. C., August 4, 1870. *CPEU,* CXLVII.

31. Bancroft to Fish, Berlin, January 18, 1871. Fish Papers, LXXV. See also Moritz Busch, "Prince Bismarck as a Friend of America and as a Statesman," *NAR,* CXXXI (1880), 6. The *Berliner National Zeitung* of October 23, 1870, however, made some disparaging remarks about this "peddlers' diplomacy" (Krämerpolitik).

32. Sorel, II, 14.

33. See Chapter IV, Table III.

34. The exports from the United States to Germany declined from $41,541,761 in the fiscal year 1869-70 to $34,610,021 in 1870-71. U. S. Census Bureau, *The Foreign Commerce and Navigation of the United States* (Washington, D. C., 1870 and 1871), 1869-70, p. 198; 1870-71, p. 191.

35. New York *Times,* August 30, 1870.

prejudices. Those Americans who sympathized with Germany now remembered the day when Louis Napoleon broke his oath of office and trampled on the Second Republic; they remembered his double-faced policy during the trying years of the Civil War; and they recalled his defiant challenges to the Western Hemisphere, particularly the recent attempt to establish a Catholic monarchy in Mexico. The time of reckoning had finally arrived for the scheming French emperor whom they held capable of forcing a war on the innocent and peace-loving German people.[36]

Many other factors strengthened the German position in the United States. In 1870, fifteen times as many German-born immigrants as French enriched their adopted country.[37] Many of them had volunteered in the Union army and, in contrast to France, their fatherland had lent moral and financial support to the Northern cause.[38] As the Republican administration acknowledged these friendly manifestations with gratitude, the Republican party showed a keen interest in the German-American voting potential. It was no coincidence that Carl Schurz, the German-born Republican member of the Senate Foreign Relations Committee, earned a reputation as an effective propagandist for the German cause in America as well as a successful mobilizer of the immigrant vote. His *Westliche Post* was only one of many German language newspapers disseminating political views which helped both the Prussian war effort and the Republican party.[39] It is impossible to determine how much the sizable German element in New York and Chicago, among many other communities, influenced the editorial attitudes of local American newspapers. It stands to reason that from the point of view of subscriptions and advertisements they could hardly ignore it.[40]

36. The Cincinnati *Gazette* of August 12, 1870, published Bancroft's despatch to that effect.

37. Immigrants born in Germany numbered 1,690,533; those born in France, 116,402. *U. S. Census, 1950, Population, II, Characteristics of the Population*, Pt. 1, Chap. B, p. 98.

38. C. E. Schieber, *Transformation of American Sentiment toward Germany, 1870-1914* (Boston, 1923), p. 4.

39. J. B. Ravold, *Français et Allemands aux États-Unis d'Amérique pendant l'année terrible* (Nancy, 1883), p. 7. The author laments that "the Republican press, in order to appeal to the German vote, echoed the Teutonic journalists." On the opposite side, the *Berliner National Zeitung* of September 18, 1870, described the Republican party as being supported by decent and educated citizens, while the Democrats catered to the mob.

40. The French consul in San Francisco complained that the *Alta Californian* "still manifests hatred and bad faith towards us." He estimated that German businessmen offered the American press twenty times as many chances for advertisements as the French. Breuil to Favre, San Francisco, March 23, 1871. *CPCEU*, XXXVIII. In

Having only recently fought a war for national unity, Northerners were quite naturally disposed to side with the people striving for unification. They agreed basically with the Providence *Press* that the main issue of the war could be summarized in the statement: "Prussia fights for nationality, Napoleon for empire."[41] Occasionally the gloomy prediction was voiced that Germany would in time employ its military system as an instrument of aggression. But this view did not fit into the American image of the Germans as a vigorous and progressive people leading Europe towards the most rational and solid liberty. The new Reich was expected to replace the imperialistic Caesarism of Napoleon with the parliamentary institutions of a peace-promoting constitutional government. "Germany's military system," wrote the New York *Times*, "implies a nonaggressive policy."[42]

It is not surprising that Germans living in the United States, like those in Newark, N. J., interpreted the war as one "between Germanism and the Latin races, between peaceful, democratic development of German civilization and the dying Celto-Romanism."[43] Even the *Times* not only misjudged Prussia-Germany and its political and military leaders, but also echoed racial and religious prejudices. It eulogized Teutonic love of liberty and peace. "The Latin races," it commented, "have done their part—and not always an inglorious one —in the world's history. Now more earnest and moral and free races must guide the helm of progress. Protestantism and parliamentary government must lead European advancement."[44]

The influence of religious views on the attitudes towards the two belligerents had been considerable. Napoleon's aid to the Pope in the Roman question and the contention that he was supported by "Jesuits, ultramontanes, and infallibilists"[45] accounted for some of the antagonism against him in the United States. One of the underlying causes of the war, some Americans thought, could be traced to the alarm with which the Church in France watched the growth of Protestant

---

Chicago, too, the French consul noted the effects of the absence of a major French business undertaking or banking house. Niboyet to Gramont, Chicago, July 22, 1870. *CCC Chicago*, I.

41. August 4, 1870. In an editorial of August 26, 1870, the New York *Times* severely criticized the French people for being "dazzled by the tinsel of an empire resting upon treachery and prolonged by fraud." In contrast, "the German people want unity for the sake of Germany, and not to make Germany a scourge to other nations."

42. September 5, 1870.

43. Place to Gramont, New York, July 18, 1870. *CPCEU*, XXXVIII.

44. The New York *Times*, August 16, 1870.

45. Bancroft to Davis, Berlin, September 7, 1870. J. C. Bancroft Davis Papers.

Germany. As the worldly champion of Catholicism, they argued, France would not tolerate a powerful Lutheran pope in the person of King William of Prussia. Similar opinions were echoed in Germany. The *Gazette of Augsburg,* for instance, wrote that "on the Rhine we did not only fight France, we attacked Rome and the Catholic clergy."[46] For this reason the Germans felt that Protestant Britain had let them down by remaining passive.[47] French Protestants too tried to translate religious solidarity into political sentiments. When after the fall of the Second Empire a deputation of Paris pastors went to thank Washburne for the recognition of the new republic, they took pride in the fact that "a great Protestant nation is the first to stretch its hand out to France at this moment of peril and pain."[48] In turn, Washburne did not miss this opportunity to refer to them as representatives of the great moral force which would assure the future of France.

This patriotic religious minority lived in a world of illusion if it looked to American Protestants for as much as moral support. To them, France was a Catholic country, and it was judged as such. The Presbyterian Reformed Synod of the United States adopted resolutions which saw in France's plight a "righteous retribution for the martyrdoms of St. Bartholomew's Day."[49] In their sermons clergymen speculated that if France had made the "right" choice at the time of the Reformation, its fate would have been a happier one. In the Presbyterian Church at Washington, D. C., Reverend Charles B. Boynton went so far as to describe the war of 1870 as "an attempt on a giant scale to arrest the progress of civil and religious freedom and to bring first Europe and then the world under the control of the Romish Church by the military power of France."[50] Carried away by what amounted to fanatic prejudice, he warned his congregation that a defeat of Protestant Prussia would be followed by a Catholic crusade against the Western Hemisphere. This exaggeration of the religious significance of the war was particularly deplored by those who followed it as a politico-military event.

It would not be entirely correct to divide American reactions to this conflict according to regional, religious, racial, and party prefer-

46. Quoted in L. de Saint-Vincent, *Les protestants et la guerre de 1870* (Paris, 1907), p. 204. The author interpreted the war as a struggle between Protestantism and Catholicism.

47. Bancroft to Fish, Berlin, July 23, 1870. *DDGDS,* (MF) XLIV-16.

48. *Journal des Débats,* September 22, 1870.

49. Gazley, p. 355.

50. Charles B. Boynton, *The War in Europe: Its Religious and Political Significance* (Washington, D. C., 1870), p. 3.

ences. Still, a certain pattern did shape up indicating the tendency of the great majority of Northerners, Republicans, and Protestants to favor the Germans,[51] while Southerners, Democrats, and Catholics were more sympathetically inclined towards the French.

Regardless of descent or religion, the disastrous turn of events filled with pain the hearts of those Americans who liked the French people. This sentiment prevailed strongly in the South. The people of the Southland, among them General Robert E. Lee,[52] saw in the French defense of homes and country a parallel to their own recent experience. Moreover, Southerners as well as the Northern minority represented by the New York *World* and the Boston *Post* distrusted the Prussians. In their judgment, the Prussian monarchists were ambitious, and their government represented a strictly military system.[53]

The Irish as well as the French in America staunchly supported Catholic France. Their demonstrations and collections developed into keen competition with those of the Germans. When a German in Illinois, for instance, offered $200.00 for the first seizure of a French battle flag, a Frenchman in California promptly raised the award to $500.00 for the capture of a German flag. Taking a cue from the German-Americans after the election of 1870, the French organized themselves for effective political action. L'Union Républicaine de Langue Française, with headquarters in New York, led a major propaganda drive. It appealed to the antimonarchical sentiments of the American people and hoped to sway public opinion by picturing the Prussian king as the merciless conqueror of the recently established French republic.[54] These attempts of European immigrants to transplant their bitter Old World partisanship gave Congressional leaders cause for concern. They pleaded for harmony among all citizens and reminded them that the United States owed much to both belligerents and was interested in the peace and prosperity of both.[55]

III

The capture of Napoleon and his forces by the swiftly advancing German war machine called for a re-evaluation of the situation. Now that the suspected and hated Second Empire was swept into the rub-

51. Gazley, pp. 316 ff.

52. D. S. Freeman, *Robert E. Lee* (New York, 1935), IV, 485. Napoleon appears to have considered offering Lee a military command. Gannon, p. 120.

53. Schieber, pp. 14-18; White, *American Opinion of France,* pp. 174-75.

54. Ravold, pp. 10-16.

55. J. Keim, *Forty Years of German-American Political Relations* (Philadelphia, 1919), p. 10.

bish heap of history, Americans were confronted with a new condition. They had never abandoned their friendly feelings for the French people. The proclamation of a French republic was likely to strengthen them. At first, however, it was received with understandable scepticism.[56] Writing from the American legation at Brussels, Henry Sanford questioned the wisdom of the republicans in assuming power at a most critical moment in French history. As he saw the latest developments, a great tactical mistake had been made. The liberal cause would have been served better if the imperial dynasty had been left with the responsibility for the war and the odium attendant upon a humiliating peace.[57]

President Grant's instructions to recognize the new republic reached the American legation in Paris on September 7.[58] In its lonely isolation France was particularly grateful for this renewed evidence of encouragement, coming, as it did, at a time when the rest of Europe remained silent.[59] It was precisely for this reason that George Bancroft, the American minister to Prussia, counseled against recognition. He thought that it was unwise for the United States, in effect, to decide for Europe what constituted the valid government of France. He feared, moreover, that it might disqualify the Grant administration from playing the role of impartial mediator should the opportunity for it present itself.[60] Inasmuch as the recognition had already taken place when his recommendations arrived in Washington, Bancroft had no choice but to accept the *fait accompli*.

When on September 20 the *Journal Officiel* belatedly published the full text of Grant's neutrality proclamation, many Frenchmen preferred to rationalize that this enunciation of American policy had lost its meaning with the disappearance of the regime against which it was originally directed. Appreciative as the government of National Defense was of America's recognition, it counted on more than moral support from the United States.[61] In the name of the solidarity of free peoples French newspapers advocated an alliance with the trans-

56. The Washington *Chronicle* commented on September 6, 1870: "To meet the responsibilities of a republican government requires a degree of intelligence and moral discipline which the French people have never manifested." The *Nation* of October 27, 1870, warned that "the French Republic is in reality nothing more than a number of men trying to establish one."

57. Sanford to Fish, Brussels, September 15, 1870. Fish Papers, LXXII.

58. Hoffman, p. 164.

59. Jules Favre, *Gouvernement de la défense nationale* (Paris, 1871), I, 389-91. *Le Rappel* of September 15, 1870, reports about a cordial mass demonstration in front of the American legation in Paris.

60. Bancroft to Fish, Berlin, September 12, 1870. *DDGDS*, (MF) XLIV-16.

61. E. Poujade, *La diplomatie du Second Empire* (Paris, 1871), pp. 160-64.

Atlantic sister-republic.[62] One paper suggested that as an additional inducement to such a pact the Union be offered a naval base in the Mediterranean.[63] Some enthusiasts actually envisioned an American expeditionary force.[64] All these expectations, of course, turned out to be illusions. If there was any doubt about this in Paris, French diplomats in the United States warned their countrymen not to engage in wishful thinking. America, they cautioned, will encourage republicanism abroad, but it "has too much Anglo-Saxon blood in its veins ever to fight a war for an idea."[65]

Neither the prejudiced nor the desperate seemed to be capable of understanding that the United States could not be expected to sacrifice its sons in a foreign war so soon after its own bloody conflict. Realistically, the Grant administration turned a deaf ear to all propositions of a belligerent nature. It made no difference with whom they originated. For the German-Americans, too, demanded an offensive and defensive alliance.[66]

Although military participation was out of the question, diplomatic intervention merited at least consideration. For the United States was not an entirely disinterested party to this conflict. It had moral obligations towards France and Germany which it could best honor by offering its good offices. Indeed, a policy of silence threatened to weaken the Union's standing as a potential moral factor in world affairs. A prolonged war was also not in the interest of the United States. To suffer the temporary interruption of immigration from Europe was one matter; to watch the reservoir of immigrants being slaughtered and Europe's economic strength sapped was another.[67] Any German attempt, furthermore, to crush France as a power was regarded as a deadly blow to its latest experiment with republican institutions. For these reasons the American press favored mediation.[68] On September 5, the Secretary of State too wrote to Carl

62. Among the most enthusiastic advocates of such an alliance were *Le Rappel* (September 10, 1870) and *L'Électeur Libre* (September 10, 13, and 20, 1870).

63. The New York *Times* of September 27, 1870, referred to this suggestion in *La Liberté*.

64. These hopes were entertained by friendly demonstrators in front of the American consulate at Pau in the southwest of France. *Journal des Débats,* September 15, 1870.

65. Niboyet to Favre, Chicago, November 30, 1870. *CCC,* Chicago, I. See also Berthemy to Favre, Washington, D. C., September 10, 1870. *CPEU,* CXLVII. And J. Valfrey, *Histoire de la diplomatie du gouvernement de la défense nationale* (Paris, 1871), I, 12.

66. Place to Gramont, New York, July 18, 1870. *CPCEU,* XXXVIII.

67. Sanford to Fish, Brussels, September 14, 1870. Fish Papers, LXXII.

68. The New York *Times* of September 8, 1870, asked: "Will the United States exhibit an almost criminal indifference to the fate of republicanism in France, leaving monarchies to plead for peace?"

Schurz that "the further prosecution of the war will be folly, madness, and cruelty combined."[69] Bismarck felt increasingly more uncomfortable because he anticipated and dreaded diplomatic pressures from various neutral powers. That his close American friend, the noted diplomat and historian John L. Motley, recommended moderation to him in an ex-officio communication merely confirmed his view that republican France could count on America's moral support.[70]

Discussion about peaceful intervention ceased being a matter of theoretical speculation when on September 8, French Foreign Minister Jules Favre requested the Grant administration to join other powers in an effort to mediate the conflict. The President desired an early end of the war and instructed Fish to ascertain Germany's disposition to a possible tender of good offices.[71] Neither the German government nor the American minister in Berlin replied to the telegraphic inquiry with equivocation.[72] Bismarck rejected all foreign interference. Bancroft was equally emphatic in his advice to abstain—as had all other powers—from taking a well-intentioned step that could only embarrass the United States. According to him, only armed intervention might possibly impress the Prussians.

This reaction profoundly affected American foreign policy. Henceforth Grant ruled out any association for collective action or any conciliatory American mission unless asked by both belligerents.[73] Even then he would merely talk with them about peace rather than serve as a mediator. The President followed this course so uncompromisingly that he also declined Jules Favre's request to authorize Washburne unofficially to ask Bismarck for Prussia's peace terms. Despairing that the American government appeared to be completely disinterested in their dilemma, the French made another appeal on October 1. This time they urged it to exercise its influence in Berlin for a peace with honor.[74] But the United States stood by its traditional policy of nonintervention. This policy had really lost its tradition

69. Gannon, p. 138.

70. Dora Neill Raymond, *British Policy and Opinion during the Franco-Prussian War* (New York, 1921), pp. 175-76. Consult also Otto von Bismarck, *Gedanken und Erinnerungen* (Stuttgart, 1898), II, 99; H. von Poschinger, *Conversations with Prince Bismarck* (New York, 1900), p. 37; and J. Schroeder and P. B. Gilbert, eds., *Lettres de Bismarck à sa femme pendant la guerre de 1870* (Paris, 1903), pp. 107, 120.

71. Fish to Bancroft, Washington, D. C., September 9, 1870. *GIDS,* (MF) LXXVII-66.

72. Bancroft to Fish, Berlin, September 11 and 12, 1870. *DDGDS,* (MF) XLIV-16.

73. Berthemy to Favre, Washington, D. C., September 15, 1870. *CPEU,* CXLVII. See also Sorel, I, 312-13. This French historian criticizes the apparent willingness of the United States to recognize the legitimacy of the German conquests.

74. French Foreign Ministry to Berthemy, Tours, October 1, 1870. *CPEU,* CXLVII.

when Secretary of State William L. Marcy offered to mediate the Crimean War. For Secretary Fish to invoke it again irritated French statesmen as much as his apparent lack of understanding that the United States could no longer afford to be unconcerned with the balance of power in Europe.[75] Gradually they came to suspect the President and his Secretary of State of harboring unfriendly feelings towards France, even towards republican France. These suspicions were painfully deepened when Fish made the hurtful statement to their envoy that he found it "difficult to comprehend how France could repudiate the responsibility for the war."[76]

The foreign policy of the United States with respect to the Franco-Prussian War was determined by self-interest and historic considerations as key figures in the government interpreted them. While the Secretary of State tried to observe a strict impartiality, the President's personal sympathies admittedly inclined towards the Germans. He manifested them so openly that he did not hesitate personally to attend a dedication of a Steuben monument, erected by the German colony in Washington. The French thought that even the forthcoming Congressional election did not excuse the impropriety of a neutral head of state being present at the delivery of speeches offensive to France.[77]

The most outspoken American Germanophile was the diplomat and historian George Bancroft. The distinguished German historian Leopold von Ranke referred to him as "one of us Germans."[78] The American minister in Berlin enjoyed the friendship of Bismarck as well as the trust of Prussia's prominent society. These feelings were mutual.[79] With all the eloquence at his command he advocated the closest co-operation between Berlin and Washington, from the immediate as well as the long range point of view. The King of Prussia, he observed, had done everything to avoid the outbreak of the war, as it was to be expected of a peace-loving people. In his judgment, Germany would emerge from the contest as the most powerful state in Europe. This fact and the confidence the United States could place in its good will would make it an ideal friend. As far as Bismarck was concerned, he loved to give the American republic

75. The French Foreign Minister commented on the margin of Treilhard's Washington despatch of December 6, 1870: "When the interests of the United States will require it, it will be glad to make alliances with France and Russia." *CPEU*, CXLVII.

76. Berthemy to Favre, Washington, D. C., October 23, 1870. *CPEU*, CXLVII.

77. *Ibid.*

78. De Wolfe Howe, *George Bancroft*, II, 272.

79. Moritz Busch, *Graf Bismarck und seine Leute während des Krieges mit Frankreich* (Leipzig, 1884), I, 219. See also Louis Lea Snyder, *Die persönlichen und politischen Beziehungen Bismarcks zu Amerikanern* (Darmstadt, 1932).

prominence in the eyes of Europe as a balance to Great Britain. Bancroft suggested, furthermore, that the foreign policy interests of Germany and the United States were running parallel, while they were often in direct conflict with those of France. Prussia's attitude during the Civil War and the Maximilian affair illustrated this as much as its adoption of the American principle by which private property would be protected at sea in time of war. He also noted that Germany desired to follow the enlightened policy of the United States in Asia, while France intrigued in that region for power "through the unctuous demands of its Jesuit missionaries."[80]   Finally, he discovered another bond between Germany and the United States in the federative system, in contrast to the centralization of all types of government in France. More than that, according to him, no other state in Europe, "England not excepted,"[81] possessed such solid and enduring republican institutions as Germany. It was unfortunate that the pro-German predilections of this scholar-diplomat made him a partisan rather than objective observer.

In his *L'année terrible* Victor Hugo[82] gave unrestrained expression to France's bitter disappointment. He wept for an America which abandoned France during its agonizing crisis and strangely manifested its republican solidarity by stooping so low as to kiss the heel of the German Caesar.

IV

Under these circumstances, even the hopeless private peace missions of prominent American citizens served the purpose of keeping alive the image of the sympathetic America the French used to like. The first of these missions was undertaken by I. L. O'Sullivan, a former minister of the United States to Portugal. After the fall of the empire he decided to explore the chances for peace by first ascertaining the maximum and minimum conditions of both sides. He left Paris on September 11, armed with Washburne's introduction to General Sheridan at the Prussian headquarters, a safe-conduct from Jules Favre and another from the prefect of the Paris police. He did not get very far before he discovered that the role of the self-appointed peacemaker is a harrassing one. The Prussians did not permit him to see Bismarck, and on his way back to Paris French officers arrested him as a German spy in American disguise. Not until his passports had been

---

80. Bancroft to Fish, Berlin, October 18, 1870. Fish Papers, LXXIII.
81. Bancroft to Fish, Berlin, October 17, 1870. *DDGDS,* (MF) XLIV-16.
82. Victor Hugo, *Oeuvres complètes—L'année terrible* (Paris, 1880), IX, 101-4.

authenticated was he free again to publish his recent experiences in French newspapers.[83]

The mission of General Ambrose E. Burnside assumed real significance because he actually held several conferences with the Prussian and French leaders. Although he did not act in an official capacity, his known closeness to President Grant and the co-operation given him by Washburne surrounded his diplomatic discussions with an air of high expectations. The majority of the French government, and particularly Léon Gambetta, were opposed to accepting the good offices of this private American citizen who spoke with no other authority than his professional prestige.[84] It yielded very reluctantly to the urgings of General Louis Trochu and Jules Favre, who were convinced that Burnside's solicitude was motivated by the belief that a diplomatic bridge between Berlin and Paris might open the way to peace. Favre, moreover, welcomed any opportunity enabling him to resume the negotiations with Bismarck which at Ferrières had left matters at an intolerable impasse.[85]

That the Prussian statesman agreed to see the American general, after having received the king's permission to do so, looked like a promising concession. It is not at all clear, however, whether in this instance Bismarck wished to give Americans rather than the English credit for an eventual peace or whether he wanted to use this mission for a Machiavellian purpose. General Philip H. Sheridan leaned towards the opinion that the shrewd Prussian count merely "fed the vanity" of Burnside for which he hoped to be rewarded with conversational observations about the conditions in besieged Paris.[86]

Between October 1 and 14 General Burnside and his aide-de-camp, Colonel Forbes, talked with General Trochu and Jules Favre in Paris, and with Bismarck in Versailles.[87] Although the French leaders de-

83. *Journal des Débats*, September 29–October 1, 1870. O'Sullivan sent a report to the Secretary of State on October 6, 1870. Fish Papers, LXXIII. For other references to this attempted peace mission see M. Busch, *Tagebuchblätter* (Leipzig, 1899), I, 387; and Hoffman, pp. 166-68.

84. L. J. Trochu, *Oeuvres posthumes* (Tours, 1896), I, 308-10.

85. Maurice Reclus, *Jules Favre, 1809-1880* (Paris, 1912), pp. 379-80.

86. Philip Henry Sheridan, *Personal Memoirs* (New York, 1902), II, 428-29. The Prussians granted General Sheridan permission to observe the war on their side. The French had previously turned down a similar request. H. von Poschinger, *Fürst Bismarck und die Diplomaten* (Hamburg, 1900), p. 395.

87. For the most detailed source regarding these talks see *Rapports de Jules Favre sur les négociations avec le général américain Burnside*, October 3, 9, 10, and 11, 1870. CP Prusse, CCCLXXIX. See also Burnside to Favre, Versailles, October 11, 1870. CP Prusse, CCCLXXIX. And Burnside to Washburne, Versailles, October 11, 1870. Washburne Papers, LXXI.

clined to send a written communication to the man of "blood and iron," they asked their visitors to convey certain verbal messages to him. Foreign Minister Jules Favre, for instance, wanted Bismarck to know that he was ready to receive any communication from him or to meet with him personally. Determined as France was to defend its soil to the utmost, the French statesman was convinced that an equitable understanding could be arranged to end this inhuman and useless war. As a preliminary to the working out of a lasting peace he asked for only two conditions: an armistice, followed by the election of a constituent assembly. If these conditions were not accepted, then France would fight to the finish. Indicative of the insecure political situation in which the beleaguered French leaders found themselves was their anxious desire to learn, moreover, what Bismarck's intentions were with respect to Napoleon. Did he intend to restore him to power or would he recognize the government of National Defense as the legitimate authority of France?

Busy as Count Bismarck was, he took time out for four conferences with the famous Civil War general. He appreciated the excellent cigars which Washburne had sent him and tried to accommodate his guests as best he could. He gave them positive assurances that he had rejected all overtures of Napoleon and was prepared to treat with the emergency government of France. In the course of these conversations the Germans gave the outward appearance of conflicting views between their military and political leaders. General Helmuth von Moltke, who attended one of these conferences, firmly opposed the granting of any armistice before all his military objectives were fully achieved. In view of this attitude Bismarck's approval of a conditional armistice made it appear that he was a civilian who bargained away military advantages for the sake of peace. In reality, his conditions left France little choice but to reject his terms and exposed it therefore to an embarrassing position before the court of world opinion. He was willing to grant an armistice of two days for the purpose of holding an election, preceded by a semi-armistice of as much as one month for the officials organizing the voting machinery. No food supplies were to be shipped to Paris during these forty-eight hours, and Alsace and Lorraine were to be excluded from participation in the election. It was contended that they should not have a voice in an assembly charged to make a pronouncement regarding their cession to Germany.

None of these terms was acceptable to the French, who wanted a durable peace, not a brief truce followed by renewed bloodshed. They were willing to submit all questions to arbitration, provided the Prussians would recognize that France could not compromise its territorial integrity or the fate of the starving population of Paris. Realizing the hopelessness of getting essential concessions from either side, the well-intentioned American general went home with little more than the polite gratitude of Favre and others who appreciated his gesture.[88] General Trochu, fatigued and disillusioned, left no doubt that he did not belong to this group. With tears coming to his eyes, he told Burnside very bluntly that neither he nor the American government had strengthened the cause of France.[89] Burnside had tried to render France a service—and failed. This, Elihu Washburne thought at the end of the war, was more than history would say about General Trochu, who failed to organize an all-out energetic effort to save France.[90]

V

As Frenchmen would have overwhelmingly preferred to see Bancroft, the advocate of close German-American ties, resume his writing of history rather than influence its making,[91] the *Berliner National Zeitung*[92] judged Washburne as unfit to play a role in the most important development of the century. In his capacity as caretaker of the German interests in France and as the envoy of a neutral power in a militarily besieged country, he was literally on the spot. His tasks were most difficult. The French at first suspected him because he was Germany's "agent." The Germans accused him of being partial to the country of the ancestors of his wife Adèle Gratiat. They attributed to his influence America's recognition of the French republic and the discernible shift of public opinion.

One of the first storms of criticisms he faced had its origin in the expulsion of German residents living in France. The Germans in the fatherland and in America were outraged and took Washburne to task for tolerating such a cruelty without a protest. Bancroft, too, asked Washington to make an energetic remonstrance and was disappointed when it did not even express sympathy for these unfortunate victims of the war.[93] The State Department explained to Baron von

88. Favre to Burnside, Paris, October 14, 1870. *CP Prusse*, CCCLXXIX.

89. Trochu, I, 309.

90. Washburne to Fish, Paris, January 30, 1871. Fish Papers, LXXVI. For additional information about the Burnside mission consult Benjamin Perley Poore, *The Life and Public Services of Ambrose E. Burnside* (Providence, R. I., 1882), pp. 286-93; and E. B. Washburne, *Franco-German War* (Washington, 1878), pp. 81-82.

91. *Le Rappel*, September 23, 1870.

92. October 18, 1870.

93. Bancroft to Davis, Berlin, September 5, 1870. J. C. Bancroft Davis Papers.

Gerolt that it could do nothing about this expulsion because the French had a legal right to order it for their own protection as well as that of the endangered lives of the enemy aliens in their midst. When Gerolt continued to press this matter, he was curtly lectured that no foreign minister could be permitted to advise the State Department as to the management of its internal affairs.[94]

Washburne and his staff worked seemingly endless hours certifying some 30,000 passports, procuring 9,500 railroad tickets, and helping thousands of destitute Germans.[95] To expedite these cases, he engaged the additional services of a clerk from the North German consulate who was familiar with the wishes of Prussian subjects. Not the least important of his efforts was to impress upon the French authorities their duty to protect the German residents from the wrath of the French people. Preoccupied with these constructive activities, the American diplomat had no time to worry about his critics.

His conscience was also clear in another matter. The Prussians had made an exception by permitting him to receive and send closed diplomatic bags via Versailles under the condition not to make outside information available to the isolated capital. Because he observed this pledge, Parisians found fault with the strictness of his professional code.[96] He could have abandoned Paris altogether when his government authorized him to leave the starving city. But he rose to the occasion. He stayed on, suffering with the rest of the population mounting tensions and hardships. For the first time in his life he, too, ate mule meat, one of the luxurious delicacies one could still buy for a price.[97] "During these terrible times," he wrote to his wife, "I have sighed for home more than ever. I would be delighted to bid a final adieu to public life."[98]

It was inexcusable on the part of Washburne that he did not return to his post at Paris as soon as he was aware of the July crisis. However, once the war began, he discharged his enlarged responsibilities to the best of his ability. He earned not only the gratitude of the various governments whose interests he looked after during the war,[99] but he also gained the confidence and respect of Frenchmen. Much as he

94. Davis to Fish, Washington, D. C., August 13, 1870. Fish Papers, LXXI.

95. Adolf Hepner, *America's Aid to Germany in 1870-1871* (St. Louis, 1905), pp. 7-9.

96. Robert Henrey, ed., *Letters from Paris, 1870-1875* (London, 1942), pp. 108-9.

97. Washburne to Fish, Paris, December 17, 1870. Fish Papers, LXXIV.

98. Hunt, p. 251.

99. See the letter from Bismarck to Washburne, Berlin, June 13, 1871, in Washburne, *Recollections*, II, 239-40.

disliked Napoleon III, he was sympathetic toward republican France.[100] He became increasingly impatient with the military masters of Germany who mercilessly "bombarded the great city without notice."[101] Living in the besieged city, there was little he could have done beyond what he tried. He would have been willing to accommodate the French government and serve as a diplomatic bridge between Paris and Berlin. But President Grant and Hamilton Fish tied his hands in this respect. The French government knew that Washburne was favorably disposed to American mediation. Jules Favre ascribed Burnside's mission as having been "exclusively due to the cordial influence of Washburne."[102] But this influence proved to be less powerful in Washington than that of Bancroft who devoted his literary talents to dissuading the Grant administration from any intervention in the war.

The heroic defense of Paris made such a deep impression upon an increasing number of American citizens that they hoped their government would help to find a basis for a negotiated peace. Such well-informed diplomatic observers as John Jay in Vienna, Henry Sanford in Brussels, and Elihu B. Washburne regretted that Prussia had not concluded a peace after Sedan.[103] Contemporary American observers learnt unofficially that Bismarck shared the view that a great opportunity had then been lost, due to the position taken by the military authorities of Prussia.[104] At the end of September, Secretary of State Fish instructed Bancroft to contribute as much as he could toward a settlement which would assure security to Germany without humiliating America's earliest ally. Fish had no intention of expressing any opinion with regard to specific peace terms, except that they should not be extreme. As he saw it, stubborn insistence on the territorial integrity of France or a drive for German hegemony over Europe would block the road to lasting peace.[105]

In his annual message to Congress the President himself declared that if "the United States can hasten the return of peace by a single

100. Washburne to his son, Paris, September 9, 1870. Washburne Papers, LXXI. See also Gannon, pp. 172-74.

101. Washburne, *Recollections*, I, 329.

102. *Rapports de Favre sur les négociations avec Burnside*, Paris, October 9, 1870. *CP Prusse, CCCLXXIX*. See also *L'Électeur Libre*, September 16, 1870.

103. Stolberg-Wernigerode, *Germany and the United States*, p. 121.

104. Reade, Jr., to Fish, Southampton, January 27, 1871. Personal and confidential. Fish Papers, LXXVI.

105. Fish to Bancroft, Washington, D. C., September 30, 1870. *GIDS*, (MF) LXXVII-66. See also Max Montgelas, "England, Amerika und Belgien zum Kriegsausbruch 1870," *Berliner Monatshefte*, XII (1934), 1057.

hour, that action will be heartily taken."[106] This sounded more impartial than Grant's inner convictions justified. He really believed in the contention that France had recklessly provoked the war with the intention of dismembering Germany and that it was reasonable, therefore, to penalize the guilty party. He showed full understanding for German demands for frontier adjustments which would forestall another resumption of France's historic drive towards the Rhine.[107] That this was the long-range objective of the Prussians was attested to by Leopold von Ranke. Thiers met the German scholar in Vienna on his return from St. Petersburg, where he had gone to enlist Russia's assistance. In the course of a conversation he asked Ranke: "With whom are you fighting now that Napoleon has been discarded?" "With Louis XIV,"[108] was the prompt answer.

For these reasons Grant was not disposed in October of 1870 to lend strong support to London's readiness to plead for an armistice. The opinion that France and Germany should be left alone to even their ancient scores was also shared by Bancroft.[109] He believed, what the Duke de Gramont describes as perfidious insinuations, that prior to the war Ambassador Vincent Benedetti had proposed a deal to Bismarck.[110] Benedetti allegedly offered French consent to German unification in exchange for France's annexation of Belgium and Luxemburg.[111] Germany, Bancroft wrote to Under Secretary of State Davis, disclaims any territory as such. But it had to seek guaranties for the day when France would annex Belgium and then threaten the Rhenish Provinces.[112] He attributed Bismarck's original demands for Metz, Toul and Verdun to the sense of moderation of the great Prussian statesman. The relativity of such an opinion may perhaps be best illustrated by a public letter of an American citizen who asked: ". . . since France is so revolutionary and such a disturber of the peace of Europe, why would it not be well for the Great Powers to divide France between them?"[113]

106. Richardson, *Messages*, VI, 4051 (December 5, 1870).

107. Nevins, p. 409.

108. Bancroft to Fish, Berlin, December 11, 1870. Fish Papers, LXXIV.

109. Bancroft to Davis, Berlin, September 5, 1870. J. C. Bancroft Davis Papers.

110. Circular of the Duke de Gramont to the diplomatic agents of France, Paris, August 3, 1870, in Washburne to Fish, Paris, August 5, 1870. DDFDS, (MF) XXXIV-T-70.

111. Bancroft maintained that he saw a note to that effect "in Benedetti's own handwriting." Bancroft to Fish, Berlin, July 27, 1870. DDGDS, (MF) XLIV-16.

112. Welschinger, *La guerre de 1870*, p. 5. These views prompted Hugo to dedicate a poem to Bancroft in which he summed up the sentiments of many Frenchmen: "A dwarf who adds his venom to his littleness still remains a dwarf." Hugo, IX, 77-78.

113. New York *Times*, August 23, 1870. See also Gazley, pp. 410 ff.

Not all Americans accepted the argument that, because in the past France had never hesitated to extend its own frontiers, victorious Germany was now entitled to reverse this process. The imposed dismemberment of France, it was feared, would bear the fruit of hatred and of future war. Speaking with acknowledged authority in the field of foreign affairs, Senator Charles Sumner, the powerful chairman of the Senate Foreign Relations Committee, publicly protested against the demanded cession of Alsace and Lorraine. The unity of France, he contended, was as sacred as that of Germany. He too held the Second Empire responsible for the events leading to the final catastrophe. But he was looking forward to a peace that would not perpetuate chronic irritation. Germany's security, he suggested, could be achieved through the complete disarmament of France. He expected the rest of Europe to follow suit once it recognized the many economic and political blessings of a nonmilitaristic order of society.[114]

Another approach to a peace settlement originated with the New York *Times*.[115] It had the distinction of being capable of implementation. The *Times* observed that the blockade of the Baltic and North Seas by the French fleet demonstrated that Germany's long-range security would be much more enhanced by outlying colonies than by the acquisition of neighboring territories. The ability of German ships to strike from their colonial bases against the commerce of its enemies might yet be a lifesaver for the Reich. The *Times* also suggested that the French Republic would find it easier to survive the diminution of its colonial empire than the cession of Alsace and Lorraine.

The detachment of these border provinces, the American diplomat I. L. O'Sullivan warned, "cannot be anything else than smouldering war *en permanence.*"[116] In a letter to Bancroft he outlined a peace plan which, in his judgment, offered Germany security without offending the national dignity of France. He proposed the establishment of a territorial barrier between France and Germany, stretching from Belgium to Switzerland. The permanent neutrality of this strip of land was to be guaranteed by all European powers. Whatever the merits of these suggestions may have been, they had no chance of even being considered by the "realistic" statesmen of Europe. Nor did

114. Charles Sumner, *The Duel between France and Germany* (Boston, 1911). This lecture was delivered at Boston on October 26, 1870. Sumner would not have opposed a moderate indemnity payment to Germany. Treilhard to Favre, Washington, December 29, 1870. *CPEU*, CXLVII.

115. August 30, 1870.

116. O'Sullivan to Bancroft, Paris, October 8, 1870. Fish Papers, LXXIII.

they reflect the views of the American government which took no part in the making of the final peace settlement.

The decision of the United States to permit these European affairs to take their natural course was not influenced by foreign powers. It has, furthermore, not been substantiated that, as a means of diverting England from possible intervention on the continent, Prussia encouraged the Grant administration at this time to press the Alabama Claims.[117] That also Russia sought to take advantage of this crisis in order to bring about a revision of the Treaty of 1856 merely indicated that the fate of France concerned these powers less than their own special interests. The one time that Grant intervened in the war was at a time when the protection of American interests in China was involved. For their sake he took the initiative in an effort to prevent a clash between French and German ships in Chinese waters.[118]

VI

America's official aloofness from this historic conflict contrasted sharply with many individual missions of mercy. Many American aid societies rendered help to the wounded and needy of both belligerents. The volunteer services of American doctors were in the noblest tradition of the medical profession. The American Ambulance in Paris gained the reputation as a model field hospital. There, as elsewhere, Americans saved the lives of great numbers of soldiers.[119] Touched by the cry of hunger and sorrow the President approved at the end of the war a Congressional resolution authorizing the use of a naval vessel to transport breadstuffs to Europe.[120] Citizens and organizations throughout the United States made generous contributions to alleviate the suffering of many destitute French families. These humanitarian manifestations were, of course, appreciated. However, the French never forgave President Grant for having abandoned them during the war and for having offended them at the end of it when he sent the customary congratulations to the emperor of the

117. Raymond, pp. 270-71.

118. J. Fuller, "Hamilton Fish," in Bemis, ed., *The American Secretaries of State,* VII, 154. In contrast to Berlin, Paris rejected the State Department's suggestion. However, French and German representatives in Japan had on their own accord agreed upon a provisional neutrality. Stolberg-Wernigerode, *Germany and the United States,* p. 117.

119. Among the several interesting studies which describe these activities in detail are: Thomas W. Evans, *History of the American Ambulance Established in Paris during the Siege of 1870-1871* (London, 1873), pp. 15-16, 56-66; W. MacCormac, *Souvenirs d'un chirurgien d'ambulance* (Paris, 1872), pp. 14-18; and P. Myrdacz and J. Steiner, *Sanitätsgeschichte das deutsch-französischen Krieges* (Wien, 1896), p. 147.

120. *Cong. Globe,* 41 Cong., 3 sess., Pt. 2, pp. 869-70, 1163.

German Reich. When Grant died in 1885, French commentators still referred to him as one of the most unjust and deadliest enemies of France.[121]

The fairness of this judgment does not pass the test of history. Grant's first responsibility was to the welfare of his countrymen. While his personal sympathies were no secret, his official policy took account of the domestic and power-political realities of the republic he headed. They added up to nonintervention. In Europe, the military rulers of Germany were determined to dictate their own terms of peace. How much would these men of iron have been softened by even the most persuasive arguments of the American President?

Within the space of a few years France and the United States went through wars which shook their national foundations. After 1871 it proved to be historically vital to France that the Federal Union had emerged intact from its sectional conflict. As the future demonstrated, with the rise of imperial Germany, France needed a friendly and strong America more than ever.

121. Theodore Stanton, "Le général Grant et la France," *Revue de Paris* (November 1, 1894), pp. 183-202. See also Georges Weill, *Histoire des États-Unis de 1787 à 1917* (Paris, 1919), p. 158.

Conclusion

THE MYTH OF THE UNINTERRUPTED historic friendship between France and the United States has been perpetuated in spite of the overwhelming evidence against it. The two countries moved from one controversy to another during the period from the July Revolution to the end of the Franco-Prussian War and established a long record of wars that did not occur. Domestic and world conditions, not considerations of friendship, dictated the avoidance of these wars.

In this deterioration of Franco-American relations fear played a much greater role than deep-rooted conflicts or ill-will. Monarchists were haunted by the spectre that a greatly strengthened United States would bring about the triumph of democratic principles in Europe. They were afraid, moreover, that the phenomenal development of the American Union would in time compel France to bow to Anglo-American preponderance.

One cannot escape the observation that France set itself the task of taming the extraordinary capacity of the American people for moving toward ever more ambitious goals. Century-old political habits had left France unprepared to adopt a generous instead of a basically negative policy toward one of the most energetic nations of modern times. Not keeping pace with the speed of the dynamic growth of the United States in territory, population, ships, and industrial might, France tried to stop and contain America. It made every effort to enlist the cooperation of Great Britain in support of this policy. This, too, contributed to the alienation between Paris and Washington. For even the appearance of an Anglo-French coalition in matters affecting the Western Hemisphere caused considerable concern in the United States. The combined might of these two maritime powers constituted a potential threat to the progress and security of the American republic.

The United States opposed, therefore, joint moves of the entente in American affairs. It protested against joint naval action in Caribbean waters and warned against contemplated concerted intervention in the Mexican War and in the conflict between the North and the South. It refused to receive joint messages of the entente's ministers. It turned down proposed tripartite agreements regarding Texas, Hawaii, and Cuba; and it declined to become a party to the international convention on neutral rights. The United States usually abstained from cooperation with France and other powers in order to isolate and separate European power combinations which it considered detrimental to its interests. It also realized that it would have been outweighed in the company of the other powers.

To evaluate the effect of the entente on American affairs is by no means a simple task. Aside from the fact that its members were not on equally cordial terms throughout the period under consideration, American problems were not its chief concern. In retrospect it appears to have been a blessing in disguise for the United States. For the historic rivalry between France and England continued to be a dominant underlying factor in the relations of the entente. Neither France nor England wanted the other to gain advantages from the United States or in the Western Hemisphere. Among other reasons, during the crucial decades of the 1840's and 1860's this rivalry contributed, therefore, to the frustration of separate or joint interventions in North America.

That contemporary Americans interpreted the significance of the entente in diametrically different ways attests to its considerable flexibility. During the Civil War, for example, the Secretaries of State of both the North and the South deplored the existence of an understanding between France and England concerning this conflict. Seward and Benjamin were anxious to separate the two powers, but for opposite reasons. Thinking in traditional terms, Seward believed that if the maritime powers should decide to intervene, they would do so jointly or not at all. Benjamin and Slidell came by the middle of 1862 to the conclusion that if intervention depended on the co-ordination of the policies of France and England, it would not come off. They pinned their hopes on the separate action of the French Emperor.

The United States was the beneficiary not just of the rivalry between London and Paris, but of the principle of balance of power which governed the affairs of the Old World. Whenever possible, Washington tried to take advantage of the troubles of Europe. In 1845 complications in Algeria and Morocco and tensions between

London and Paris made intervention in such a remote region as Texas impractical. The Suez Canal and Balkan questions and trouble in India and China made it almost certain in the late 1850's that the European governments would leave America to itself. And in the 1860's the growing political ferment in Europe restrained Napoleon's ambitions in the New World.

It should also be remembered that trade relations between the United States and the entente powers were a powerful deterrent to intervention. Europe had much to gain from a prosperous America. Furthermore, its military superiority notwithstanding, forceful intervention in the affairs of the United States would have been costly and difficult for both or either of the maritime powers. Nor did Louis Philippe and Napoleon III dare ignore the potentially dangerous admiration of French republicans for the model republic. In fact, public opinion in both countries would have made it very difficult for the governments really to go to extremes in Franco-American relations. The sentimental attachments between the American and French peoples were still deep enough to be taken into account by their respective policy makers.

That the United States was fully aware of these power-political realities is evidenced by its defiant firmness in the face of major and minor crises alike. If anything, Anglo-French opposition stirred Americans to a greater determination than ever to pursue their program of Manifest Destiny. It is noteworthy, however, that after the acquisition of California, Washington decided—not entirely voluntarily—to consolidate its position. Stronger and richer than before the Mexican War, the United States backed down in the 1850's in Cuba and Hawaii and agreed to a compromise regarding Central America. By this realistic appraisal of the limitations of its power, it removed some of the most explosive problems as possible causes of a conflict. And although it delivered evidently effective threats to France in the course of the Civil War and the Maximilian affair, it really searched for diplomatic solutions of existing frictions.

Throughout this period France disregarded the wisdom of abstaining from quarrels unless willing and able to fight them with determination. Time and again, it challenged and antagonized the United States but hesitated each time to follow through with decisive action. This vacillation and indecision was not unique with Napoleon III. Louis Philippe and Guizot had shown the same weakness in the conduct of French diplomacy, whatever the reasons for the final reversal of policy may have been. This frequently demonstrated incapacity to execute a determined policy invariably benefited the United States.

Nevertheless, these half-hearted attempts to check its development further deepened the psychological reluctance of Americans to become entangled with foreign governments. They continued to play a relatively passive role in international relations in spite of their growing might. France and the other European nations preferred it this way. They saw no reason to hasten the day when America would actively intervene in their conflicts. Under these circumstances, it was quite inconsistent on the part of France to look to the United States for aid and assistance in the Franco-Prussian War.

The foreign service of France during these decades would fare very badly indeed were it to be judged by the performance of its ministers to the United States. For these gentlemen sent very misleading estimates to their home government. They misjudged conditions in connection with Texas, Mexico, and the Civil War. They also grossly exaggerated the global ambitions of the United States by constantly describing it as being set on world conquest. By comparison, the militia diplomats of the Federal republic appraised the likely moves of France in America with remarkable realism and accuracy. The principal exception to these comments occurred during the Franco-Prussian War. Then, Bancroft's bias permeated his despatches from Berlin, while French diplomats in the United States informed their government about American attitudes and likely policies in a sober and enlightening manner.

On balance, the United States outmaneuvered France. It achieved most of its objectives in spite of French opposition and obstruction. But even more important than the immediate accomplishments was the future destiny of the two nations. France believed in the greatness of its nation; yet it somewhat lacked the dynamic drive and enterprising spirit needed to play the leading role in the modern world. Its interests centered in Europe—and Europe even then was not the world. It did not understand, moreover, that what the United States stood for symbolized the trend of the future: commercialism and the political emancipation of the masses. France paid dearly for failing to grasp in the mid-nineteenth century that the devotion of human energies to the elevation of the masses and the promotion of the political rights of the people had become the ever-urgent demand of modern times, over and above the external rivalry of states.

Napoleon III might look with contempt at American materialism. He might pity the hard-working pioneers of a society that adored wealth. He might scoff at the checks and balances of their political institutions and interpret their democracy as the despotism of the mob. Still, in this New World men and women worked for their own higher standard of living, not for the war machine and power of the state. Their very vitality secured the stability of their society which, together with their geographical insulation, guaranteed a security France could hardly imagine. The materialism which fertilized the soil of American democracy bore the fruit of freedom, and freedom meant strength.

In time, some of the worst fears of France were realized. Monarchies did make way for republics. The Anglo-American nations did outdistance France and the Latin countries. The United States did replace Europe as the leader of the world. This evolution did not develop quite as rapidly as worried Frenchmen anticipated. Nor did it bring about the dreaded results they had prophesied. Instead of the encroaching, law-flouting, revolutionary disturber of the social order, the United States matured into a law-upholding defender of a peaceful and stable world order. Instead of becoming a conqueror, it helped to free France and others from conquerors. Instead of materialistic selfishness, it displayed an unprecedented generosity towards foreign nations.

The political leaders of France in the mid-nineteenth century correctly foresaw the main course of America's future, which they loathed and tried to retard. But they demonstrated little understanding of the basically constructive nature of the American experiment with its new approaches to the problems of society.

Bibliography

I. MANUSCRIPT SOURCES
OFFICIAL PAPERS

A. *Material in the Archives du Ministère des Affaires Étrangères*

Correspondance politique

Amérique Centrale, 1853-59

Angleterre, 1844-47, 1861-64

Argentina, 1846, 1859

Autriche, 1861-62, 1866

Brésil, 1853-62

Équateur, 1852-58

Espagne, 1861-62

États-Unis, 1830-71

Mexique, 1845-47, 1861-66

Pérou, 1854-58

Prusse, 1861-62, 1870-71

Russie, 1861-64

Texas, 1833-46

des consuls, États-Unis, 1848-71

Correspondance consulaire et commerciale.

Boston, 1851-69

Chicago, 1860-71

New Orleans, 1841-64

New York, 1836-70

Philadelphia, 1850-70

San Francisco, 1849-71

Washington, D. C., 1831-73

Mémoires et documents

États-Unis, 1790-1865

France, No. 2120. (Lettres de Drouyn de Lhuys à Walewski, 1852-55)

Papiers Thouvenel, VIII, XIII, XVII (Lettres de Flahaut, Mercier et Sartiges à Thouvenel, 1860-62)

B. *Material in the Archives de France*

F 12- 2689-93, 3168, 6313-15, 6529. These bundles of documents contain material on Franco-American trade relations.

C. *State Department Diplomatic and Consular Correspondence*

Instructions to U.S. ministers to Austria, 1837-71

Instructions to U.S. ministers to France, 1830-71

Instructions to U.S. ministers to Great Britain, 1861-64
Instructions to U.S. ministers to German States and Germany, 1835-74
Instructions to U.S. ministers to Mexico, 1854-67
Instructions to U.S. ministers to Spain, 1848-63
Instructions to special missions, 1850-71
Despatches from U.S. ministers to China, 1856-60
Despatches from U.S. ministers to France, 1830-71
Despatches from U.S. ministers to Germany, 1870-71
Despatches from U.S. ministers to Great Britain, 1848-65
Despatches from U.S. ministers to Mexico, 1859-67
Notes to the French legation in Washington, 1830-70
Notes from the French legation in Washington, 1830-71
Notes to the German legation in Washington, 1853-71
Notes from the German legation in Washington, 1869-70
Notes from the French Foreign Office to the U.S. legation in Paris, 1830-70
Reports from special agents, 1830-60
Consular instructions, 1830-70
Consular despatches, 1830-70. They include letters from U.S. consuls in Algiers, Bordeaux, Guadeloupe, Le Havre, Marseilles, Martinique, Nantes, Paris, St. Pierre, and Tripoli.

D. *U. S. Presidential Correspondence* (in National Archives)
Ceremonial letters from France to the President of the United States, 1830-61
Communications to foreign sovereigns from the President of the United States, 1830-61

E. *U. S. Naval Records* (in National Archives)
Correspondence of the Mediterranean Squadron Cruise, 1848-60
Letters received by the Secretary of the Navy from captains, 1870
Letters received from commanding officers of squadrons, Atlantic, 1870-71

F. *Letter Books of the Confederate Department of State* (in MSS Division, Library of Congress)
Judah P. Benjamin to John Slidell, 1862-64
John Slidell to Judah P. Benjamin, 1862-64
Henry Hotze's diplomatic correspondence, 1862-64

PRIVATE PAPERS

(In MSS Division, Library of Congress, unless otherwise indicated)
Bancroft, George
Bigelow, John (New York Public Library)
Clayton, John M.
Davis, J. C. Bancroft

Dayton, William L. (Princeton University)
Everett, Edward (Massachusetts Historical Society)
Faulkner, Charles J. (University of Virginia)
Fish, Hamilton
Hughes, John (St. Joseph's Seminary, Dunwoodie, N.Y.)
Marcy, William L.
Polk, James
Rives, William C.
Sanders, George N.
Seward, William H. (Rochester University)
Washburne, Elihu B.
Webb, James Watson (Yale University)

II. PRINTED SOURCES

A. *United States*:

Compilation of Reports of the Committee on Foreign Relations, 1789-
   1901. 8 vols. Washington, D. C., 1901. Published as *U. S.
   Senate Doc.*, 56 Cong., 2 sess., No. 231.
Congressional Globe, 1833-72.
House Ex. Doc., 27 Cong., 3 sess., No. 197. Report of the commissioner
   sent to Europe in 1843 to negotiate a loan for the United States.
———, 34 Cong., 1 sess., No. 47. Report on the commercial relations
   of the United States with all foreign nations in 1855.
———, 39 Cong., 1 sess., No. 93. Material relating to the French
   evacuation from Mexico.
———, 40 Cong., 1 sess., No. 30. Correspondence between the Department of State and the U. S. minister to Mexico in 1867.
———, 41 Cong., 2 sess., No. 27. Material relating to the foreign
   indebtedness of the United States.
Journal of the Congress of the Confederate States of America, 1861-
   65. 7 vols. Washington, D.C., 1904-5. Published as *Senate Doc.*,
   58 Cong., 1 sess., No. 234, vols. 25-31.
Register of Debates in Congress, 1830-37.
Senate Doc., 61 Cong., 2 sess., No. 279. Relating to affairs in Hungary,
   1849-50.
Senate Ex. Doc., 40 Cong., 1 sess., No. 20. Correspondence relating
   to the Maximilian affair.
Senate Misc. Doc., 37 Cong., 3 sess., No. 38. Concurrent resolution of
   February 28, 1863, relating to foreign intervention in the Civil War.
Senate Report, 42 Cong., 2 sess., No. 183. Report on the sale of arms
   to France during the Franco-Prussian War.
Senate Resolution, 38 Cong., 1 sess., No. 13. Relating to the French
   evacuation from Mexico.

U. S. Census Bureau. *The Foreign Commerce and Navigation of the United States, 1856-71.* Washington, D.C., 1856-71.

———. *Statistical Abstract of the. United States, 1878 and 1946.* Washington, D.C., 1878 and 1946.

———. *U. S. Census, 1950, Population, II, Characteristics of the Population,* Pt. 1. Washington, D.C., 1953.

U. S. Commissioners to the Paris Universal Exposition in 1867. *Reports.* Washington, D.C., 1870.

U. S. Department of Agriculture. *Agricultural Reports, 1843-72.* Washington, D.C., 1843-72.

U. S. Navy Department. *Official Records of the Union and Confederate Navies in the War of Rebellion.* Ser. II. Washington, D.C., 1922.

Malloy, W. M. (ed.). *Treaties, Conventions, . . . between the United States of America and other Powers, 1776-1909.* 2 vols. Washington, D.C., 1910.

Miller, H. (ed.). *Treaties and other International Acts of the United States of America.* 8 vols. Washington, D.C., 1931-1948.

Manning, W. R. (ed.). *Diplomatic Correspondence of the United States. Inter-American Affairs, 1831-1860.* 12 vols. Washington, D.C., 1932.

Nasatir, A. P. *French Activities in California. An Archival Calendar Guide.* Stanford, Calif., 1945.

Richardson, J. D. (ed.). *A Compilation of the Messages and Papers of the Confederacy.* 2 vols. Nashville, Tenn., 1906.

Richardson, J. D. (ed.). *A Compilation of the Messages and Papers of the Presidents.* 10 vols. Washington, D.C., 1896.

Winkler, E. W. (ed.). *Secret Journals of the Senate, Republic of Texas, 1836-1845.* Austin, Texas, 1911.

B. *France:*

Annuaire diplomatique de l'empire français, Paris, 1858-1869.

Département de l'agriculture, du commerce et des travaux publics. *Annales du commerce extérieur,* Paris, 1854-66.

Douanes, Direction générale. *Tableau général du commerce et de la navigation,* Paris, 1849-59.

Commission chargé de réunir, classer, et publier les papiers aux Tuileries. *Papiers et correspondance de la famille impériale.* Paris, 1870-71.

C. *Mexico:*

Lefêvre, E. (ed.). *Documents officiels receuillis dans la secrétairerie privée de Maximilien.* 2 vols. Bruxelles, 1869.

D. *Collections of Conversations, Diaries, Letters, and Speeches*

Baker, G. E. (ed.). *The Works of William H. Seward.* Boston, 1884.

Basler, R. P. (ed.). *The Collected Works of Abraham Lincoln.* New Brunswick, N.J., 1955.

Bismarck, O. von. *Die Gesammelten Werke.* Berlin, 1928.

Curtis, G. W. (ed.). *The Correspondence of John Lothrop Motley.* 2 vols. New York, 1889.

Favre, Jules. *Discours parlementaires.* 4 vols. Paris, 1881.

Ford, W. C. (ed.). *A Cycle of Adams Letters, 1861-1865.* 2 vols. New York, 1920.

Hawkins, R. L. (ed.). *Newly Discovered French Letters of the Seventeenth, Eighteenth and Nineteenth Centuries.* Cambridge, Mass., 1933.

Pierce, E. L. (ed.). *Memoirs and Letters of Charles Sumner.* 4 vols. Boston, 1893.

Poschinger, H. von. *Conversations with Prince Bismarck.* New York, 1900.

Quaife, M. M. (ed.). *The Diary of James K. Polk.* 4 vols. Chicago, 1910.

Russell, John. *The Later Correspondence of Lord John Russell, 1840-1878.* Edited by G. P. Gooch. 2 vols. London, 1925.

Schroeder, J. and Gilbert, P. B. (eds.). *Lettres de Bismarck à sa femme pendant la guerre de 1870.* Paris, 1903.

Senior, N. W. *Conversations with Distinguished Persons during the Second Empire from 1860 to 1863.* 2 vols. London, 1880.

Thiers, A. *Discours parlementaires.* Paris, 1880-81.

Thouvenel, L. *Le secret de l'empereur—correspondance confidentielle et inédite échangée entre M. Thouvenel, le Duc de Gramont et le Général Comte de Flahaut, 1860-1863.* 2 vols. Paris, 1889.

Welles, E. T. (ed.). *The Diary of Gideon Welles.* 3 vols. Boston, 1911.

Wellesley, H. R. C. *Secrets of the Second Empire: Private Letters from the Paris Embassy.* Edited by F. A. Wellesley. New York, 1929.

Wellesley, V. and Sencourt, R. *Conversations with Napoleon III.* London, 1934.

Wilson, J. G. (ed.). *General Grant's Letters to a Friend, 1861-1880.* New York, 1897.

III. NEWSPAPERS AND PERIODICALS

NEWSPAPERS

A. American (in the Library of Congress)

Cincinnati *Gazette,* 1870
Jackson *Mississippian,* 1854
New Orleans *Courrier de Louisiane,* 1848
    Daily Picayune, 1848

New York *Courrier des États-Unis*, 1848-62
   Globe, 1845
   Herald, 1862
   Journal of Commerce, 1849-59
   Times, 1852-71
   World, 1863
Philadelphia *Pennsylvania Inquirer*, 1852-53
Providence *Press*, 1870
Richmond *Daily Dispatch*, 1861-64
Springfield *Illinois State Journal*, 1863
Washington, D.C., *Chronicle*, 1870
   Globe, 1835-45
   National Intelligencer, 1835-65

B. French (in the Bibliothèque Nationale, Paris)
   Charivari, 1852-54
   Le Constitutionel, 1835-66
   L'Électeur Libre, 1870
   Le Figaro, 1890, 1898
   Gazette de France, 1848-52
   Journal des Débats, 1835-70
   Le Moniteur, 1846-70
   La Patrie, 1845-57
   La Presse, 1846-60
   Le Rappel, 1870
   Le Siècle, 1851-53
   La Semaine Financière, 1857-60
   Le Temps, 1861-71
   L'Univers, 1848-54

C. German
   Berliner National Zeitung, 1861-71

PERIODICALS

A. American
   American Journal of International Law
   American Historical Review
   American Railroad Journal, 1852-61
   Bankers' Magazine, 1850-57
   California Historical Society Quarterly
   Catholic Historical Review
   Catholic Magazine, 1848
   Commercial and Financial Chronicle
   De Bow's Review, 1846-70
   Harper's Magazine, 1856-65

Hispanic American History Review
The Index (London), 1862-64
Journal of the History of Ideas
Journal of Modern History
Journal of Political Economy
Journal of Southern History
Merchant's Magazine and Commercial Review, 1855-60
Mississippi Valley Historical Review
North American Review, 1835-70
Pacific Historical Review
Pacific Northwest Quarterly
U.S. Democratic Review, 1846-52

B. French

Journal des économistes, 1841-68
Revue contemporaine, 1862
Revue d'histoire diplomatique, 1887-1950
Revue historique, 1920-55
Revue indépendante, 1844
Revue de littérature comparée, 1928
Revue des deux mondes, 1835-1940
Revue de Paris, 1894-1920
Revue rétrospective, 1848
Revue des sciences politiques, 1885-1940

C. German

Preussische Jahrbücher, 1861-62

IV. MEMOIRS, THESES, BOOKS, AND ARTICLES
(With brief comments)

Chapter I. *Republican Ideology and Diplomacy.*

"Absolutism versus Republicanism: The State of Europe," *U.S. Democratic Review*, XXXI (1852), 592-600.

Blanc, Louis. *Histoire de la révolution de 1848.* 2 vols. Paris, 1870. An account by the leader of the Socialist movement in France.

Broglie, Albert de. "1852 et la révision de la constitution," *RDDM* (May 15, 1851), pp. 593-610.

Callahan, J. *Cuba and Its International Relations.* Baltimore, 1899.

Calman, Alvin. *Ledru-Rollin and the Second French Republic.* New York, 1922. Discusses the views and activities of this radical republican.

Castelar, Emilio. "The Republican Movement in Europe," *Harper's New Monthly Magazine* (June-November, 1872), pp. 47 ff.

Cauvin, Henri. "La France est monarchique," *Constitutionel*, December 5, 1852.

Chinard, Gilbert. "L'Amérique et la révolution de 1848," *French-American Review*, I (1948), 264-72.

———. "Comment l'Amérique reconnut la République de 1848," *French-American Review*, I (1948), 83-109.

Collins, R. W. "Catholicism and the Second French Republic, 1848-52." Unpublished Ph.D. dissertation, Columbia University, 1923. An enlightening analysis of the vital role played by French Catholics in the rise and fall of the Second Republic.

Copans, Simon J. "French Opinion of American Democracy, 1852-1860." Unpublished Ph.D. dissertation, Brown University, 1942. An extensive survey of French opinion sources.

Curti, Merle E. *Austria and the United States, 1848-1852*. Northampton, Mass., 1926. A valuable contribution to American history during the era of the mid-nineteenth-century revolutions.

———. "John C. Calhoun and the Unification of Germany," *AHR*, XL (1935), 476-78.

———. "The Impact of the Revolutions of 1848 on American Thought," *Proceedings of the American Philosophical Society*, XCIII (1949), 209-215.

———. "George Sanders—American Patriot of the Fifties," *South Atlantic Quarterly* (January, 1928), pp. 79-87.

———. "Young America," *AHR*, XXXII (1926), 34-55.

Curtis, Eugene N. *The French Assembly of 1848 and American Constitutional Doctrine*. New York, 1918. Discusses French arguments regarding the advisability of adopting certain principles of the American Constitution.

———. "American Opinion of the French Nineteenth-Century Revolutions," *AHR*, XXIV (1924), 249-70.

Cuvillier-Fleury, A. *Portraits politiques et révolutionnaires*. Paris, 1852. Articles from the *Journal des Débats*.

Dansette, A. *Explication de la Deuxième. République*. Paris, 1942. Emphasizes the significance of social and economic problems.

———. *Deuxième République et Second Empire*. Paris, 1942.

Dautry, Jean. *Histoire de. la révolution de 1848 en France*. Paris, 1948. A detailed presentation of the problems and accomplishments of this revolution.

Delassus, Henri. *Le problème de l'heure présente*. Lille, 1904. Comments on the desire of French republicans to establish the United States of Europe under French leadership.

Lucas-Dubreton, J. *Lamartine*. Paris, 1951. A modern biography of the poet-statesman of the Second Republic.

Durkin, J. T. "Four Letters to Fordham on the Republic of 1848," *Thought* (March, 1941), pp. 40-50.

Ettinger, A. A. *The Mission to Spain of Pierre Soulé*. New Haven,

Conn., 1932. An interesting work on the eccentric American diplomat who was close to the revolutionary leaders of Europe.

Farmer, Paul. "Some Frenchmen Review 1848," *Journal of Modern History,* XI (1948), pp. 320-25.

"French Ideas of Democracy and a Community of Goods," *NAR* (October, 1849), pp. 277-325.

Garros, Louis. *Le coup d'état du 2 décembre.* Paris, 1952.

Gazley, J. G. *American Opinion of German Unification, 1848-1871.* New York, 1926. Chapter VII deals with American opinion of France.

Gershoy, Leo. "Three French Historians and the Revolution of 1848," *Journal of the History of Ideas* (January, 1951), pp. 131-46.

Goiran, Henri. "La révolution de 1848 à New York," *La République Française,* V, 17-37.

Grandfort, M. de. *The New World.* New Orleans, 1855. A French visitor's prejudiced view of the United States.

Greer, Donald M. *L'Angleterre, la France et la révolution de 1848.* Paris, 1925.

Guérard, Albert. *Beyond Hatred: The Democratic Ideal in France and America.* New York, 1925. A stimulating comparative study.

Guichen, E. de. *Les grandes questions européennes et la diplomatie des puissances sous la seconde république française.* Paris, 1925.

Guillemin, H. *La tragédie de quarante-huit.* Paris, 1948.

Guizot, François de. *De la démocratie en France.* Paris, 1849. A severe critique of democracy as a political system.

Howe, M. A. DeWolfe. *The Life and Letters of George Bancroft.* 2 vols. New York, 1908.

Laboulaye, Édouard. *Considérations sur la constitution.* Paris, 1848.
———. *De la constitution américaine.* Paris, 1850.

Lamartine, A. de. *Histoire de la révolution de 1848.* Paris, 1849. A detailed account by the leader of the revolutionary government.

Livermore, Abiel A. *The War with Mexico Reviewed.* Boston, 1850. A critical analysis.

McKay, Donald C. *The National Workshops: A Study in the French Revolution of 1848.* Cambridge, Mass., 1933. Stresses the social and economic aspects of the revolution.

Manuel, F. E. "An American's Account of the Revolution of 1848," *Journal of Modern History* (September, 1934), pp. 294-307.

Maurois, André. *A History of France.* New York, 1956.

May, A. J. *Contemporary American Opinion of the Mid-Century Revolutions in Central Europe.* Philadelphia, 1927.

Mitchell, Donald G. *The Battle Summer: Being Transcripts from Personal Observation in Paris during the Year 1848.* New York, 1850.

Noël, Octave. *Histoire du commerce du monde.* Paris, 1906.

Normanby, Constantine H. P. *A Year of Revolution.* London, 1857.

Ormesson, W. d'. *La grande crise mondiale.* Paris, 1933.

Palm, Franklin C. *England and Napoleon III.* Durham, N. C., 1948.

Pierre, Victor. *Histoire de la République de 1848.* Paris, 1873. Stresses the political aspects of the republic's history.

Poussin, G. T. *Les États-Unis d'Amérique.* Paris, 1874. An informative survey by one of the French ministers to the United States.

Pouthas, Charles. *Les révolutions de 1848 en Europe.* Paris, 1952. A valuable contribution to the history of these revolutions.

Powell, J. H. *Richard Rush: Republican Diplomat, 1780-1859.* Philadelphia, 1942. Biography of the American minister to France at the time of the February Revolution.

Rauch, Basil. *American Interest in Cuba, 1848-1855.* New York, 1948.

Reardon, John. "Evidences of Anti-Isolationism in American Foreign Policy, 1789-1850." Unpublished Ph.D. dissertation, Georgetown University, 1953. Refers to United States policy with respect to the republican movements in Europe.

Rush, Richard. *Recollections of a Residence. at the English and French Courts.* London, 1872.

Schodt, Eddie W. "American Policy and Practice with Respect to European Liberal Movements, 1848-1853." Unpublished Ph.D. dissertation, University of Colorado, 1952. Discusses the conflict in American policy between the desire to encourage liberal movements in Europe and the traditional emphasis on noninterference in the domestic affairs of other nations.

Schouler, James. *History of the United States of America.* New York, 1891.

Scott, Robert. "American Travellers in France, 1830-1860." Unpublished Ph.D. dissertation, Yale University, 1940. An interesting opinion study paying attention to the different reactions of American Catholics and Protestants.

Sencourt, R. *Napoleon III: The Modern Emperor.* London, 1933. An important reappraisal of Napoleon III.

———. *The Life of Empress Eugénie.* New York, 1931.

Soltau, Roger. *French Political Thought in the Nineteenth Century.* New Haven, Conn., 1931. Throws light on the question of monarchism versus republicanism.

Ticknor, George. *Life, Letters and Journals.* 2 vols. Boston, 1876.

Tocqueville, A. de. *Souvenirs.* Paris, 1893.

Van Deusen, G. G. *Horace Greeley: Nineteenth Century Crusader.* Philadelphia, 1953.

Walsh, Robert. *Notes on the American Constitution.* Keeseville, Ky., 1849.

White, Elizabeth B. *American Opinion of France from Lafayette to Poincaré.* New York, 1927. A helpful standard work.

Whitridge, A. *Men in Crisis: The Revolutions of 1848.* New York, 1949.

Wikoff, Henry. "My First Week in Paris," *Democratic Review* (September, 1849).

Willson, Beckles. *America's Ambassadors to France, 1777-1927.* New York, 1928. Particularly helpful for biographical details.

Wilson, James H. *The Life of Charles A. Dana.* New York, 1907.

Wright, G. "A Poet in Politics: Lamartine and the Revolution of 1848," *History Today,* VIII (1958), 616-27.

Chapter II. *Franco-American Diplomatic Relations, 1830-1860.*

Adams, E. D. *British Interests and Activities in Texas, 1838-1846.* Baltimore, 1910. Based on British sources.

Alaux, Gustave. "La République Dominicaine et l'Empereur Soulouque," *RDDM* (April 15, 1851), pp. 459-501.

Bacourt, A. F. de. *Souvenirs of a Diplomat.* New York, 1885. Recollections of a French minister who spent unhappy years in Washington.

Barbé-Marbois, F. *Histoire de la Louisiane.* Paris, 1829.

Barral-Montferrat, H. D. "La doctrine de Monroe et les évolutions successive de la politique étrangère aux États-Unis," *Revue d'histoire diplomatique* (1903), pp. 594-619. Denounces the ambitious pretensions of the United States.

Belly, Félix. "La question de l'isthme américain," *RDDM* (July 15, 1860), pp. 328-68.

Belmont, Perry. "La question cubaine, 1852-1856," *Revue d'histoire diplomatique* (April-June, 1935), pp. 235-41.

Blue, George Vern. "France and the Oregon Question," *Oregon Historical Quarterly,* XXXIV (1933), 39-59, 144-163. A scholarly analysis.

————. "The Project for a French Settlement in the Hawaiian Islands, 1824-1842," *Pacific Historical Review,* II (1933), 85-99.

Bourgeois, Émile. *History of Modern France.* 2 vols. Cambridge, Eng., 1919. A good reference study.

Bradley, H. W. *The American Frontier in Hawaii: The Pioneers, 1789-1843.* Stanford, Calif., 1942. One of the leading books on this topic.

————. "Hawaii and the American Penetration of the North-Eastern Pacific, 1800-1845," *Pacific Historical Review,* XII (1943), 277-86.

Brookes, Jean I. *International Rivalry in the Pacific Islands, 1800-1875.* Berkeley, Calif., 1941. A valuable monograph.

Brooks, N. C. *A Complete History of the Mexican War.* Baltimore, 1849.

Cady, John F. *The Roots of French Imperialism in Eastern Asia.* Ithaca, N. Y., 1954. An enlightening analysis of French missionary, mercantile, naval, and political interests in Eastern Asia.

———. *Foreign Intervention in the Rio de la Plata, 1838-1850.* Philadelphia, 1929. Throws light on French ambitions in South America.

Callahan, J. M. *American Relations in the Pacific and the Far East, 1784-1900.* Baltimore, 1901.

Chase, Mary K. *Négociations de la République de Texas en Europe, 1837-1845.* Paris, 1932. Discusses the activities of Texan agents in Europe.

Clark, B. C. *Remarks upon United States Intervention in Hayti.* Boston, 1853. Critical of United States policy.

Clyde, P. H. *United States Policy toward China, 1839-1939.* Durham, N. C., 1940. A source compilation.

Cochut, A. "Le Chili en 1859," *RDDM* (December 15, 1859), pp. 822-61.

Cordier, Henri. *L'expédition de Chine de 1857-58.* Paris, 1905. The work of a leading French authority on the Far East.

———. *L'expédition de Chine de 1860.* Paris, 1906. A detailed monograph.

———. *La France et la Cochinchine, 1852-1858.* Leide, 1906.

Cucheval, A. "Le Texas et les États-Unis," *RDDM* (July 15, 1844), pp. 233-82.

Democratic Party, National Committee of. *General Cass and the Quintuple Treaty.* Washington, D. C., 1848.

Dennett, Tyler. *Americans in Eastern Asia.* New York, 1922. Still very useful.

De Voto, Bernard. *The Year of Decision: 1846.* Boston, 1943.

Dommartin, H. Du Pasquier de. *Les États-Unis et le Mexique— L'intérêt européen dans l'Amérique du nord.* Paris, 1852. Recommends an active French policy to prevent Mexico's absorption by the United States.

Dutot, S. *France et Brésil.* Paris, 1859.

Edwards, H. R. "Diplomatic Relations between France and the Republic of Texas, 1836-1845," *Southwestern Historical Quarterly,* XX (1917), 209-41, 341-57.

Ettinger, A. A. "The Proposed Anglo-American Treaty of 1852 to Guarantee Cuba to Spain," *Transactions of the Royal Historical Society,* XIII (London, 1930), 149-85.

Fairbank, John K. *The Trade and Diplomacy on the China Coast, The Opening of the Treaty Ports, 1842-1854.* Cambridge, Mass., 1953.

Faivre, J. P. *L'expansion française dans le Pacifique de 1800 à 1842.* Paris, 1953. Traces the slow progress of France in the Pacific.

Galbraith, John S. "France as a Factor in the Oregon Negotiations," *Pacific Northwest Quarterly,* XLIV (1953), 69-73.

Garber, P. N. *The Gadsden Treaty.* Philadelphia, 1923.

Gessler, C. *Hawaii.* New York, 1937.

Goyau, Georges. *La France missionnaire dans les cinq parties du monde.* 2 vols. Paris, 1948. A detailed account of the role and problems of French missionaries.

Graebner, N. A. *Empire on the Pacific—A Study in American Continental Expansion.* New York, 1955.

Griffin, E. *Clippers and Consuls.* Ann Arbor, Mich., 1933. Two important factors during the expansionist period.

Grimblot. "Du Texas et son annexation aux États-Unis," *Revue Indépendante* (August 25, 1844), pp. 596-615.

Gubbins, J. H. *The Progress of Japan, 1853-1871.* Oxford, Eng., 1911.

Guizot, F. *Histoire parlementaire de France.* Paris, 1864. A major reference work.

Harcourt, Bernard d'. "Négociations relatives à un projet d'établissement colonial français en 1845," *Revue d'histoire diplomatique,* I (1887), 525-47. Discusses Guizot's effort to extend French influence to the Philippine Islands.

Hill, L. F. *Diplomatic Relations between the United States and Brazil.* Durham, N. C., 1932. Detailed monograph.

Holinski, Alexandre. *La Californie et les routes interocéaniques.* Bruxelles, 1853.

Hooley, O. E. "Hawaiian Negotiation for Reciprocity, 1855-1857," *Pacific Historical Review,* VII (1938), 128-46.

Huberich, C. *The Trans-Isthmian Canal: A Study in American Diplomatic History, 1825-1904.* Austin, Texas, 1904.

Janes, H. L. "The Black Warrior Affair," *AHR,* XII (1907), 280-98.

Joinville, Prince François de. *Notes sur l'état des forces navales de la France.* Paris, 1844. Boasts of French naval superiority.

Jomini, A. G. *Diplomatic Study on the Crimean War.* London, 1882.

Judd, L. F. *Honolulu, 1828-1861.* New York, 1880.

Julien, Charles A. *Histoire de l'Océanie.* Paris, 1951. Traces the power struggle of the maritime powers in Oceania.

King-Hall, Stephen. *Western Civilization and the Far East.* London, 1924.

Knight, M. M. *The Americans in Santo Domingo.* New York, 1928.

Koskinen, Aarne A. *Missionary Influence as a Political Factor in the Pacific Islands.* Helsinki, 1953. An outstanding analysis of the interrelation between religion and politics in the Pacific theater.

Kuykendall, R. S. *The Hawaiian Kingdom, 1778-1854.* Honolulu, 1938. One of the leading books on this topic.

——, and Day, A. G. *Hawaii: A History.* New York, 1948.

Lafond, Georges. *L'effort français en Amérique latine.* Paris, 1917.

Logan, R. W. *The Diplomatic Relations of the United States with Haiti, 1776-1891.* Chapel Hill, 1941.

McCleary, John W. "Anglo-French Naval Rivalry, 1815-1848." Unpublished Ph.D. dissertation, Johns Hopkins University, 1947. The effect of this rivalry on American affairs was important.

McKay, Donald C. *The United States and France.* Cambridge, Mass., 1951. A good general survey with emphasis upon the developments in the twentieth century.

McLemore, R. A. "The Influence of French Diplomatic Policy on the Annexation of Texas," *Southwestern Historical Quarterly,* XLIII (1940), 342-47.

Martin, K. L. P. *Missionaries and Annexation in the Pacific.* London, 1924.

Merk, Frederick. "The British Corn Crisis of 1845-46 and the Oregon Treaty," *Agricultural History,* VIII (1934), 95-123.

Metcalf, H. B. "The California French Filibusters in Sonora," *California Historical Society Quarterly,* XVIII (1939), 3-21.

Mofras, E. Duflot de. *Exploration du territoire de l'Orégon, des Californies et de la Mer Vermeille.* 2 vols. Paris, 1844. Publication ordered by Louis Philippe.

Morse, H. B. *The International Relations of the Chinese Empire.* London, 1910.

Nasatir, A. P. "The French Consulate in California, 1843-1856." *California Historical Society Quarterly,* XI (1932), 195-223, XII (1933), 155-172.

Parks, E. T. *Colombia and the United States, 1765-1934.* Durham, N. C., 1935.

Paxson, Frederick L. "A Tripartite Intervention in Hayti, 1851," *University of Colorado Studies,* I (1902), 323-30.

Peters, H. E. *The Foreign Debt of the Argentine Republic.* Baltimore, 1934.

Piggot, F. *The Declaration of Paris, 1856.* London, 1919.

Powell, J. H. *Richard Rush: Republican Diplomat, 1780-1859.* Philadelphia, 1942.

Pratt, Julius W. "James K. Polk and John Bull," *Canadian Historical Review,* XXIV (1943), 133-48.

Rathgeber, H. J. "Early French Trade and Settlement in California." Unpublished Master's thesis, University of California, Berkeley, 1940.

Raymond, X. "Diplomatie anglo-américaine," *RDDM* (April 15, 1853), pp. 298-333.

Recluse, É. "Les républiques de l'Amérique du sud, leurs guerres et leur projet de fédération," *RDDM* (October 15, 1866), pp. 953-80.

Renouvin, Pierre. *La question d'Extrême-Orient, 1840-1940.* Paris, 1946.

———. *La politique extérieure du Second Empire.* Paris, 1940.

Reynand, Pellisier de. "Le droit maritime selon le congrès de Paris," *RDDM* (February 15, 1857).

Rippy, J. F. *The United States and Mexico.* New York, 1931. A standard work.

Rives, G. L. "Mexican Diplomacy on the Eve of War with the United States," *AHR*, XVIII (1913), 275-94.

Robertson, William Spence. "French Intervention in Mexico in 1838," *Hispanic American Historical Review*, XXIV (1944), 222-52.

Rouhaud, H. *Les régions nouvelles—histoire du commerce et de la civilisation au nord de. l'océan Pacifique.* Paris, 1868.

Savage, C. *Policy of the United States towards Maritime Commerce in War.* Washington, D. C., 1934.

Schmitz, J. W. *Texas Statecraft, 1836-1845.* San Antonio, Texas, 1941. An outstanding work on the subject, presented from the point of view of Texas.

Scribner, R. L. "The Diplomacy of William L. Marcy." Unpublished Ph.D. dissertation, University of Virginia, 1949.

Sédès, Jean-Marie. *Histoire des missions françaises.* Paris, 1950.

Sherman, W. R. *The Diplomatic and Commercial Relations of the United States and Chile, 1820-1914.* Boston, 1926.

Simpson, F. A. *The Rise of Louis Napoleon.* London, 1950.

Sioussat, St. George L. "John C. Calhoun," in Bemis, S. F., ed., *The American Secretaries of State and their Diplomacy.* New York, 1928. Vol. V, 127-236.

Smith, Justin H. "The Mexican Recognition of Texas," *AHR*, XVI (1910), 36-55.

———. *The Annexation of Texas.* New York, 1911. A standard work.

Smith, B. *Yankees in Paradise.* New York, 1956. A well written book. Presents interesting details on the rivalry between Catholic and Protestant missionaries.

Stevens, S. K. *American Expansion in Hawaii, 1842-1898.* Harrisburg, Pa., 1945. Among the leading books on the subject.

Takekoshi, Yosoburo. *The Economic Aspects of the History of the Civilization of Japan.* London, 1930.

Tansill, Charles C. *The United States and Santo Domingo, 1798-1873.* Baltimore, 1938.

Treat, P. J. *Diplomatic Relations between the United States and Japan, 1853-1895.* 2 vols. Stanford, Calif., 1932.

Treudley, M. *The United States and Santo Domingo, 1789-1866.* Worcester, Mass., 1916.

Van Alstyne, R. "Great Britain, the United States, and Hawaiian Independence, 1850-55," *Pacific Historical Review,* IV (1935), 15-24.

White, Elizabeth B. *American Opinion of France from Lafayette to Poincaré.* New York, 1927.

Willis, R. K. "French Imperialists in California," *California Historical Society Quarterly,* VIII (1929), 116-29.

Willson, Beckles. *John Slidell and the Confederates in Paris, 1862-1865.* New York, 1932.

Woodford, Frank B. *Lewis Cass, the Last Jeffersonian.* New Brunswick, N.J., 1950. Biography of a respected Secretary of State and United States minister to France.

Worley, J. K. "The Diplomatic Relations of England and the Republic of Texas," *Texas Historical Association Quarterly,* VI (1905), 1-40.

Chapter III. *Franco-American Incidents, 1830-1860.*

Bemis, Samuel Flagg. *John Quincy Adams and the Union.* New York, 1956.

Dyer, B. *Zachary Taylor.* Baton Rouge, La., 1946. Touches on Poussin incident.

Gazley, J. G. *American Opinion of German Unification, 1848-1871.* New York, 1926.

Learned, H. B. "William Learned Marcy," in Bemis, S. F., ed., *The American Secretaries of State and their Diplomacy.* New York, 1928. VI, 205-208. Discusses Soulé incident.

Marion, Marcel. "Un épisode oublié des relations pécuniaires franco-américaines," *RDDM* (November 1, 1926), pp. 46-64. Reviews the spoliation claims incident.

McLemore, R. A. *Franco-American Diplomatic Relations, 1816-1836.* Baton Rouge, 1941. Presents a detailed account of the claims controversy.

Peck, Charles. *The Jacksonian Epoch.* New York, 1890.

Pincetl, St. J., Jr. "Relations de la France et des États-Unis pendant la Seconde République, 1848-1851." Unpublished Ph.D. dissertation, Université de Paris, 1950. Devotes an entire chapter to the Poussin incident.

Roux, Georges. *Thiers.* Paris, 1948.

Van Deusen, Glyndon G. *The Jacksonian Era, 1828-1848.* New York, 1959.

Webster, Charles K. "British Mediation between France and the United States, 1834-1836," *English Historical Review,* XLII (1927), 58-78.

Webster, S. "Marcy and the Cuban Question," *Political Science Quarterly,* VIII (1893), 1-32.

Williams, Mary W. "John Middleton Clayton," in Bemis, S. F. (ed.). *The American Secretaries of State and their Diplomacy.* New York, 1928. V, 19-31.

Chapter IV. *Economic Relations, 1830-1871.*

Amé, Léon. *Étude sur les tarifs de douanes et sur les traités de commerce.* 2 vols. Paris, 1876. A scholarly work.

Becqué, É. *L'internationalisation des capitaux.* Montpellier, 1912.

Blumenthal, Henry. "The California Societies in France, 1849-1855," *Pacific Historical Review,* XXV (1956), pp. 251-60.

Bonaparte, Napoléon Joseph. *Visites et études de S.A.I. le prince Napoléon . . . aux produits collectifs des nations qui ont pris part à l'exposition de 1855.* Paris, 1856. Offers detailed data on the international exposition of 1855.

Boucher, Henri. *La marine marchande américaine de 1585 au 11 novembre 1918.* Paris, 1923.

Cameron, R. E. "French Foreign Investments, 1850-1880." Unpublished Ph.D. dissertation, University of Chicago, 1952. Concentrates on the later period for which more material is available.

Capefigue, J. *Histoire des grandes opérations financières.* Paris, 1858-1860.

Carey, Henry C. *The French and American Tariffs Compared.* Philadelphia, 1861. A defense of the Morrill tariff.

Clapham, J. H. *The Economic Development of France and Germany, 1815-1914.* Cambridge, Eng., 1936.

Clément, A. "Des crises commerciales," *Journal des économistes* (February 15, 1858), pp. 161-91.

Clough, Shepard B. *Economic History of Europe.* Boston, 1941.

——. *France—A History of National Economics, 1789-1939.* New York, 1939. A comprehensive work.

Cochut, A. "Production et commerce du coton," *RDDM* (October 15, 1853), pp. 293-318.

Cole, A. H. "Evolution of the Foreign Exchange Market of the United States," *Journal of Economic and Business History,* I (1929), 384-421.

Courcelle-Seneuil, J. G. "Crise commerciale aux États-Unis," *Journal des économistes* (January, 1855), pp. 112-15.

Cowdin, E. C. *Paris Universal Exhibition of 1867.* Albany, 1868.

Cummings, R. O. "American Interest in World Agriculture, 1861-1865," *Agricultural History,* XXIII (1949), 116-23.

Curti, Merle. "America at the World Fairs, 1851-1893," *AHR,* LV (1950), 833-56.

Dauphin, B. Paul. *Émission et circulation des titres des sociétés étrangères en France.* Paris, 1907.

Depew, Charles M. *One Hundred Years of American Commerce, 1795-1895.* 2 vols. New York, 1895.

Dewey, Davis R. *Financial History of the United States.* New York, 1920.

Duncan, B. "Franco-American Tobacco Diplomacy, 1784-1860," *Maryland Historical Magazine,* LI (1956), 273-301.

Dunham, A. L. *The Anglo-French Treaty of Commerce of 1860.* Ann Arbor, Mich., 1930. The standard work.

———. *The Industrial Revolution in France, 1815-1848.* New York, 1955.

———. "Unrest in France in 1848," *Journal of Economic History,* Supplement VIII (1948), 74-84.

Feis, Herbert. *Europe: The World's Banker, 1870-1914.* New Haven, Conn., 1930.

French, Henry F. "Observations on English Husbandry" in *Report of the Commissioner of Patents for the Year 1860.* Washington, D. C., 1861. Vol. II, pp. 161-65. A comparative essay on agriculture.

Guillaume, Louis. *L'épargne française et les valeurs mobilières étrangères.* Paris, 1907. Estimates French savings and relates them to foreign investments.

Haight, F. A. *A History of French Commercial Policies.* New York, 1941.

Hartmann, J. *Die Wirtschaftspolitik Napoleons III.* Berlin, 1938.

Hayden, R. "The States' Rights Doctrine and the Treaty-Making Power," *AHR,* XX (1917), 566-85. Important in connection with alien property and inheritance questions.

Hobson, C. K. *The Export of Capital.* London, 1914. A standard work.

Horn, J. E. "Le protectionisme en Amérique," *Journal des économistes* (August, 1862), pp. 325 ff.

Hubbard, C. "Exposition Universelle de 1855," *Journal des économistes* (October, 1855), pp. 54-66.

Hutchins, J. G. B. *The American Maritime Industries and Public Policy, 1789-1914.* Cambridge, Mass., 1941.

Jenks, L. H. *The Migration of British Capital to 1875.* New York, 1927.

Juglar, C. *Des crises commerciales.* Paris, 1889. Stresses the international character of the major crises.

Knowles, L. C. A. *Economic Development in the Nineteenth Century.* London, 1932.

Lacour-Gayet, J. *Histoire du commerce.* Vol. V. Paris, 1952. A major reference work.

Landes, D. S. "French Entrepreneurship and Industrial Growth in the Nineteenth Century," *Journal of Economic History*, IX (1949), 45-61.

Lavollée, Charles. "Commerce extérieur de la France d'après les documents officiels," *RDDM* (April 15, 1859), pp. 978-97.

Lebeuf, E. B. "Du commerce de la France pendant la période décennale 1847-1856," *Journal des économistes* (April 15, 1859), pp. 50-66.

Levasseur, E. *Histoire du commerce de la France de 1789 à nos jours.* Paris, 1912.

Lévy, R. G. "La fortune mobilière de la France à l'étranger," *RDDM* (March 15, 1897), pp. 415-45. A valuable contribution to the study of French foreign investments.

Lewis, Cleona. *America's Stake in International Investments.* Washington, D. C., 1938. The standard work.

Loeb, Charles G. *Legal Status of American Corporations in France.* Paris, 1921.

McGrane, R. C. *Foreign Bondholders and American State Debts.* New York, 1935.

Marion, Marcel. *Histoire financière de la France depuis 1715.* Vol. V. Paris, 1928.

Martin, G. *Histoire économique et financière.* Paris, 1927.

Medberry, J. K. *Men and Mysteries of Wall Street.* Boston, 1870.

Meekison, V. V. "Treaty Provisions for the Inheritance of Personal Property," *American Journal of International Law*, XLIV (1950), 313-32.

Morrow, Dwight D., Jr. "The Impact of American Agricultural Machinery on France, 1851-1914, with some Consideration of the General Agricultural Impact until 1880." Unpublished Ph.D. dissertation, Harvard University, 1957.

Noël, Octave. *Histoire du commerce extérieur de la France.* Paris, 1879.

———. *Histoire du commerce du monde.* Paris, 1906. Presents convenient statistical summaries.

Pohly, Claire. *Les exportations de la France vers les nouveaux pays industriels, 1860-1935.* Genève, 1939.

Reybaud, L. "L'exposition de l'industrie de 1855," *RDDM* (December 15, 1855), pp. 1284-1321.

Riley, Mary L. *The Imprint of France on the United States.* New York, 1948.

Rodet, D. L. "Tarif et tendances du commerce des États-Unis," *RDDM* (July 1, 1843), pp. 139-59.

Rosenberg, Hans. *Die Weltwirtschaftskrisis von 1857-1859.* Stuttgart, 1934.

Say, Léon. *Rapport sur le paiement de l'indemnité de guerre.* Paris, 1874. Goes into the question of French savings and investments.

Sée, Henri. *Histoire économique de la France—Les temps modernes.* Paris, 1942. Among the leading French studies.

Simon, M. "Cyclical Fluctuations and the International Capital Movements of the United States, 1865-1897." Unpublished Ph.D. dissertation, Columbia University, 1955.

Théry, E. *Les valeurs mobilières en France.* Paris, 1897.

Tenré, L. *Les états américaines en vue de l' exposition universelle de Paris.* Paris, 1867.

Tisserand, Eugène. *Considérations générales sur l'agriculture.—exposition universelle de 1867.* Paris, 1867.

Tramond, J., and Reussner, A. *Élements d'histoire maritime et coloniale contemporaine, 1815-1914.* Paris, 1947.

Usher, J. M. *Paris: Universal Exhibition, 1867.* Boston, 1868.

U. S. Department of Agriculture. "Breeds of Draft Horses," *Farmers' Bulletin,* No. 619 (Washington, 1954).

Vitu, A. *Guide financière.* Paris, 1864.

Van Vleck, G. W. *The Panic of 1857.* New York, 1943. Considers England's silver shipments to the East as a major cause of the depression.

Viallate, Achille. *L'activité économique en France de. la fin du XVIIIe siècle à nos jours.* Paris, 1937.

Walker, W. H. "Franco-American Commercial Relations, 1815-1850." Unpublished Ph.D. dissertation, University of Iowa, 1928.

Waltershausen, A. Satorius von. *Die Entstehung der Weltwirtschaft.* Jena, 1931.

Weiss, H. B. *The Pioneer Century of American Entomology.* New Brunswick, N. J., 1936.

White, H. D. *The French International Accounts, 1880-1913.* Cambridge, Mass., 1933.

Chapter V. *The Civil War and France.*

Adams, Charles F. *Seward and the Declaration of Paris.* Boston, 1912.

———. *The Crisis of Foreign Intervention in the War of Secession, September-November, 1862.* Boston, 1914.

Adams, E. D. *Great Britain and the American Civil War.* New York, 1925. An authoritative book on the subject.

Aldis, O. F. "Louis Napoleon and the Southern Confederacy," *NAR,* CXXIX (1879), 342-60. A Northern exposé of Napoleon's intrigues.

Andrews, R. M. "Archbishop Hughes and the Civil War." Unpublished Ph.D. dissertation, University of Chicago, 1935.

Bancroft, F. *The Life of William H. Seward.* 2 vols. New York, 1900.

Baroux, Abbé. *Lettre à J. Denève.* Orléans, 1863.

Barrillon, François G. *Politique de la France et de l'humanité dans le conflit américain.* Paris, 1861. Recommends French intervention.

Belliot des Minières, E. *La question américaine.* Paris, 1862. Favors the South.

Belperron, Pierre. *La guerre de sécession, 1861-1865.* Paris, 1947. A recent French account of the American Civil War.

Bemis, George. *Hasty Recognition of Rebel Belligerency and Our Right to Complain of It.* Boston, 1865.

Bernstein, S. *Essays in Political and Intellectual History.* New York, 1955. Chapter VIII is an essay on "French Diplomacy and the American Civil War."

Bigelow, John. *France and the Confederate Navy, 1862-1868.* New York, 1888. Revealing on Napoleon's duplicity.

Bigelow, Poultney. "John Bigelow of Ulster County and His Relations with William H. Seward," *Ulster County Historical Society Proceedings* (1932), pp. 32-42.

Bonham, M. L., Jr. "The French Consuls in the Confederate States," *Studies in Southern History and Politics.* New York, 1914. Pp. 83-104.

Bulloch, James D. *The Secret Service of the Confederate States in Europe.* 2 vols. New York, 1884. The author was the naval representative of the Confederate States in Europe.

Callahan, James M. *The Diplomatic History of the Southern Confederacy.* Baltimore, 1901.

Capers, H. D. *The Life and Times of C. G. Memminger.* Richmond, Va., 1893. A useful biography of the Confederate Secretary of the Treasury.

Case, Lynn M. *French Opinion on the United States and Mexico, 1860-1867.* New York, 1936. The significance of this book lies in the fact that it is based on the reports of the attorney generals.

Cate, W. A. *Lucius Q. C. Lamar.* Chapel Hill, 1935.

Clapp, Margaret. *Forgotten Citizen: John Bigelow.* Boston, 1947. A brilliant biography of a distinguished American diplomat in France.

Claussen, M. P. "Peace Factors in Anglo-American Relations, 1861-65," *Mississippi Valley Historical Review,* XXVI (1940), 511-22.

Cohen, V. H. "Charles Sumner and Foreign Relations." Unpublished Ph.D. dissertation, University of Oklahoma, 1951. The record of an influential figure in American diplomatic history.

Coulter, E. M. *The Confederate States of America, 1861-1865.* Baton Rouge, 1950. One of the distinguished volumes in the *A History of the South* series.

Cowell, John W. *La France et les États-Confédérés.* Paris, 1865.

Davis, Jefferson. *The Rise and Fall of the Confederate Government.* 2 vols. New York, 1881.

De Leon, Edwin. *Thirty Years of My Life on Three Continents.* London, 1890. The autobiography of the Confederate propaganda agent in France.

Donner, B. "Carl Schurz and the Civil War," *The Wisconsin Magazine of History,* XX (1936), No. 2.

Durham, A. L. *The Anglo-French Treaty of Commerce of 1860.* Ann Arbor, Mich., 1930.

———. "The Development of the Cotton Industry in France and the Anglo-French Treaty of Commerce of 1860," *Economic History Review,* I (1928), 281-307.

———. "Government Aid to Industry in the French Economic Reforms of 1860," *Economic Journal* (May, 1927), pp. 291-306.

Eaton, Clement. *A History of the Southern Confederacy.* New York, 1954. A good brief account.

Einstein, Lewis. *Napoleon III and American Diplomacy at the Outbreak of the Civil War.* London, 1905. An address by the Third Secretary of the American embassy in London, read before the Société d'Histoire Diplomatique at Paris.

———. "Napoléon III et les préliminaires diplomatiques de la guerre civile aux États-Unis," *Revue d'histoire diplomatique* (1905), pp. 336-48.

Sister Evangeline, "Seward and the Maritime Question." Unpublished Master's thesis, St. John's University, 1941.

Evans, Thomas W. *Memoirs—The Second French Empire.* New York, 1905. This American dentist, who practiced in Paris, was close to the imperial family.

Fröbel, Julius. *Amerika, Europa und die politischen Gesichtspunkte der Gegenwart.* Berlin, 1859. A remarkable analysis of the United States as a factor in world affairs.

Gasparin, A. de. *Une parole de paix—sur le différend entre l'Angleterre et les États-Unis.* Paris, 1862. Written by a friend of the North.

Golder, F. A. "The Russian Fleet and the Civil War," *AHR,* XX (1915), 802.

Grandguillot, A. P. *La reconnaissance du sud.* Paris, 1862.

Hassard, John R. G. *Life of the Most Reverend John Hughes, D.D.* New York, 1866.

Haut, Marc de. *La crise américaine.* Paris, 1862. Favors recognition of the South.

Henderson, W. O. "The Cotton Famine on the Continent, 1861-65," *Economic History Review,* IV (1933), 195-207.

Hendrick, Burton J. *Statesmen of the Lost Cause.* Boston, 1939.

Hobson, C. K. *The Export of Capital.* London, 1914.

Huntley, Stephen McQueen. *Les rapports de la France et la Confédération pendant la guerre de sécession.* Toulouse, 1932.

Jones, Robert Owen. "British Pseudo-Neutrality during the American Civil War." Unpublished Master's thesis, Georgetown University, 1952.

Jordan, Donaldson, and Pratt, Edwin J. *Europe and the American Civil War.* Boston, 1931. Helpful on European opinion during the Civil War.

Korolewicz-Carlton, Richard. "Napoléon III, Thouvenel et la guerre de sécession." Unpublished Ph.D. dissertation, Université de Paris, 1951. Analyzes French policy during the first two years of the war. Stresses Thouvenel's contribution to the preservation of French neutrality.

Laboulaye, Édouard. *Upon Whom Rests the Guilt of the War?* New York, 1863. In support of the Union's cause.

Legoyt, A. "De la crise cotonnière," *Journal des économistes* (March, 1863), pp. 425-49.

Lonn, Ella. *Foreigners in the Confederacy.* Chapel Hill, 1940. Informative.

———. *Foreigners in the Union Army and Navy.* Baton Rouge, 1951. Informative.

Lothrop, Thomas K. *William Henry Seward.* New York, 1898.

Lutz, Ralph. *Die Beziehungen zwischen Deutschland und den Vereinigten Staaten während des Sezessionskrieges.* Heidelberg, 1911.

Lynch, M. C. "The Diplomatic Mission of John Lothrop Motley." Unpublished Ph.D. dissertation, Catholic University, 1944.

McGuire, G. "The Mission of Archbishop Hughes to Europe, 1861-62." Unpublished Master's thesis, Columbia University, 1946.

McVeigh, Donald R. "Charles James Faulkner in the Civil War," *West Virginia History,* XII (1951), 129-41.

Mason, Virginia. *The Public Life and Diplomatic Correspondence of James M. Mason.* Roanoke, Va., 1903.

Meade, R. D. *Judah P. Benjamin, Confederate Statesman.* New York, 1943. Enlightening biography of the Confederate Secretary of State.

Moreau, Henri. *La politique française en Amérique, 1861-1864.* Paris, 1864. Favorable to the North.

Nouette-Delorme, Émile. *Les États-Unis et l'Europe.* Paris, 1863. Recommends recognition of the South as a means of protecting the interests of Europe against the growing power of the United States.

O'Daniel, Victor F. "Archbishop John Hughes—American Envoy to France, 1861," *Catholic Historical Review,* III (1917), 336-39.

Ollivier, Émile. *L'empire libéral.* Paris, 1900.

Owsley, F. L. *King Cotton Diplomacy.* Chicago, 1931. One of the outstanding books on Civil War diplomacy.

Pecquet Du Bellet, P. *The Diplomacy of the Confederate Cabinet of Richmond and Its Agents Abroad.* New York, 1865. A critical contemporary source.

Pollard, E. A. *The First Year of the War.* Richmond, Va., 1862.

Pomeroy, Earl S. "French Substitutes for American Cotton, 1861-1865," *Journal of Southern History,* IX (1943), 555-60.

Prévost, F. and Pecquet, P. *Le blocus américain—droit des neutres.* Paris, 1862.

Randall, J. G. *The Civil War and Reconstruction.* Boston, 1953. A leading book on this subject.

Robertson, J. R. *A Kentuckian at the Court of the Tsars.* Berea, Ky., 1935. A biography of Cassius Marcellus Clay.

Sandburg, Carl. *Abraham Lincoln—The War Years.* 4 vols. New York, 1939.

Sears, Louis M. "A Neglected Critic of our Civil War," *Mississippi Valley Historical Review,* I (1915), 532-45. The critic is E. Forçade of the *RDDM.*

————. "A Confederate Diplomat at the Court of Napoleon III," *AHR,* XXVI (1921), 255-281.

Seward, F. W. *Reminiscences of a War-Time Statesman and Diplomat, 1830-1915.* New York, 1916.

Simms, Henry H. *Life of Robert M. T. Hunter.* Richmond, Va., 1935.

Snoy, J. Charles. "Les répercussions internationales de la guerre de sécession, 1861-1865," *Revue générale* (September 15, 1929), pp. 284-300.

Stock, Leo Francis. "Catholic Participation in the Diplomacy of the Southern Confederacy," *Catholic Historical Review,* XVI (1930), 1-18.

Stovall, Pleasant A. *Robert Toombs.* New York, 1892.

Teichmann, W. C. *Englands und Frankreichs Stellung zum Bürgerkriege in den Vereinigten Staaten von Amerika, 1861-1865.* München, 1885.

Temple, Henry W. "William H. Seward," in Bemis, S. F. (ed.)., *The American Secretaries of State.* New York, 1928. VII, 3-115.

Thompson, S. B. *Confederate Purchasing Operations Abroad.* Chapel Hill, 1935.

Todd, H. H. "The Building of the Confederate States Navy in Europe." Unpublished Ph.D. dissertation, Vanderbilt University, 1941.

Todd, Richard C. *Confederate Finance.* Athens, Ga., 1954.

"Die Trent Angelegenheit, 1861-1862," *Preussische Jahrbücher* (1862), VIII, 630-36.

Véron, Eugène. "Dissolution de l'union américaine, ses causes et ses conséquences," *Revue nationale et étrangère* (February, 1861), pp. 321-45.

Walpole, Spencer. *The History of Twenty-Five Years.* 2 vols. London, 1904.

Weill, Georges. *Histoire des États-Unis de 1787 à 1917.* Paris, 1919.

West, W. Reed. *Contemporary French Opinion on the American Civil War.* Baltimore, 1924. A standard source.

Willson, Beckles. *America's Ambassadors to France, 1777-1927.* New York, 1928.

———. *John Slidell and the Confederates in Paris, 1862-65.* New York, 1932.

Woldman, A. A. *Lincoln and the Russians.* Cleveland, 1952.

Chapter VI. *The Maximilian Affair.*

Arnaud, René. *La Deuxième République et le Second Empire.* Paris, 1929.

Aubry, Octave. *The Second Empire.* New York, 1940.

Bigelow, John. *Retrospections of an Active Life.* 5 vols. New York, 1909-1913. A valuable contemporary source.

Blanchot, Charles. *L'intervention française au Mexique.* Paris, 1911. Detailed account.

Bratianu, G. *Napoléon III et les nationalités.* Paris, 1934. Contends that the very prosaic cause of the intervention was the determination of prominent Frenchmen to protect their threatened financial interests in Mexico.

Callahan, John. *Evolution of Seward's Mexican Policy.* Morgantown, W. Va., 1909. Still useful.

Campbell, H. Murray. *The French Intervention and the Empire of Maximilian, 1862-67.* Mexico City, 1951. Very critical of Napoleon III.

Case, L. M. *French Opinion on the United States and Mexico, 1860-1867.* New York, 1936.

Clapp, Margaret. *Forgotten Citizen: John Bigelow.* Boston, 1947.

Clark, Chester Wells. *Franz Joseph and Bismarck—The Diplomacy of Austria before the War of 1866.* Cambridge, Mass., 1934.

Corti, Egon Caesar. *Maximilian and Charlotte of Mexico.* Translated from the German by Catherine A. Phillips. 2 vols. New York, 1928. A leading work.

———. *Die Tragödie eines Kaisers.* Wien, 1949. Adds new material to the previously published biography of Maximilian.

Coulter, E. M. *The Confederate States of America, 1861-65.* Baton Rouge, 1950.

Delord, Taxile. *Histoire du Second Empire.* 6 vols. Paris, 1869-76. A detailed contemporary source.

Duniway, Claude A. "Reasons for the Withdrawal of France from Mexico," *AHA Annual Reports,* I (1902), 315-28. Contends that developments in Europe influenced Napoleon's decision to withdraw from Mexico.

Ferris, N. L. "The Relations of the United States with South America during the American Civil War," *Hispanic American Historical Review,* XXI (1941), 51-78. The threat of the French intervention in Mexico helped to solidify the relations between North and South America.

Fleury, M. *Memoirs of the Empress Eugénie.* New York, 1920. Describes Eugénie's role in bringing about the Mexican expedition.

Frazer, Robert W. "Maximilian's Propaganda Activities in the United States, 1865-1866," *Hispanic American Historical Review,* XXIV (1944), 4-29.

Garnier-Pagès, L. A. *Discours sur la politique extérieure.* Versailles, 1868.

Gaulot, Paul. *L'Empire de Maximilien.* Paris, 1890.

————. *L'expédition du Mexique, 1861-67.* Paris, 1906. Discusses the difficulties French troops and Maximilian encountered in Mexico.

Gerrity, Francis Xavier. "American Editorial Opinion of French Intervention in Mexico, 1861-1867." Unpublished Ph.D. dissertation, Georgetown University, 1952. A useful opinion study.

Hanna, K. A. "The Role of the South in the French Intervention in Mexico," *Journal of Southern History,* XX (1954), 3-21.

Henry, Paul. *Napoléon III et les peuples.* Paris, 1943. Comments on Seward's skillful handling of the Mexican affair.

Hill, Lawrence. *Diplomatic Relations between the United States and Brazil.* Durham, N. C., 1932. Touches on Webb's role in connection with the French evacuation from Mexico.

Hyde, H. M. *Mexican Empire: The History of Maximilian and Carlota of Mexico.* London, 1946. A good general account.

Jerrold, Blanchard. *The Life of Napoleon III.* London, 1882. Touches on Webb's relationship with Napoleon.

Kératry, E. de. *La créance Jecker—les indemnités françaises et les emprunts mexicains.* Paris, 1868. A contemporary discussion of French interests in the Mexican bonds question.

————. *L'élévation et la chute de l'empereur Maximilien.* Paris, 1867.

Kingsley, Vine Wright. *French Intervention in America.* New York, 1863. Presents evidence challenging Napoleon's contention that he had no permanent ambitions regarding Mexico.

Lally, Frank Edward. *French Opposition to the Mexican Policy of the Second Empire.* Baltimore, 1931. Discusses the difficult position in which Napoleon found himself as a result of the Mexican adventure.

Loliée, F. *The Life of an Empress*. London, 1908. Touches on Eugénie's part in promoting the Mexican scheme.

Lynch, M. C. "The Diplomatic Mission of John Lothrop Motley," Unpublished Ph.D. dissertation, Catholic University, 1944.

Martin, P. F. *Maximilian in Mexico: The Story of the French Intervention, 1861-1867*. New York, 1914.

McCormack, Robert Blaine. "James Watson Webb and French Withdrawal from Mexico," *Hispanic American Hist. Rev.*, XXXI (1951), 274-286.

Nolte, F. *L'Europe militaire et diplomatique au dix-neuvième siècle, 1815-84*. Paris, 1884.

Paléologue, Maurice. *Les entretiens de l'impératrice Eugénie*. Paris, 1928. A good biography of Eugénie.

———. *The Tragic Empress*. New York, 1928.

Perkins, Dexter. *The Monroe Doctrine, 1826-1867*. Baltimore, 1933. Contains important details on the Mexican affair.

Prévost-Paradol, L. A. *Quelques pages d'histoire contemporaine*. Paris, 1871. A retrospective critique.

Rippy, J. F. *The United States and Mexico*. New York, 1931. A brief general study.

Rothan, G. *Souvenirs diplomatiques—la France et sa politique extérieure en 1867*. Paris, 1887. A useful contemporary source.

Schnerb, Robert. *Rouher et le Second Empire*. Paris, 1949. The biography of one of the most influential statesmen of the Second Empire.

Schofield, John M. *Forty-Six Years in the Army*. New York, 1897. Contains General Schofield's own story of his mission to France.

Sencourt, Robert. *The Life of the Empress Eugénie*. New York, 1913.

Springer, Max. "Napoleon III, ein Vorläufer des modernen Imperialismus," *Archiv für Politik und Geschichte*, IX (1927), 443-56.

Stolberg-Wernigerode, Albrecht zu. *Bismarck und die Verständigungspolitik, 1864-66*. Berlin, 1929. Goes into Bismarck's interest in the Mexican affair.

Teichmann, W. C. *Englands und Frankreichs Stellung zum Bürgerkriege in den Vereinigten Staaten von Amerika, 1861-1865*. München, 1885.

Willson, Beckles. *America's Ambassadors to France, 1777-1927*. New York, 1928.

Chapter VII. *The United States and the Franco-Prussian War, 1870-1871.*

Bigelow, John. *Retrospections of an Active Life*. 5 vols. New York, 1909-1913.

Bismarck, Otto von. *Gedanken und Erinnerungen.* Stuttgart, 1898. Bismarck's memoirs.

Boynton, Charles B. *The War in Europe: Its Religious and Political Significance.* Washington, D. C., 1870. A strongly anti-French and anti-Catholic sermon by a Presbyterian minister in Washington, D. C.

Busch, Moritz. *Graf Bismarck und seine Leute während des Krieges mit Frankreich.* 2 vols. Leipzig, 1884. Contains references to the Burnside mission.

————. "Prince Bismarck as a Friend of America and as a Statesman," *NAR,* CXXXI (1880), 1-13, 157-76.

————. *Tagebuchblätter.* Leipzig, 1899. Touches on the Burnside mission.

Carroll, E. M. *French Public Opinion and Foreign Affairs, 1870-1914.* New York, 1931.

Case, Lynn M. *French Opinion on War and Diplomacy during the Second Empire.* Philadelphia, 1954. A scholarly investigation of French opinion.

Codwin, E. C. *France in 1870-71.* New York, 1872. An address delivered at Cooper Union, N. Y.

Desmarest, J. *La défense nationale, 1870-1871.* Paris, 1949. A modern French work on the Franco-Prussian War.

Evans, Thomas. *History of the American Ambulance Established in Paris during the Siege of 1870-71.* London, 1873. An interesting account of the humanitarian services rendered by Americans in Paris.

Favre, Jules. *Gouvernement de la défense nationale.* Paris, 1871. The French statesman's story of the war.

Freeman, D. S. *Robert E. Lee.* 4 vols. New York, 1935.

Fuller, J. V. "Elihu B. Washburne," in Bemis, S. F. (ed.), *The American Secretaries of State,* VII, 119-22.

————. "Hamilton Fish," in Bemis, S. F. (ed.), *The American Secretaries of State,* VII, 125-214.

Gannon, Francis X. "A Study of Elihu Benjamin Washburne: American Minister to France during the Franco-Prussian War and the Commune." Unpublished Ph.D. dissertation, Georgetown University, 1950. A critical appraisal of Washburne's diplomatic career.

Gazley, J. G. *American Opinion of German Unification, 1848-1871.* New York, 1926.

Grund, J. P. "Bismarck and Motley," *NAR,* CLXVII (1898), 361-76, 481-96, 569 ff.

Guerlac, Othon. "Le suicide de Prévost-Paradol à Washington et l'opinion américaine." *Revue de littérature comparée,* VIII (1928), 100-112.

Henrey, Robert (ed.). *Letters from Paris, 1870-1875.* London, 1942. Written by a political informant to the head of the London House of Rothschild.

Hepner, Adolf. *America's Aid to Germany in 1870-71.* St. Louis, 1905. A detailed record.

Hoffman, Wickham. *Camp, Court, and Siege.* New York, 1877. The observations of the chargé d'affaires of the American legation in Paris at the time of the outbreak of the war.

Hugo, Victor. *L'année terrible,* in *Oeuvres complètes.* Paris, 1880.

Hunt, G. *Israel, Elihu, and Cadwallader Washburn.* New York, 1925. A brief biography.

Keim, J. *Forty Years of German-American Political Relations.* Philadelphia, 1919.

Lord, R. H. *The Origins of the War of 1870.* Cambridge, Mass., 1924. A standard work. Critical of Bismarck's maneuvers prior to the war.

MacCormac, W. *Souvenirs d'un chirurgien d'ambulance.* Paris, 1872.

Montgelas, Max. "England, Amerika und Belgien zum Kriegsausbruch 1870," *Berliner Monatshefte,* XII (1934), 1054-59.

Myrdacz, P., and Steiner, J. *Sanitätsgeschichte des deutsch-französischen Krieges.* Wien, 1896.

Nevins, Allan. *Hamilton Fish.* New York, 1936. An elaborate biography of the Secretary of State at the time of the Franco-Prussian War.

Oncken, Hermann. *Napoleon III and the Rhine.* New York, 1928. An eminent German historian's attempt to interpret the war as a continuation of France's historic drive towards the Rhine.

Pingaud, A. "La politique extérieure du Second Empire," *Revue historique,* CLVI (1927), 41-68. Discusses Napoleon's vacillations and indecision as manifested by his changing alliances.

Poore, Benjamin Perley. *The Life and Public Services of Ambrose E. Burnside.* Providence, R. I., 1882.

Poschinger, H. von. *Fürst Bismarck und die Diplomaten, 1852-1890.* Hamburg, 1900.

Poujade, E. *La diplomatie du Second Empire.* Paris, 1871. Comments upon France's disappointment about the attitude of the United States during the war of 1870.

Ravold, J. B. *Français et Allemands aux États-Unis d'Amérique pendant l'année terrible.* Nancy, 1883. Denounces the pro-German sympathies in the United States during the war.

Raymond, Dora Neill. *British Policy and Opinion during the Franco-Prussian War.* New York, 1921.

Reclus, Maurice. *Jules Favre, 1809-1880*. Paris, 1912. Biography of the French Foreign Minister after the fall of the Second Empire.

Roux, G. *Thiers*. Paris, 1948. Biography of the distinguished French statesman of the nineteenth century.

De Saint-Vincent, L. *Les protestants et la guerre de 1870*. Paris, 1907. Interprets the war as a struggle between Protestantism and Catholicism.

Scherer, E. "On the Franco-Prussian War—Nine Letters Written Anonymously to the New York *World*," *University of Arizona Bulletin*, VII (1936), No. 4.

Schieber, Clara E. *Transformation of American Sentiment toward Germany, 1870-1914*. Boston, 1923.

Sheridan, Philip Henry. *Personal Memoirs*. 2 vols. New York, 1902. General Sheridan was the official American observer on the Prussian side in the Franco-Prussian War.

Smith, William A. "Napoleon III and the Spanish Revolution of 1868," *Journal of Modern History*, XXV (1953), 211-233. Excellent background material.

Snyder, Louis Lea. *Die persönlichen und politischen Beziehungen Bismarcks zu Amerikanern*. Darmstadt, 1932. Discusses Bismarck's close relations with his American friends.

Sorel, Albert. *Histoire diplomatique de la guerre franco-allemande*. 2 vols. Paris, 1875. A leading French study on the war.

Stanton, Theodore. "Le général Grant et la France," *Revue de Paris* (November 1, 1894), pp. 183-202. Defends Grant against French criticism.

Stolberg-Wernigerode, Albrecht zu. *Bismarck und die Verständigungspolitik, 1864-66*. Berlin, 1929.

Stolberg-Wernigerode, Otto zu. *Germany and the United States of America during the Era of Bismarck*. Philadelphia, 1937. A standard work.

Sumner, Charles. *The Duel between France and Germany*. World Peace Foundation, 1911. A lecture delivered in Boston on October 26, 1870.

Trochu, Louis J. *Oeuvres posthumes*. Tours, 1896. Memoirs of General Trochu.

Valentin, Veit. *Bismarcks Reichsgründung im Urteil englischer Diplomaten*. Amsterdam, 1937. Touches on German-American relations prior to 1870 which were of concern to France.

Valfrey, J. *Histoire de la diplomatie du gouvernement de la défense nationale*. 2 vols. Paris, 1871. Comments on the lack of realism of those Frenchmen who hoped for American military intervention.

Wachter, A. *La guerre franco-allemande de 1870-71*. 2 vols. Paris, 1895. Comments on the Burnside mission.

Washburne, E. B. *Recollections of a Minister to France, 1869-1877.* 2 vols. New York, 1887.

——. *Franco-Prussian War.* Washington, 1878. Washburne's war correspondence.

Weill, Georges. *Histoire des États-Unis de 1787 à 1917.* Paris, 1919.

Welschinger, Henri. *La guerre de 1870—causes et responsabilités.* 2 vols. Paris, 1910. A French historian's interpretation of the war. Very critical of Germany and the United States.

White, Elizabeth B. *American Opinion of France from Lafayette to Poincaré.* New York, 1927.

Index